IAN HAMILTON FINLAY

A visual primer by Yves Abrioux
with introductory notes and commentaries
by Stephen Bann

REAKTION BOOKS

Published by Reaktion Books Ltd
1–5 Midford Place, Tottenham Court Road
London W1P 9HH, UK

First published 1985, this revised and expanded
second edition first published 1992

Copyright © Yves Abrioux and Stephen Bann, 1985, 1992

Designed by Ron Costley
Photoset by Wilmaset,
Birkenhead, Wirral
Printed and bound in Great Britain by
Balding and Mansell plc,
Wisbech, Cambs

A CIP record for this book is available from the British Library

ISBN 0 948462 35 3

The publisher acknowledges subsidy
from the Scottish Arts Council
towards the publication of this volume.

IAN HAMILTON FINLAY

A visual primer

Contents

Acknowledgements *page* vi
Preface to Second Edition vii
Preface to First Edition ix
Biographical Notes 1
    Artists Books – Collaborations – Poem Cards –
    Little Spartan War – Blades – Homages – Friendship

PART I

1 Stonypath: The Garden and the Temple 39
    introduced by Stephen Bann
    The Garden 39
    The Temple 65
2 Literacy Traditional and Modern 71
    introduced by Stephen Bann
    Short Stories and Rhyming Poems 71
    Metaphors and Metamorphoses,
    Tugs and Barges, Found Poems 77
    One-Word Poems, An Inland Garden, Elegy 93
3 Neoclassical 105
    introduced by Stephen Bann
    Heroic Emblems 105
    Deliberate Forms 111
    Landscape Improvements 121
    The Third Reich Revisited 141
    introduced by Ian Hamilton Finlay
    Idylls 145
    introduced by Stephen Bann

PART II

1 What's in a Name? 159
    Juan Gris
2 Near and Far 165
    The Pastorals of Mars – Firtrees and Pines –
    First Suprematist Standing Poem –
    The Immeasurable – Nature Over Again After Poussin
3 The Word 182
    The Word
4 Metaphor, Rhyme, Citation 189
    Rhymes for Lemons
5 Civilizing Dada 198
    Letters and Numbers

6 The Destructive Element 204
    Military Honours
7 Hieroglyph, Allegory, Portrait 213
    Portraits
8 Neopresocratic 218
    Lyres – Tags – Chant for a Regional Occasion –
    Definitions and Translations – Signs/Axioms –
    Fragments – Sea Poppy II
9 Sundials 232
    Sundials
10 Et in Arcadia Ego 241
    Arcady – Watteau
11 Sublimity, Terror, Awe 250
    Saint-Just – Revolution – Pastoral – Third Reich –
    Arrosoir – Adorno's Hut
12 The Objects of Allegory 293
    Allegories – Osso
13 Translating the Classics 299
    Translations – Revolutionary Heads – Grove

Notes and References 309
Bibliography 312
Index 318

Acknowledgements

Owners of works not mentioned in the captions are listed here:

The Arts Council of Great Britain *Strawberry Camouflage* p. 186; Professor Stephen Bann *Unnatural Pebbles* p. 112 left; Angela Boyce *Piranesi* p. 111; David Brown *Terra/Mare* p. 24; Simon Cutts *Talismans and Signifiers* p. 114 left; Eastbourne Art Gallery *Drift* p. 187; Rod Gathercole *Secret* p. 188; Glasgow Art Gallery and Museums, Kelvingrove, Glasgow *Clay the Life* p. 269; Graeme Murray Gallery, Edinburgh *Talismans and Signifiers* p. 114 middle and right and p. 115, *Japanese Stacks* p. 116, *Classic Landscape* p. 217; Kröller-Müller Rijks-museum, Otterlo, Netherlands *Windflower* p. 10; the Most Honourable the Twelfth Marquis of Lothian, K.C.V.O., D.L. *The Monteviot Proposal* p. 123; Musée de la Révolution Française, Château de Vizilles, France *Guillotine Teapot* p. 279; Les Musées de la Ville de Strasbourg, *Adorno's Hut* p. 292; Museum Moderner Kunst, Vienna *Hommage à Bara* p. 277, *Two Drums* p. 277; Victoria Miro *Dove, dead in its snows . . .* p. 154; National Galleries of Scotland, Edinburgh *Et in Arcadia Ego* p. 243; Scottish Arts Council *Big 'E' at Midway* p. 215; John Stoller *Marble Paper Boat* p. 25; The Tate Gallery, London *Starlit Waters* p. 187; Victoria Miro Gallery, London *Beautiful, Fanatical . . .* p. 118, *'Now the Names of the Twelve are these . . .'* p. 118, *Corday, Lux* p. 119, *Events Are a Discourse* p. 120, *The Sea's Leaves, The Strawberry's Waves* p. 154, *The World Has Been Empty Since the Romans* p. 269, *Shaded Path* p. 305; Sol Lewitt Collection / Wadsworth Atheneum, Hartford, Connecticut, USA *Unnatural Pebbles* p. 112 right and p. 113; Werkstatt Kollerschlag, Austria *Cythera* p. 156.

Photographs

We should particularly like to thank David Paterson, without whom this book could not have been realized in its present form, as well as all the other photographers listed here. In certain cases, the publishers have been unable to ascertain the authorship of photographs.

Marius Alexander, pp. 7 bottom, 66, 68 top, 68 bottom right, 69, 70 top, 141, 244 top, 260, 302; courtesy Christine Burgin Gallery, New York, p. 268; Geremy Butler, p. 223; Carlisle Museum and Art Gallery, p. 95; Ian Hamilton Finlay, p. x top; courtesy Glasgow Art Gallery and Museum, p. 269 bottom; Martyn Greenhalgh, pp. 59, 60, 61, 149; Andrew Griffiths, pp. 13 middle and top, 67, 124, 125, 262; Ronald Gunn, p. 187 bottom; courtesy Harris Museum and Art Gallery, Preston, p. 306 top; Ralph Hinterkeuser, pp. 154 top, 155; Sean Hudson, pp. 114, 115; Benjamin Katz, p. 298; courtesy Galerie Jule Kewenig, pp. 117, 150, 154 top, 155, 292, 298, 307; courtesy Kröller-Müller Rijksmuseum, Otterlo, Netherlands, pp. 126, 127; Hani Latif, pp. 112, 113, 217 bottom; Dieter Leistner, p. 307; Jannes Linders, p. 16 bottom; courtesy James Lingwood and the TSWA-Four Cities Project, p. 140; courtesy Leisure and Amenities Department, Borough of Luton, pp. 136, 137, 138, 139; Karl-Heinz Müller, p. 117; Monika Nikolic, pp. 129, 272; David Paterson, pp. x bottom, 3 top, 10, 11, 13 bottom, 18, 19, 24, 25, 41, 42, 43, 44, 45, 46, 47, 48, 49, 50, 51, 52, 53, 54, 55, 56, 57, 58, 68 bottom left, 70 bottom, 101, 102, 103, 111, 121, 164, 175, 176, 178, 179, 180, 181, 188, 197 top right, 200, 215, 217 top, 224, 230, 234, 235 bottom and top left, 236, 237, 244 bottom, 259, 262 bottom, 263; Antonia Reeve, pp. viii, 14 bottom, 17 top, 62, 63, 64, 116, 118, 119, 120, 146 top, 154 bottom, 258, 267, 271, 276, 277, 278, 279, 292; courtesy Stuart Collection, University of California at San Diego, p. 306 bottom; Marco Schibig, pp. 130–131; Ken Schles, p. 268; Tom Scott, pp. 186 top, 243; John Stathatos, p. 30; Jim Styles, p. 235 top right; Diane Tammes, pp. 3 bottom, 6, 239 top; courtesy Victoria Miro Gallery, pp. 17 bottom, 151, 269 top, 305; Elke Walford, p. 150; Peter Walser, pp. 228, 229; John Webb, p. 186 bottom; Kurt Wyss, p. 128.

All printed items were published by the Wild Hawthorn Press when not otherwise credited.

Preface to Second Edition

In the seven years since the first edition of this book was published, Ian Hamilton Finlay's basic approach has not changed. Indeed, his militantly neoclassical standpoint has been repeatedly reaffirmed in numerous one-man exhibitions on revolutionary and idyllic themes. Permanent installations and contributions to major international exhibitions have given his trenchant analysis of contemporary aesthetics – and ethics – a higher public profile.

This new edition documents Finlay's production over the past few years. It includes a greatly expanded selection of revolutionary iconography, accounting for the artist's intense involvement with this theme throughout the 1980s (Part II, Chapter 11). An entirely new visual section has been added to Part I to illustrate Finlay's current celebration of the idyll. These works, many of which are elaborations of earlier poems, testify to the overall coherence of the voluminous and greatly varied oeuvre that Finlay has produced since his first poems and stories were published in the 1950s. The clarity and purity of his aesthetic continues to express a serenity that few contemporary artists can rival, though the weapons of polemic are kept close at hand and may be seized at any moment to defend the ideal.

Two completely new chapters have been added to Part II. Chapter 12 discusses the way Finlay uses allegorical procedures to intensify the interchange between his work and burning issues in the history and culture of our century. Chapter 13 maps out the artist's translation (or transportation) of classical values into various countries and across seas and oceans, in response to commissions and invitations from different parts of the world.

The author and the publishers would like to thank Ian Hamilton Finlay for his co-operation. We would also especially like to thank Pia Simig, whose help has been invaluable in the making of this new revised and expanded edition.

February 1992

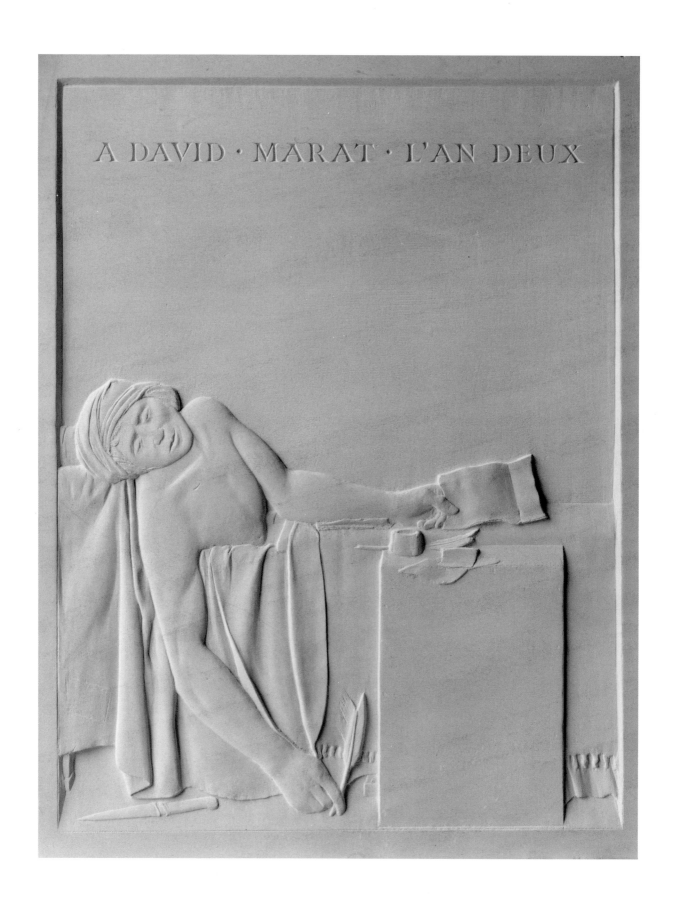

A David · Marat · L'An Deux, 1991
stone relief, with Neil Talbot

Preface to First Edition

Ian Hamilton Finlay's status as an important and original artist is now widely recognized. Although his native Scotland has been reluctant to acknowledge his worth, Finlay's international reputation has grown immeasurably in recent years. He has completed important commissions and participated in major exhibitions, both at home and abroad.

It remains that Finlay's work is not easy to classify. It covers numerous fields and involves many collaborators, ranging from traditional craftsmen to architects and other contemporary artists. Finlay has also had recourse to modern industrial techniques. Different aspects of his production have at some time or other received special attention. Thus, in some quarters, Finlay is still chiefly known as Britain's foremost concrete poet. For others, he is primarily a gardener: his garden has received visitors from all over the world and has been recognized as an important British garden. In France, Finlay is highly respected by experts in the field of landscape design. A number of commissions testify to the relevance of his investigations into the way in which art impinges on architecture and the environment. Or again, if Finlay's name is familiar to a wider public in the UK, this is doubtless due to media coverage of his long-running and at times spectacular conflict with Strathclyde Region and the Scottish Arts Council – a battle which has itself engendered works of art.

This *Primer* reflects the diversity of Finlay's oeuvre. It reproduces works which are not readily available, frequently because they originally appeared in limited editions, on the lists of small publishers – primarily under the imprint of Finlay's own Wild Hawthorn Press. The impact of a number of Finlay's booklets relies very much on their scale, on the quality of their paper and on the process of turning the pages. Their reproduction here is therefore qualified by the difficulty of achieving the same effect in the form of this book. The *Primer* also includes reproductions of Finlay's non-printed works, which are increasingly finding their way into private and public collections all over the world.

What has perhaps not sufficiently been recognized is the overall coherence of Finlay's work. One of the purposes of this book is to suggest where this lies. The *Primer* is divided into two parts, preceded by Biographical Notes. Part I is almost exclusively visual. It opens with an extended selection of photographs (many of them specially commissioned) of what remains Finlay's prime achievement – the Garden and Temple at Little Sparta, Stonypath, in southern Scotland. There follows a selection of works, chiefly from the 1950s to the early 1970s, which show how Finlay's most intensive phase of overtly modernistic 'experimentation' in fact constitutes a thorough examination of the basis of literacy (both artistic and literary) in the contemporary world. Part I closes with examples of the 'neoclassical rearmament' which is now Finlay's major preoccupation, and which is a vigorous response to the contemporary cultural context.

Part II of the book consists of an illustrated essay built round a number of more or less familiar notions: aura, citation, rhetoric, metaphor, image and allegory, the sublime . . . It touches on Finlay's relationship with different art forms (sculpture, photography, portrait painting, etc.) and aesthetic movements (cubism, dada, neoclassicism, the idea of the avant-garde). Finlay still rightly likes to regard himself as a poet. Much of his work hovers on the borderline between poetry and some other medium. It can be argued that his production as a whole is best regarded as a highly original poetic statement on the state of European culture. Herein lies the source of the literary standpoint often adopted in the text, and of the detailed attention given to the verbal energies displayed by Finlay's work. His reactivation of traditional themes and motifs (sundials, Arcady) owes much of its success to the particular discursive force evolved by Finlay over the years.

Ian Hamilton Finlay patiently answered a number of queries and made useful suggestions. Both he and Sue Finlay valiantly hunted out material I required. My task would have been impossible without their kind co-operation. My thanks go also to Stephen Bann, who let me see some early publications of Finlay's in his collection, and who listened to my reflections and ruminations over the years. No one can hope to give an account of Finlay's work without repeatedly having recourse to the authoritative running commentary that Dr Bann has been providing for twenty years. My text provides ample evidence of my debt to him on this score too.

The introductory notes in Part I were written by Stephen Bann (with the exception of the *Third Reich Revisited*), and Dr Bann provided a commentary to the Speer project, as well as allowing some previous commentaries to be reprinted.

The Temple Pool, 1968   The Temple Pool, 1979

BIOGRAPHICAL NOTES

1925: Born in Nassau, Bahamas. Returned to Scotland as a child; boarding school; father lost his fortune made from bootlegging with a schooner; poverty in Glasgow; education ended at the age of thirteen with the outbreak of war and evacuation to the Orkneys.[1]

Read many books on cubism when he was about fourteen.[2]

Briefly attended Glasgow School of Art before being called up; almost never went; read books on cubism and surrealism. Hitch-hiked to London, which he first entered astride a torpedo or a bomb in the back of a truck.

1942: At seventeen, army service for three and a half years. Finlay was a sergeant in the RASC and saw service in Germany. He became friendly with the artists Colquhoun, MacBryde, John Minton, often staying with them while he was in the army.

End of World War II: Worked as a shepherd in the Orkneys. Had a dream of 'Sweet Philosophy', in which he found visionary happiness in discoursing with classically-clad philosophers in a kind of bright green-grassed grove; wanted to study philosophy, but this was not possible.

Agricultural labouring and writing, first short stories and then short plays. Most of the short stories were published in the *Glasgow Herald* in the mid-1950s, before appearing in book form. Finlay's short plays date from the late 1950s; some were broadcast by the BBC.

The protagonists of Finlay's stories are mostly children and country or fishing folk. For all their surface simplicity and economy of means, the stories have the symbolic power associated with Russian exponents of the genre (Sologub, Andreyev), or with the Joycean epiphany. At the same time, their prose rhythms place them within an unjustly neglected strain of Scottish writing (John Macnair Reid, Ian Macpherson). Such fruits of the 'non-classical tradition of the north'[3] have not received the attention they deserved. However, one may wonder whether the community and culture implied by their form still exist. Finlay recognized the problem and

subsequently reformulated the themes of some of his earlier stories and poems in a more obviously modernistic idiom.

Late 1950s: Move to Edinburgh, followed by a sojourn in the Orkneys as a labourer; rhyming poems period.

Like the short stories, Finlay's rhyming poems embody both the accents of native Scottish speech and a strict formal concern. Described by Mike Weaver as a collection of 'sophisticated folk poems',[4] *The Dancers Inherit the Party* was admired in America by such poets as Robert Creeley, Robert Duncan and Lorine Niedecker. However, the book was not at all well received in Scotland.

1961: The Wild Hawthorn Press founded by Finlay and Jessie McGuffie. The Press, which at the outset published works by a number of contemporary artists, came over the years to concentrate exclusively on Finlay's own production. From the start, it was notable both for the uncompromising quality of its publications and for the possibilities it offered for formal innovation. The first book to be published at the Wild Hawthorn Press was *Glasgow Beasts, an a Burd*, poems by Finlay written in Glaswegian dialect.

1962: Founded the periodical *Poor. Old. Tired. Horse.*, offset at the Wild Hawthorn Press. It ran to twenty five issues, the last of which appeared in 1968. *Poor. Old. Tired. Horse.* was a forum for the verbal and the visual, the traditional and the modernistic, the creative and the theoretical. It introduced new kinds of poetry into Scotland and enabled Finlay to establish contacts with the outside world.

A biographical portrait in *Typographica* 8 (1963) observed that the media had made Finlay's activities sound dadaistic, and that according to a report in Radio Newsreel 'his airship, the Wild Hawthorn Zeppelin, was going to bombard the 1962 Festival Writers' Conference [in Edinburgh]; his Wild Hawthorn March was banned by the Edinburgh magistrates; and a radio broadcast put out the rumour that 50,000 supporters of the Glasgow

Ian, Sue, Eck and Ailie Finlay by the Temple Pool, 1967

Toy Fish, 1965
painted wood

Rangers [Football Club] were going to demonstrate in favour of Shimpei Kusano, the Frog Poet & the Wild Hawthorn'. The entire episode was, of course, fictional.

1963: Exhibition of toys at the home of the publisher John Calder, Ledlanet House, Fife. In the early 1960s, Finlay had felt 'an absolute need to turn from the rhythmic to the static, ... and turned towards making little toys – things of no account in themselves, yet true to [his] inspiration, which was away from Syntax toward "the Pure"'.[5] The static nature of the toys marked Finlay's transition towards concrete poetry, which he did not know at the time.

Founded the broadside *Fishsheet* for concrete poetry (one issue only).

Publication of *Rapel*, Finlay's first collection of concrete poems, and of *Standing Poem 1*, his first poem/card.

1964: *Canal Stripe Series 3*, Finlay's first published booklet-poem. The kinetic booklets in the *Ocean* and *Canal Stripe Series* were an innovation of Finlay's at the Wild Hawthorn Press, and an important contribution to the concrete poetry mode. Works from these series were also transformed into kinetic constructions. This two-pronged attack on conventional book form demonstrates the overall coherence of Finlay's formal innovations, however varied these may be. The structure of both the booklets and the constructions is semantic. They constitute significant forms.

Poster Poem (le Circus), the first in a long string of poem/prints (an innovation also introduced by Finlay), belongs to a series also featuring works by Franz Mon, Ferdinand Kriwet, John Furnival and Pierre Albert-Birot.

Move to Easter Ross, north of Inverness, where Finlay created his first poems designed to be set in an environment.

First poem in sandblasted glass shown at the Cambridge International Exhibition of Concrete Poetry in November of the same year.

1965–7: 'Under the general rubric of a "new classicism", Finlay began to investigate the inscription of the poem in the world and the transcendence of the sign through metaphor.'[6]

Summer 1966: Spent in Fife, with Sue Finlay, at Coaltown of Callange, 'a place as pastoral as its address'.[7] The 'idyllic pastoral' inspired such works as the *Coaltown*

'Panzer Leader' (von Manstein)

Frogbit, floating poem, 1968
painted wood, with Peter Grant

tye
cringle
fall
shippon
parrel
carling
bitt
gooseneck
traveller
beam
tabernacle
manger
crib

25 December

Tye Cringle, 1972
Christmas card, with Michael Harvey

of Callange Tri-kai, *Autumn Poem* and *6 Small Songs in 3's.*

Autumn 1966: Ian and Sue Finlay settled at Stonypath. They had met two years earlier; they have two children.

Stonypath was an abandoned hillside croft in the Southern Uplands of Scotland, where the Finlays immediately set about creating their world-famous garden. It consists of a stone house, agricultural buildings and about four acres of land. One of the buildings was turned into a gallery showing the work of Finlay and his collaborators. This subsequently became a Garden Temple. In 1968, Stonypath was a desolate spot, with none of the vegetation that is now so well established. The ponds did not exist. There was just one old tree in the front of the cottage. This is still standing, in a corner of the garden.

At Stonypath, Finlay began building model planes and boats.

1967: Sunken garden begun at Stonypath; pond dug behind the cottage.

International concrete poetry exhibition at the 1967 Brighton Festival. Participants from Britain, Europe and America. Finlay contributed *Star/Steer* to a collection of concrete poems published for the festival. Other works, done in collaboration with Henry Clyne, were featured in the exhibition. *Poor. Old. Tired. Horse.* 24 is a photographic record of works by various artists exhibited at different sites in the streets and gardens of Brighton – and even out at sea.

Finlay had corresponded with Eugen Gomringer, in Switzerland, and with the Brazilian concrete poets, from about 1962. He was the Scottish representative on the *comité international* of the concrete poetry movement. This 'deliberate connection with [the] literary avant-garde'[8] ceased when concrete poetry degenerated into a trite, decorative mode. Finlay's own contributions to concrete poetry demonstrate his enduring concern for cultural values. The booklet *Ocean Stripe Series 5*, produced in 1967, shows Finlay taking stock of the tradition of the avant-garde.

1967–8: Boat names and boat registration numbers in painted wood, some covered in nylon fishing net. One of these works, *Starlit Waters*, was acquired by the Tate Gallery in 1976 and was the object of a minor press campaign in the wake of the Carl Andre bricks controversy. Works from the same series are to be found in other public collections. A further set of similar works was undertaken for Finlay's Serpentine Gallery Exhibition in 1977.

1968: First one-man exhibition at the Axiom Gallery, London.

Published in 1968, the last issue of *Poor. Old. Tired. Horse.* is entirely devoted to one-word poems. The mode was devised by Finlay in the mid-1960s. Other poets were invited to contribute one-word poems to Finlay's magazine. Contributors included George Mackay Brown, Edwin Morgan, Edward Lucie-Smith, Jerome Rothenberg, Guy Davenport, Ernst Jandl, Pedro Xisto. Finlay's instructions to his fellow poets stipulated that the poem 'was to consist of one word, with a title of any length, these two elements forming, as it were, a corner which would then contain the meaning'.

Finlay observes that 'It seemed obvious to me that one could not have a literally one-word poem on the page, since any work must contain *relationship*; equally, one could (conceivably) have a one-word poem in a garden, if the surroundings were conceived as *part* of the poem. I thought of the one-word poem as a kind of native alternative to haiku (a form which *was* then in Fashion). What I didn't know then, was, that the one-*line* poem was virtually an established European form, of which examples can be found in Apollinaire. [. . .] Obviously, one-word and one-line poems, have a certain relation to concrete poetry. (I once described the sonnet as a "sewing machine for the monostich".) This opens on to two areas of questioning: first, what is the especial status of the fragment? and, why does one desire the word in itself? These questions probably have to wait until literature very belatedly recognises the concrete poem. Or perhaps they will never be answered, or asked, by literature, since they are first and foremost, metaphysical questions.'[9]

The one-word poem was never a fixed form for Finlay. *Stonechats*, the booklet containing the largest number of his one-word poems, is a collection of texts conceived as inscriptions for the garden at Stonypath. It demonstrates the importance of the one-word poem to the semiotic aesthetic which characterized Stonypath in the first years of its development. Finlay also adapted one-word poems for poem/cards by adding an image, or by replacing one of the verbal components with an image. The concentration implied by the one-word poem had brought to the forefront the importance of the relationship between constituent elements in any work, which is central to Finlay's aesthetic.

EASTERTIDE

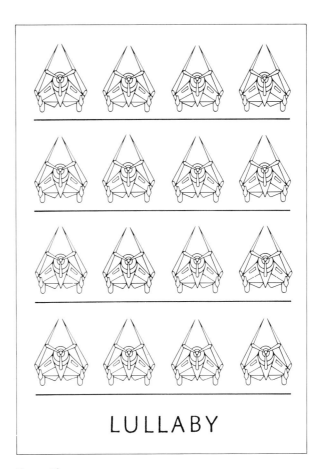

LULLABY

Eastertide, 1975
folding card, with Laurie Clark

Lullaby, 1975
card, with John Andrew

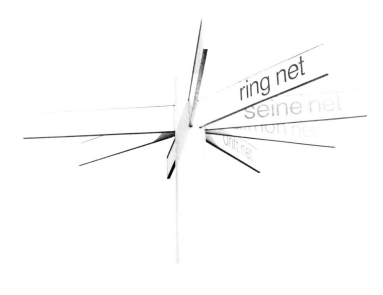

over the roof
WIND unwind MILL

garden wall
CHERRY tree STONE

bathtime
WATER baby GURGLES

Signpost, 1969
painted wood, with Peter Grant

From *The Collected Coaltown of Callange Tri-Kai*, 1968
Screwpacket Press

1969: Small loch at Stonypath formed by damming a tiny stream.

1970: Retrospective exhibition on Ian Hamilton Finlay and the Wild Hawthorn Press at the Ceolfrith Bookshop Gallery, Sunderland.

In the early 1970s, Finlay's garden at Stonypath began to assume a more coherent shape.[10] At the same time, the image of the modern warship began to replace that of the fishing-boat as Finlay's main theme, and his 'neoclassical rearmament project' began to emerge more clearly.

1971: *The Weed Boat Masters Ticket* booklet published at the Wild Hawthorn Press. This was the first of a series of question booklets, later expanded to *So You Want To Be A Panzer Leader* and *The Wild Hawthorn Art Test*. In these booklets, Finlay's intention to challenge – wittily – the literary and artistic competence of his readers is openly declared by the form.

1972: Retrospective exhibition, Scottish National Gallery of Modern Art.

Embarked on a series of large colour poem/prints with Jim Nicholson.

c. 1974: Started a series of works for the Max Planck Institute Garden, Stuttgart. The project took several years to complete.

1975–6: Ceramic works in collaboration with David Ballantyne; impresa-type medallions in collaboration with Ron Costley, and other works based on the Renaissance emblem; collaboration with the American artist Jud Fine.

1976–7: Large neon works and Battle of Midway Tableau (in collaboration with James Stoddart and James Boyd) for Finlay's Serpentine exhibition in 1977.

Much of Finlay's work is done in collaboration with a range of artists and craftsmen. Other works make use of modern industrial techniques. The garden at Stonypath owes much to the collaboration of Sue Finlay. In many cases, a single work or design is recast in radically different idioms or media. These collaborations and variations form an integral part of the evaluation of cultural forces on which Finlay is engaged.[11]

1977: Series of embroideries with Pamela Campion (earlier embroideries date from 1973).

April–May 1977: *Collaborations* exhibition, Kettle's Yard, Cambridge.

June–September 1977: *Lyre* on show at the Silver Jubilee Exhibition of Contemporary Sculpture, Battersea Park, London. Consists of an actual Oerlikon gun standing on concrete slabs and accompanied by a quotation referring to Heraclitus from Edmund Hussey's book *The Presocratics*.

September–October 1977: Exhibition at the Serpentine Gallery, London. This was divided into five rooms plus an information area. The catalogue described the first of these rooms in the following terms: 'We are to imagine a neo-classical interior, perhaps a small temple opening upon a garden at Stourhead or Stowe'. This marks the first public claim by Finlay to a religious environment as the proper setting for his work.

The publication in 1977 of Finlay's *Heroic Emblems*, with extensive commentaries by Stephen Bann, underlined the extent to which commentary and documentation form an essential part of his work. Indeed, it is a major aspect of Finlay's aesthetic that his works should induce a process of exploration and meditation on their references.

1978: Withdrawal of Serpentine travelling exhibition from the Scottish Arts Council's Charlotte Square Gallery, Edinburgh, just before the planned opening, in protest against actions of SAC officials. Finlay comments: 'Beyond the prosaic (almost pedantic, moral) level already alluded to, what I was aware of (as a "reason") was, that the absence of the works was a clearer statement of their content, than the works themselves could have been, *in that circumstance*. In short, the absence of the exhibition, *was* the exhibition, and the [Scottish] Arts Council clearly found this unacceptable though it had recently mounted (and publicly defended) an exhibition which consisted entirely of blank canvases, carefully framed. (Perhaps this was the ideal "state art" social occasion – so very near in form to my own, yet in effect its opposite.)'[12]

The cancelled exhibition can be taken to mark the opening of what, after a number of preliminary skirmishes, was to become the Little Spartan War. Within months, the SAC made it known that, while it accepted that Finlay's action in withdrawing the exhibition was entirely legal, communications between themselves and the artist would henceforth be conducted through soli-

O'ERLIKON

O'erlikon, 1973
card, with Susan Goodricke

Dryads (The Seasons), 1980
ceramic, with Roger Bunn

'A CALM IN A TEA-CUP'
After Kate Greenaway

the ABC of tea

ABCDEFGHIJKLMNOPQRSTEAUVWXYZ

Summer Vocabulary Lesson

1. Is the tea infished?
2. It is infished.
3. Suffishiently?
4. Suffishiently.

1. Is it pouring?
2. It is pouring.
3. The rain is pouring.
4. May I pour?

'A Calm in a Tea-Cup', 1973
folding card, with Richard Demarco

From *Tea-leaves and Fishes*, 1966
booklet

citors. They then instructed their solicitors not to correspond with Finlay. Subsequently, the SAC refused to allow the artist the right to add documentary material to works of his in their collection. The Crown Office intervened to prevent the Consumer Protection Department (a department of local government) from taking legal action against the SAC. Strathclyde Regional Council entered the fray by withdrawing the rates relief it had formerly granted to the gallery in Finlay's garden at Stonypath. One of the 'reasons' put forward by the Region was that the gallery did not receive an SAC grant ... In 1980 – in a move that had been in the making at least since his Serpentine exhibition – Finlay transformed his gallery into a Garden Temple. Strathclyde Region refused him the rates exemption granted by law to religious buildings. It failed even to give the Finlays the chance to put their case for mandatory relief[13] and had recourse to legal pressures to enforce its arbitrary decision. In this, it had the passive, and at times active, support of a number of judicial, administrative and elected officials, as well as public bodies, who refused to act on the matter. In September 1984, the SAC published a statement asking Strathclyde Region to avoid further action pending reassessment of the Garden Temple. The Region failed to respond. The Regional Assessor, acting at the behest of the SAC, subsequently agreed that the description 'garden temple' was a valid one, but the Region still remained unmoved – and in February 1985, the SAC refused to advise the Region as to the meaning of the term. Although Finlay protested that in so doing the SAC had violated the terms of its charter,[14] the arts establishment once again refused to take notice, and Strathclyde Region announced that it was going to go ahead with the sale of the works seized from the Temple in 1983.

If the events of 1984–5 suggest considerable confusion on the part of various British authorities, it should be recalled that Finlay's demand throughout the whole affair has always been simply for a fair chance to put his case, so that the legality of the Region's rates claim might be properly established. The conflict is not over payment as such. It is the result of Strathclyde Region's refusal to examine the grounds on which a building can appropriately, in the 1980s, be regarded as a Garden Temple. Finlay refuses to allow a bureaucracy to settle unilaterally a cultural question which it has publicly stated not even to understand.[15] It should also be underlined that no brief account of the affair can give any indication of the hardship and suffering which the

Finlays have put up with, in their refusal to yield on what they consider to be a matter of principle.

In 1978, Finlay embarked on a 'Five Year Hellenisation Plan' for his garden at Stonypath. Stonypath was subsequently renamed Little Sparta.

1978: Corresponded with Albert Speer; idea for the *Third Reich Revisited* series (first exhibited in 1982; complete showing, 1984–5).

1978 also marked the beginning of Finlay's 'Free Arts' project, an answer to the problem of the dominance of state-aided art within a pluralist democracy. The project was designed to allow everyone to have a role as a patron in a genuinely pluralist cultural economy, instead of reducing the general public to the role of consumer in an arts market dominated by the state. The scheme worked in a modest way, even if Finlay encountered reluctance on the part of artists and potential patrons to participate in a project which did not have official approval.

March 1979: 'Crates Event' at the Charlotte Square offices of the SAC. Projected by Finlay as a pastiche of the avant-garde 'event' (a type of activity the SAC likes to subsidize), it was built around the return by Finlay of two neoclassical stone reliefs which the SAC had accidentally delivered to Stonypath after acquiring them for its collection. Finlay played upon the ambiguities of bureaucratic prose, in an effort to focus upon the problem of communication between the artist and the arts administration. The SAC was not appreciative and the reliefs in question were subsequently modified to mark the occasion.

The SAC's stone reliefs were to figure once more in the Little Spartan War when, early in 1984, they were removed from the SAC headquarters and installed in the Temple at Little Sparta as war spoils. The raid was carried out by the Saint-Just Vigilantes, a group of Finlay supporters who had previously conducted a number of guerrilla activities in defence of the garden and Temple. Named after a prominent French Revolutionary leader, the Vigilantes made their first appearance in the fictional context of Finlay's *Third Reich Revisited*. Reference to the French Revolution became a prominent feature both of Finlay's garden and Temple and of the conduct of the Little Spartan War.

1978–9: *Japanese Stacks*, in various woods, with John R. Thorpe.

Concertina, 1962
folding booklet, with John Picking and Pete McGinn

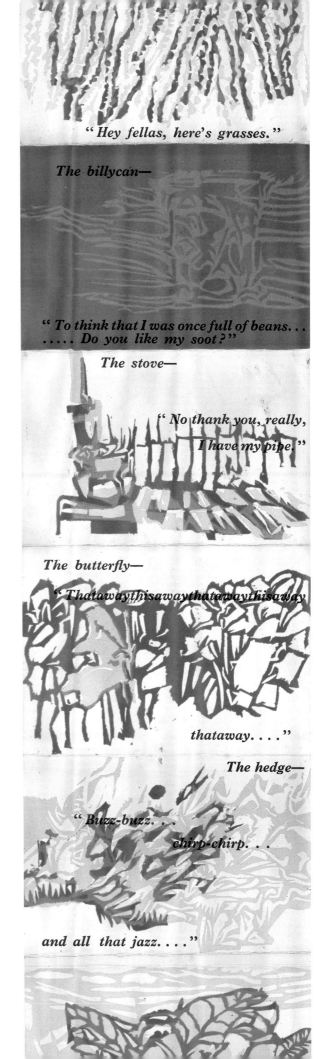

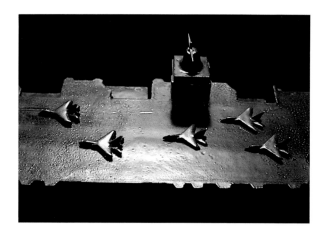

Golden Aircraft-carrier (detail), 1974
ceramic, with the Ceramic Workshop, Edinburgh

Barque, 1974, painted metal, with Michael Harvey

Windflower, 1976, neon, with Ron Costley

1980: Work started on the Sacred Grove at the Kröller-Müller Museum in Holland. Project completed in Spring 1982.

1980–1: *Nature Over Again After Poussin* travelling exhibition.

4 February 1983: After a long period of verbal skirmishing, accompanied by various attempts by Strathclyde Region to put pressure on the Finlays, the First Battle of Little Sparta took place, when the sheriff officer unsuccessfully attempted to seize works from the Garden Temple. The Saint-Just Vigilantes were successfully mobilized, and Little Sparta won the day – as the pressmen and television cameras in attendance testified. The Vigilantes had earlier drawn attention to themselves by carrying out a neoclassical poster campaign (in Latin) involving several historic buildings in Edinburgh, and also by conveying 'to the protection of the trees' dryads from the Little Sparta Temple, which the sheriff officer had placed under summary arrest.[16] A medal was struck to commemorate the First Battle of Little Sparta, and a monument was erected on the battlefield.

15 March 1983: Budget Day Raid. While the attention of the press was monopolized by events at Westminster, the Region struck again. The sheriff officer removed from the Finlays' Temple a number of works, which he placed in an undisclosed bank vault. Documentation forming an integral part of some of the pieces removed was left behind, depriving them of much of their value. Amongst the items seized (valued at twice the sum figuring on the sheriff officer's warrant) were a number of works belonging in whole or in part to various individuals and establishments. It proved impossible to ensure the cooperation of judicial or parliamentary authorities to obtain the return of these items to their rightful owners. Only the Wadsworth Atheneum of Connecticut was able to recover its property, with the threat of assistance from the US State Department. Private collectors in Britain were unable to obtain satisfaction, even after offering proof of ownership. Following the sheriff officer's raid, Little Sparta was closed to visitors for a year.

August–September 1983: Monumental stone inscription – *'The Present Order is the Disorder of the Future'* Saint-Just – exhibited at the Sculpture Show, Hayward Gallery, London.

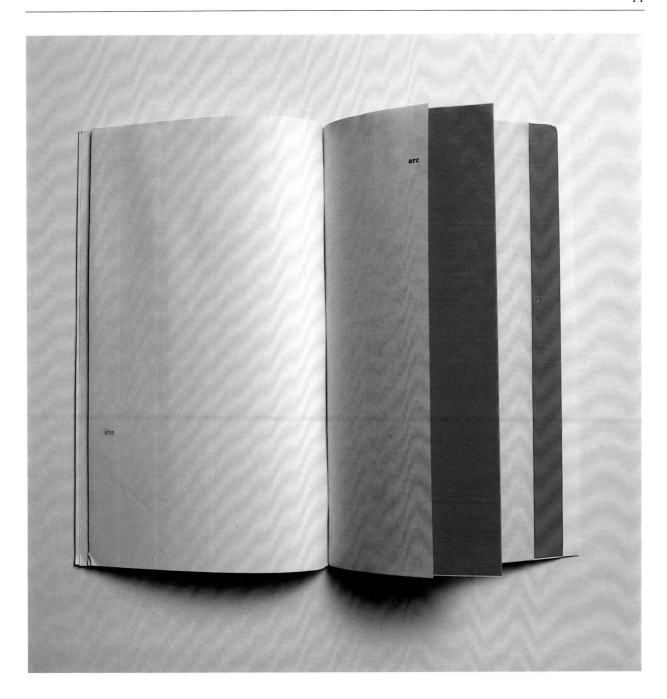

'I do set my bow in the cloud, and it shall be for a token of a covenant between me and
the earth. And it shall come to pass, when I bring a cloud over the earth, that the bow
shall be seen in the cloud: And I will remember my covenant, which is between me and
you and every living creature of all flesh: and the waters shall no more become a flood to
destroy all flesh.'   Genesis 2, 13–15

Ocean Stripe Series 3, 1965
kinetic booklet

Ian Hamilton Finlay / Jim Nicholson)

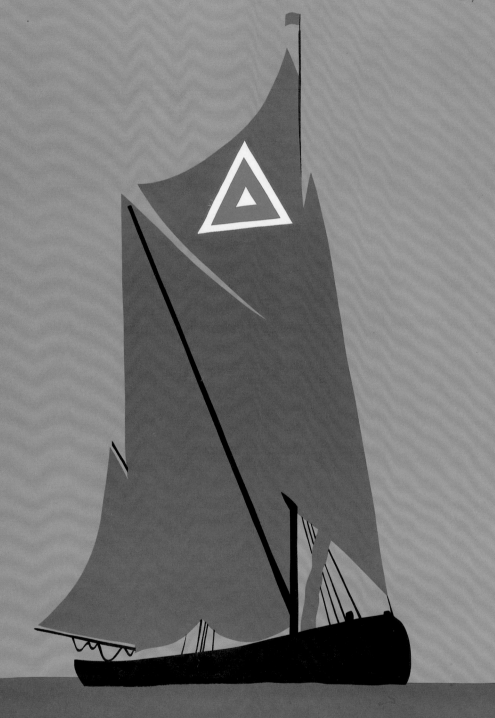

HOMAGE TO MODERN ART

1983–4: Collaborations with the architect Andrew Townsend. Goose Hut and Grotto completed at Stonypath, Little Sparta.

1984: The garden and Temple again open to visitors. The Temple, in what will probably be its definitive state, consists of a Main Room, conceived as an extension of the garden, and as a homage to the classical and pastoral values of the French Revolution; an Intermediary Room, on the theme of Virtue, Terror and Revolution, with wall-hangings and flags repeating the motif of the lyre and the Oerlikon gun; and a Dark Room. In 1984, this housed the stone relief war trophies. There is also an Office where essays, publications and other documents are stored. While the garden spread into the main room of the Temple, an increasing number of columns and capitals found a place in the garden, bringing about a movement in the opposite direction. The interpenetration of garden and Temple is now one of the chief features of Little Sparta.

Summer–Autumn 1984: Exhibition of tree-plaques in the Merian-Park, Basel, and of *Talismans and Signifiers*, and *Japanese Stacks* at the Graeme Murray Gallery, Edinburgh and subsequently in the British Council's British Show in Australia; completed *Third Reich Revisited*, together with Heroic Ephemera from the Little Spartan War, in a touring exhibition organized by Southampton Art Gallery.

Proposals for the Schweizergarten, Vienna, the Maritime Village, Swansea, and the Villa Celle, Italy – a measure of the recognition of the landscaping aesthetic developed by Finlay at Little Sparta. Indoor sculpture *9 Columns* purchased by the Kunstmuseum, Düsseldorf.

March–May 1985: *Little Sparta & Kriegsschatz* exhibitions with Sarkis at the Espace Rameau–Chapelle Sainte-Marie, Nevers, France and at the Eric Fabre Gallery, Paris. Finlay also took part in outdoor sculpture exhibitions at Geneva, and at Wageningen in Holland. Proposals for the bi-centennial celebrations of the French Revolution.

July 1985: Shortlisted for the Turner Prize.

1985: *Reflections on the French Revolution*, exhibition at the Graeme Murray Gallery, Edinburgh.

Saint-Just Vigilante sentry on the roof of Stonypath cottage

Before the battle: Finlay discusses tactics with a television news reporter

Saint-Just Vigilantes surrendering to the sheriff officer

Homage to Modern Art, 1972
screen print, with Jim Nicholson

The First Battle of Little Sparta, 4 February 1983

A Remembrance of R.L.S.
Winter

From *A Remembrance of R.L.S.*, 1987
a proposal for the Princes Street Gardens, Edinburgh
with Kathleen Lindsley

Head of Waldemar Januszczak, from 'Four Heads', 1987
plaster, wicker, with Alexander Stoddart

1986: *Marat Assassiné and other works*, exhibition at the Victoria Miro Gallery, London.

1986–87: The Follies War conducted by the Saint-Just Vigilantes in protest against the officially sanctioned trivialization of culture in *Follies: a National Trust Guide*. After having sent letters of protest to no avail to the publishers (Jonathan Cape) and the National Trust, the Vigilantes mounted an energetic propaganda campaign, the high point of which was the stickering of the offending publication on the shelves of various book-shops. The National Trust subsequently removed its name from the second edition.

1987: *A View to the Temple*, Documenta 8, Kassel; *A Remembrance of Annette* (the poet Annette von Droste-Hülshoff), Skulpture Projekte, Münster; *Monument to Feuerbach* at the summer sculpture exhibition, Antwerp; *Aphrodite of the Terror*, Edinburgh International Exhibition.

Homage to Ian Hamilton Finlay, exhibition at the Victoria Miro Gallery, London.

Installation of *Unda* on the campus of the University of California at San Diego, and of a rock inscribed with the signature of the Swiss artist Hodler at the Furka Pass, Switzerland.

Exhibitions in and around Paris: *Inter Artes et Naturam*, at the municipal museum of modern art; *Midway*, at the Bibliothèque Nationale; *Pastorals*, at the Claire Burrus Gallery; *Revolutionary Pursuits*, at the Cartier Foundation for Contemporary Art.

To mark the permanent installation of a French version of the monumental inscription *The Present Order . . .* in the grounds of the Cartier Foundation, the Parisian literary magazine *Digraphe* organized a ceremony in honour of Finlay. With the artist's approval, *Digraphe* decided to establish a French Section of the Saint-Just Vigilantes.

April 1987: Finlay officially commissioned by the French Ministry of Culture to submit a proposal for a garden commemorating the French Revolution and the Declaration of the Rights of Man. Work continued on another major Revolutionary project, celebrating the Jacobin Committee of Public Safety (1793–4), on the approaches to a new Paris orbital motorway.

1987–89: The French War. One of the works exhibited by Finlay in Paris (Spring 1987) gave rise to a vicious campaign of vilification directed against the artist. *Osso* uncompromisingly interrogated the status of the myth of nature at the end of a century in which a natural force (streaks of lightning) had been used to emblematize the horrific outpouring of Nazi violence. Certain sectors of the French art press mounted a campaign against the work, systematically misdescribing *Osso* without either naming it or providing an illustration of it. Reduced to its central fragment 'SS', the work served as an anonymous pretext for scurrilous attacks on its creator.

A disgruntled ex-collaborator of the artist joined in, releasing selected extracts of letters from Finlay. In the words of the French Ministry of Culture's official statement on the matter, these extracts were deliberately quoted out of context so as to suggest a meaning which the recipient of the letters knew was not intended by Finlay. A French court upheld this judgement in 1989.[17]

In the meantime, sections of the French media continued to pursue what, in its official condemnation of the defamatory attacks to which Finlay had been subjected, the authorities described as a campaign of disinformation.[18] According to the Ministry of Culture, the aftermath of the Occupation had made even trumped-up charges of Nazism and anti-semitism a highly emotive issue in France. (Indeed, any attempt by an artist to confront this painful chapter of modern history risks being deemed unacceptable, even in intellectual circles.)[19] Fearing that the abuse issuing from the press would 'infest' the celebration of the bicentenary of the French Revolution, the Ministry of Culture cancelled Finlay's Versailles project on 25 March 1988. A ministerial aide explained that France was not worthy of celebrating the bicentenary of its Revolution.[20] Finlay immediately suspended his second major Revolutionary project. The deep personal distress generated by the whole affair left an indelible mark on the artist and his family.[21]

April 1988: Symposium on the Garden Temple at Little Sparta, organized by Edinburgh University and preceded by a ceremony, 'Hommage à Ian Hamilton Finlay pour une révolution néoclassique', staged by the magazine *Digraphe* (April 21st).

1988: Finlay represented in the inaugural exhibition of contemporary British sculpture at the Tate Gallery Liverpool. The exhibition as a whole was named *Starlit*

CLASSICAL

NEOCLASSICAL

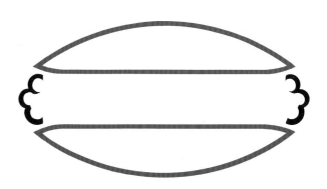

CATAMERINGUE

Classical/Neoclassical, 1987
print, with Gary Hincks

Catameringue, 1970
screen print, with Peter Grant

Wolke, 1991
neon, with Michael Harvey and Neil McLeish
Sacramento, California

'C'est dans la place . . .', 1991
neon, with Michael Harvey
Utrecht, Netherlands

Waters, after one of the Finlay pieces in the show.

Exhibition of Finlay's *Proposals* at Dunkirk. Exhibition at the Victoria Miro Gallery, London. *An Exhibition on Two Themes*, Jule Kewenig Gallery, Germany.

1989: *Bicentenary Celebrations*, Pittenweem; *Works*, Butler Gallery, Kilkenny Castle, Ireland.

1990: Exhibitions at the Hamburg Kunsthalle, the Kunsthalle Basel, and in various galleries in the USA, Germany, Italy, the UK.

Publication by the Graeme Murray Gallery, Edinburgh, of *Ian Hamilton Finlay & The Wild Hawthorn Press: a catalogue raisonné, 1958–1990*.

1991: Exhibitions in Norway, Germany, Austria and Britain.

Cythera forms the centrepiece of *Metropolis*, a major international exhibition in Berlin; two works exhibited in *Virtue and Vision*, Royal Scottish Academy.

Revolutionary Heads executed for the private library of the German architect O. M. Ungers, and work commissioned for Ungers' Karlsruhe Library. Commissions for permanent projects in Hamburg, Frankfurt and St Louis, Missouri. Also exhibitions in Lübeck and Kiel, at the Wadsworth Atheneum in the USA, in Madrid, and at the Tate Gallery, Liverpool.

A major retrospective show curated by the Graeme Murray Gallery at the Fruitmarket Gallery, Edinburgh; the exhibition travelled to Milan. Also in Edinburgh, *The Poor Fisherman*, an exhibition centred on Finlay's versions of the painting by Puvis de Chavannes, at the Talbot Rice Centre.

Official opening of the Ian Hamilton Finlay Improvements, Stockwood Nurseries, Luton – the first public garden completed by Finlay in Britain.

February–April 1992, 'Ten Maquettes for Neo-Classical Structures', Victoria Miro Gallery; 'Instruments of Revolution and other works', ICA, London.

Flute, 1991
bronze

Inter Artes et Naturam, 1988
rhododendron wood, with Keith Brookwell

Lochan Eck, Little Sparta

The Goose Hut, Little Sparta, 1982
with Andrew Townsend

'As they gazed in astonishment, and wept for the fate of their people, their old cottage, which had been small, even for two, was changed into a temple: marble columns took the place of its wooden supports, the thatch grew yellow, till the roof seemed to be made of gold . . .'   Ovid, *Metamorphoses*, Book VIII

Temple of Philemon and Baucis, 1984

a patch
on a sail

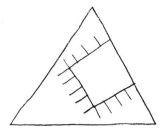

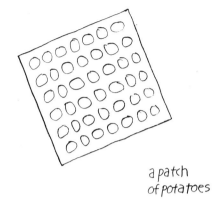

a patch
of potatoes

the patch
of a sail

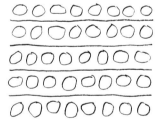

earth, patched
on potatoes

the sea, patched
with sails

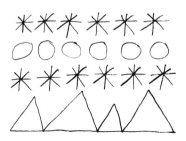

earth, patched
with potatoes

the earth, patched
with sea

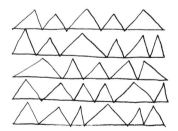

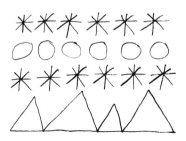

From *Ocean Stripe Series 4*, 1966
booklet, with Emil Antonucci

star potatoes
star sails

Q.1 *Which 20th Century Russian artist sometimes depicted himself as The Best Aeroplane?*

A.

Q.3 *Study the following inventory. Pick out three items to give your impression of a steam-powered herring drifter, INS 1.*

Coal-scuttle, herring-net, anchor, teapot, thimble, funnel, porthole, tea-caddy, coal-shovel, crystal-set, galley-stove, fishing-numerals, steam-pipe, fish-basket, flag.

A.

The Wild Hawthorn Art Test, 1977
booklet, with Martin Fidler

The Weed Boat Masters Ticket, Preliminary Test (Part Two), 1971
booklet, with Ian Gardner

Sombraero

Pip

Cookers and Eaters

The Mexican Navy

From *The Wild Hawthorn Wonder Book of Boats*, 1975
with Martin Fidler

The Stitch

The Windmill

The Net

The Kiss

From *Exercise X*, 1974
booklet, with George L. Thomson

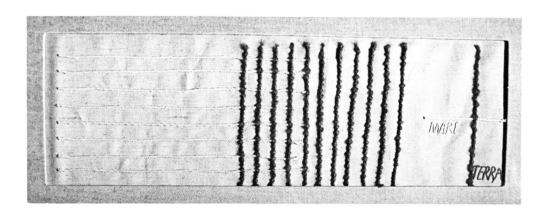

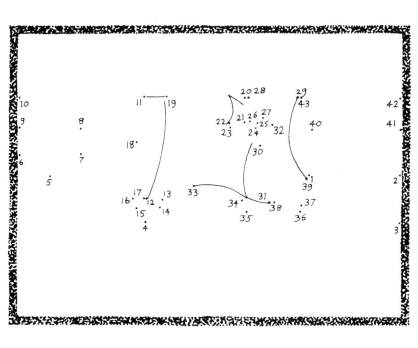

Poire/Loire, 1976
coloured pencil, with Jud Fine

Terra/Mare, 1973
embroidery, with Pamela Campion

Homage to Seurat, 1972
card, with Ron Costley

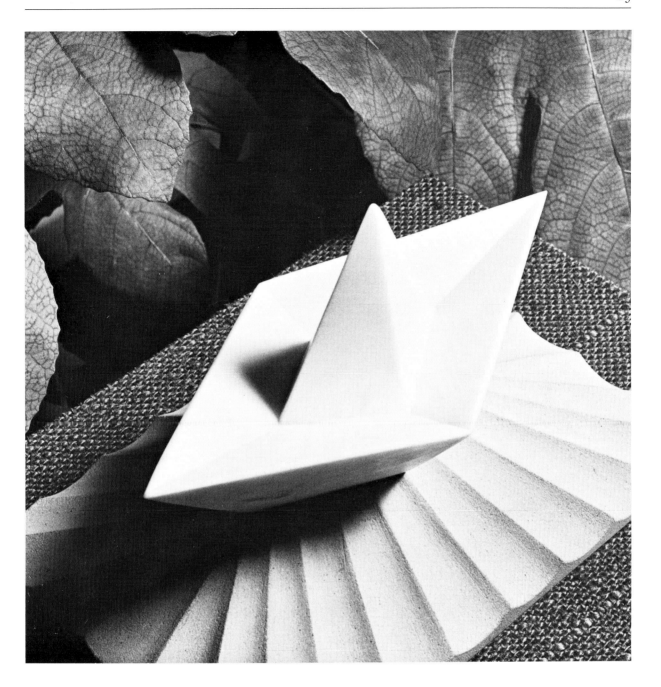

Marble Paper Boat, 1975
marble, stone, with Christopher Hall

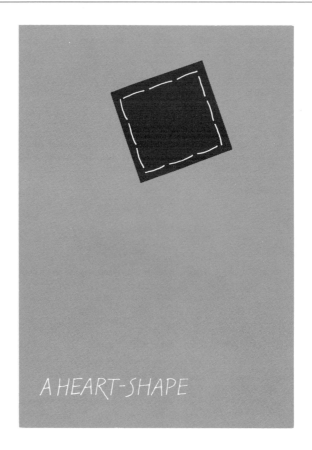

A Heart-Shape, 1971
card, with Ron Costley

A Patch . . ., 1970
card, with Ron Costley

The Sign of the Nudge, 1971
card, with Michael Harvey

National Flags Series, Valhalla, 1975
card, with Michael Harvey

AN ILLUSTRATED DICTIONARY
OF THE LITTLE SPARTAN WAR

ACHTUNG, excl. normally prefacing a pastoral warning sign.

ARCADIAN, adj. leafy, dangerous; n. a shepherd, a commando, a nymph, a satyr, a Waffen-SS man; according to Lord Byron, a blackguard.

BARK, n. the natural zimmerit texturing of the trunk & branches of a tree.

BREEZE, n. a small wind, such as rustles the branches of camouflage leaves.

CLAUDE, n. an artist of the Peace Party.

CABAL, n. a dubious conclave, as, ie. the Arts Council.

DISSIDENT, n. (if a rebel) a traditionalist; (if a reverend citizen) a rebel.

DOVECOTE, n. the barracks of the war-bird.

DRYAD, n. a tree-spirit in the likeness of a lady clothed in a camouflage-smock.

FERME ORNÉE, n. an armoured farm

INSCRIPTION, n. an arcane communication often coded in Latin.

KEEPER, n. (if of an artistic establishment) a mossy mode of Director.

MOLE, n. a creature of the underground establishment.

NEOCLASSICISM, n. a rearmament prog-ramme for architecture and the arts.

 REGION, n. an artificial place, ruled by bumpkins and bureaucrats.

 SCHUTZENPANZER, n. one of the awesome forms assumed by Pan.

 SMALL-ARM, n. a percussion instrument purporting to be a flute.

 TEMPLE, n. a sacred place; a place menaced by bailiffs.

 WATER-PISTOL, n. a pacifist weapon.

An Illustrated Dictionary of the Little Spartan War, 1983
with Nicholas Sloan, *MW Magazine*, Holland

PINK MELON JOY AND MORE
A PLAY

(Douglas Hall.) I regret that I cannot give you permission to publish any other response to your letter, even in the form of a simple answer (yes or no).

(Gertrude Stein.) All the part was distributed and the selection of more was not made before the sight was so particular that any letter had a signature.

(Lindsay Gordon.) The Region maintains that whatever the building is called it does not comply with the criteria for buildings used for religious purposes. Mr Finlay complains that he has not been given the opportunity to present his arguments which, he believes, would show that the building does comply with these criteria.

(Gertrude Stein.) Silence is not hurt by attending to taking more reflection than a whole sentence.

(The Sheriff Officer.) I have not made any arrangements to call as at the moment such a visit would be inappropriate as some of your correspondence is not being ignored.

(Gertrude Stein.) Some people are heated with linen.

(Councillor Sanderson.) A warrant sale will take place because the goods have been removed to a place of sale.

(Gertrude Stein.) A simple melancholy clearly precious and on the surface and surrounded and mixed strangely.

(Douglas Hall.) I think that all possible means to this end should be considered by all the parties concerned.

A corner of the Garden Temple, Little Sparta, after Strathclyde Region's Budget Day Raid.

Wax-drippings are from the stolen candlesticks TERROR and VIRTUE. Accompanying documentation, *la liberte ou la mort 1789* (centre), is a study of the rhetoric of the Revolution by the French poet Roche. All the works stolen were separated from their written parts (integral to them) and so were left as fragments. Photograph by John Stathatos. Published by The Committee of Public Safety, Little Sparta.

Pink Melon Joy, 1984
card

Terror/Virtue: After Strathclyde Region's assault on the Garden Temple, Little Sparta, 1983
card, with John Stathatos

Néoclassicisme Révolutionnaire, 1988
screen print, with Gary Hincks

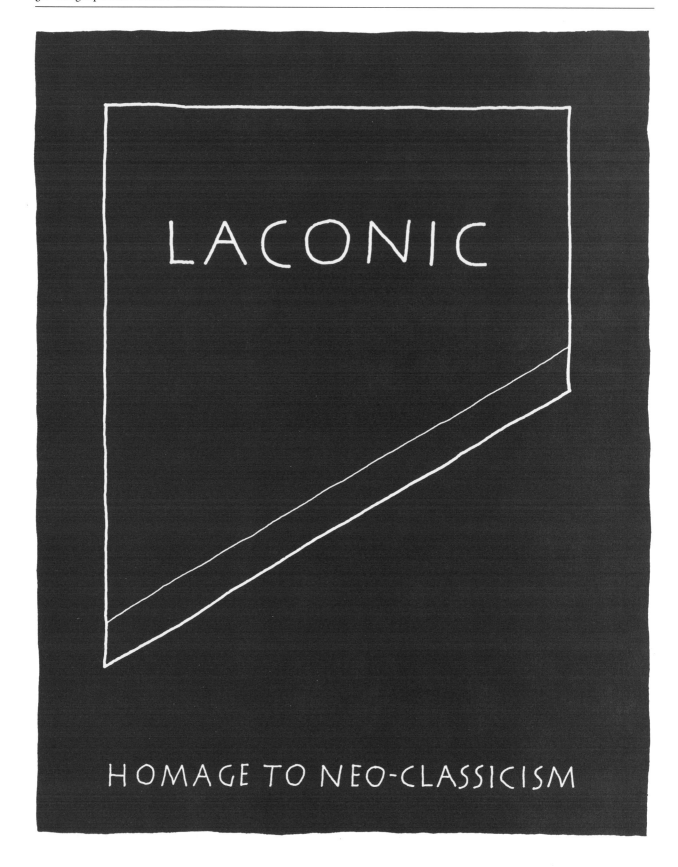

Laconic, 1987
screen print, with Ron Costley

IAN HAMILTON FINLAY · GARY HINCKS · WILD HAWTHORN PRESS · LITTLE SPARTA

COUNTERCOMPOSITION

Countercomposition, 1989
screen print, with Gary Hincks

The Harbour at Gravelines, 'in familiar mottle camouflage',
after Seurat, 1978
screen print, with Gary Hincks

Ceci n'est pas une pipe.

After Magritte, 1991
print, with Gary Hincks

Detached Sentences on Friendship

Ian Hamilton Finlay

Illustrations by
Kathleen Lindsley

WILD HAWTHORN PRESS

He who lives alone is always
on sentry duty.

With a friend we are neither
in company nor alone.

Friends who cannot speak each
other's language are spared the
degradation of small talk.

Friendship is *inclination*,
acquaintance *geography*.

The wind, roaring in the night, is
both stranger and friend.

Two is solitude, three is a crowd.

Friends who seem to have deserted
us may have deserted themselves.

Friends are placed beside each other
in battle. *Saint-Just*.

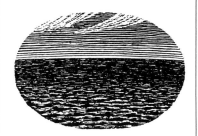

When our friends leave us, they take
away our shores.

from *Detached Sentences on Friendship*, 1991
booklet, with Kathleen Lindsley

PART I

PART I

 1 Entrance to Front Garden
 2 Roman Garden
 3 Henry Vaughan Walk
 4 Sunk Garden
 5 Mare Nostrum
 6 Raspberry Camouflage
 7 Sundial (Fragments/Fragrance)
 8 Julie's Garden
 9 'Das grosse Rasenstück'
10 Temple Pool
11 Temple of Philemon and Baucis
12 Lararium
13 Allotment (Epicurean) Garden
14 Pacific Air War Inscribed Stone
15 C. D. Friedrich Pyramid
16 Claudi Bridge
17 Xaipe after J. C. Reinhart
18 Grotto of Aeneas and Dido
19 Hypothetical Gateway to
     an Academy of Mars

20 Hillside Pantheon
21 'Silver Cloud'
22 Virgil's Spring
23 Upper Pool
24 Middle Pool
25 Apollo and Daphne
26 Nuclear Sail
27 Lochan Eck
28 Hegel Stile
29 Midway Inscription
30 'The Present Order . . .'
31 Laugier's Hut
32 Saint-Just's Column
33 O Tannenbaum
34 Tristram's Sail (Sundial)
35 Garden Temple
36 Monument to The First Battle
     of Little Sparta

drawing by Gary Hincks, 1992

1 STONYPATH
THE GARDEN & TEMPLE

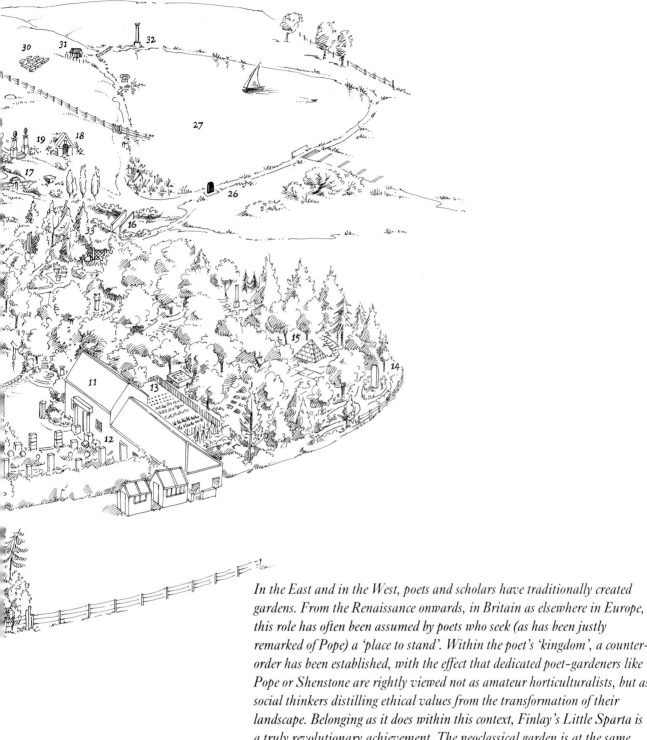

The Garden

In the East and in the West, poets and scholars have traditionally created gardens. From the Renaissance onwards, in Britain as elsewhere in Europe, this role has often been assumed by poets who seek (as has been justly remarked of Pope) a 'place to stand'. Within the poet's 'kingdom', a counter-order has been established, with the effect that dedicated poet-gardeners like Pope or Shenstone are rightly viewed not as amateur horticulturalists, but as social thinkers distilling ethical values from the transformation of their landscape. Belonging as it does within this context, Finlay's Little Sparta is a truly revolutionary achievement. The neoclassical garden is at the same time a model of society, in which each aspect of cultural activity, like each botanical specimen, has been granted its appropriate place.

From 'Unconnected Sentences on Gardening'

A garden is not an object but a process.

Installing is the hard toil of garden making, *placing* is its pleasure.

Superior gardens are composed of Glooms and Solitudes and not of plants and trees.

A liberal's compost heap is his castle.

Garden centres must become the Jacobin Clubs of the new Revolution.

Solitude in gardens is an aspect of *scale*.

Certain gardens are described as retreats when they are really attacks.

Trees are preserved by manners, not by economy wrappers.

Ecology is Nature-Philosophy *secularised*.

The murmur of innumerable bills was known to most great gardeners.

From 'More Detached Sentences on Gardening in the Manner of Shenstone'

Gardening activity is of five kinds, namely, sowing, planting, fixing, placing, maintaining. In so far as gardening is an Art, all these may be taken under the one head, composing.

Better than truth to materials is truth to intelligence.

The inscription seems out of place in the modern garden. It jars on our secularism by suggesting *the hierarchies of the word*.

Brown made water and lawns (&c.) Palladian elements, as much as Lord Burlington did, his columns and porticos.

Brown made water appear as Water, and lawn as Lawn.

The gardens of Kent and Brown were mistakenly referred to the Chinese aesthetic, just as today's thoughtful gardens are considered to be Japanese. 'Japanese garden' has come to signify no more than 'art garden'. The contemporary 'sculpture park' is not – and is not considered to be – an art garden, but an art gallery out-of-doors. It is a parody of the classical garden native to the West.

The main division of gardens is into art gardens and botanical gardens. Compared to this division all the others – 'The Garden as Music', 'The Garden as a Poem' – & etc. – are superficial.

As public sex was embarrassing to the Victorians, public classicism is to us.

Composition is a forgotten Art.

Artificial gardens – as Lamb describes them – now strike us as not at all artificial, since they have been made 'natural' by time.

Woodland Garden   General view of Temple Pool

Nuclear Sail, 1974
slate, with John Andrew

Obelisk, Upper Pool, 1982
stone, with Nicholas Sloan

Pond Inscription, by the Temple Pool, 1969
stone, with Maxwell Allan

Woodland Garden with Herm, 1982
stone, with John Andrew

Island, with Silver Cloud, Upper Pool

Aircraft carrier Bird-Table, 1972
stone

The Present Order, 1983
stone, with Nicholas Sloan

Claude Lorrain from 'Nature Over Again After Poussin', 1980
stone, with Nicholas Sloan

Claude's bridge, 1982
with Nicholas Sloan

Aircraft carrier Fountain, 1972, bronze

Caddis shell/Goddess shell, 1976, stone, with Keith Bailey

Dürer's signature, the Woodland Garden, 1980
stone, with Nicholas Sloan

Fly Navy, in the Roman Garden, 1980,
stone, with John Andrew

Elegiac inscription, by the Upper Pool, 1975
stone, with John Andrew

Epicurus Herm, 1982, stone, with John Andrew

General view: Woodland Garden

Pool inscription, 1979
stone, engraved bronze, with Keith Bailey

Terra/Mare, Front Garden, 1974
wood, with George L. Thomson

The Land's Shadows, sundial, 1974
stone, with Michael Harvey

Tristram's Sail, sundial, 1971
slate and stone, with Michael Harvey

H)our Lady, sundial, 1978
stone, with Graeme Murray and Ron Costley

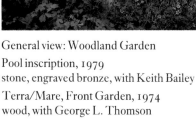

The Woodland Garden

Lettered slabs in the Front Garden, 1974
cast concrete, with Michael Harvey

'The Great Piece of Turf', Temple Pool, 1975
(see Albrecht Dürer's watercolour 'Das grosse Rasenstück')

By the Upper Pool

A corner of the Front Garden   The Front Garden: towards the Roman Garden

'Silver Cloud', 1973
inscribed marble, with Michael Harvey

Midway, 1974
slate, with Michael Harvey

Herm (Hypnos, god of sleep), 1984
with Alexander Stoddart

All the noble
sentiments of my heart,
all its most praiseworthy
impulses – *I could give them
free rein, in the midst of
this solitary wood.*

Louvet plaque, 1991
tree-plaque, with Andrew Whittle
Jean-Baptiste Louvet (1760–97), Girondist deputy, author of
the romantic novel *Faublas*. An enemy of Robespierre, soon
proscribed by the Jacobins, Louvet lived for a time a
Rousseauesque existence as a fugitive in the forest of the
Jura.

Apollo and Daphne, 1987
sheet-metal, with Ron Costley

Gate Piers, The Garden, Little Sparta, 1991
with David Edwick

Lararium with a sculpture of Apollo – Saint-Just, 1986
bronze, with Andrew Townsend and Alexander Stoddart

With yellow pears . . ., after Hölderlin's *Hälfte des Lebens*,
1985
stone, with Keith Bailey

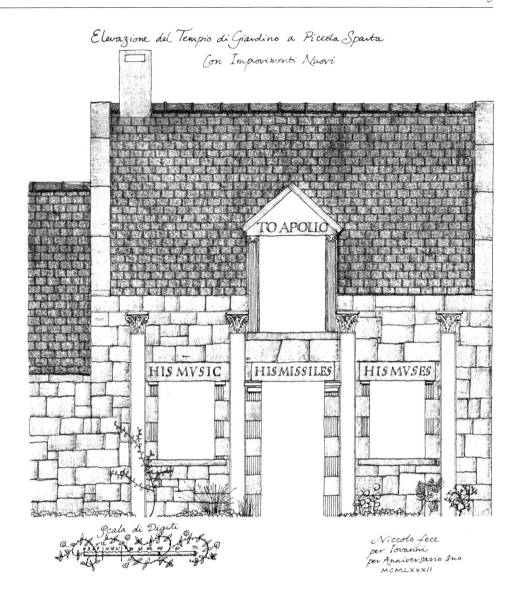

Elevazione del Tempio di Giardino a Piccola Sparta
Con Improvimenti Nuovi

TO APOLLO

HIS MVSIC   HIS MISSILES   HIS MVSES

Scala di Digiti

Niccolo fece
per Iovanni
per Anniversario suo
MCMLXXXII

The Temple

Classical writers recount that the 'Musaea' of ancient Greece, dedicated to the Muses as protectors of the Arts and Sciences, were often situated in gardens. In more recent times, the great European gardens have almost always incorporated temples; both ancient Virtue and the modern British Worthies are celebrated at Stowe, both Flora the goddess of flowers and the Sun God Apollo at Stourhead. At Little Sparta, there was first of all a simple agricultural building in the farm courtyard. Then a gallery was created there. In time, with the 'neoclassical rearmament' of the garden, this metamorphosed into a Temple, which concentrates within its solemn interior space the cultural message of the surrounding territory. Apollo has migrated far from his native Greece; he is the pale 'Hyperborean Apollo' visiting the northern regions, of whom Heine and Pater write. His modern avatar is the French revolutionary, Saint-Just.

Apollon Terroriste, 1988
resin and gold leaf, with Alexander Stoddart   Drawing by Nicholas Sloan, 1982

Inscriptions in the Garden Temple
stone

The Garden Temple, Little Sparta

In the Garden Temple

In the Garden Temple

In the Garden Temple

2 LITERACY
TRADITIONAL & MODERN

Short Stories and Rhyming Poems

Finlay's first published works were short stories, which appeared in a collected edition in 1958. In retrospect, they appear to anticipate his characteristic choice of poetic imagery. In one story, 'The Boy and the Guess', the narrator challenges a boy to find the common feature between certain well-known occupants of the sea and a 'string of sturdy little hill ponies'. By the end of the tale, we know (although we have not actually been told) that the answer lies in the equation between the hill ponies and the fishing-boats, one of which is finally seen 'skipping away' out to the open sea. By 1964, when Finlay published his first 'poster-poem', Le Circus, this equation could be made without the ploy of the guessing game. Fishing-boat and circus pony are identified in boldly juxtaposed words, as each jumps (both jump) through 'the rainbow's hoop'.

Outside this perspective, of course, the short stories have their own place in a particularly Scottish tradition. Finlay felt himself close to a number of writers of the 1920's and 1930's, such as John Macnair Reid, who had been virtually forgotten by the post-war years, and were later recalled to favour in the anthologies at least in part by his own efforts. But even at this stage his allegiances are not confined to Scotland. The dust-jacket of The Sea-Bed and Other Stories *hails him as a 'Symbolist in – roughly – the tradition' of the Russian writer Sologub.*

Finlay's rhyming poems, collected in 1960 in The Dancers Inherit the Party, *have similarly broad allegiances. When the American poet Lorine Niedecker read them, she was convinced that Finlay had read her own writings and had been influenced by them. But this was certainly not the case. Perhaps the paradox that an original form of poetic diction can be both strictly local, and yet also international in its ramifications, is only an apparent one. Finlay's poems in Glaswegian dialect, vehemently repudiated by senior Scottish figures like MacDiarmid, helped to forge a link with contemporary American poets like Robert Creeley.*

A Broken Engagement

When I was young and we had our money – we lost it afterwards – we kept a maid. That is, we kept several, one after another, but I remember only one of them, the maid Peggy, a plump, grown-up girl with rowan-berry-red cheeks, black hair, a white apron and a black dress . . .

Our house was two-storied, and Peggy must have had a bedroom in it, but the kitchen was really more her place. I mean 'her place' in the nice sense: the place you would normally go to look for her, and where, in the evening when the work was finished, she was free to amuse herself just as I was in the drawing-room upstairs. The kitchen was downstairs, in the basement. This was just under ground level and was reached by a flight of old-fashioned, steep stone stairs which were lit by a gas-lamp even by day.

I used to go down there a lot in the evening, after tea. At that hour, with the several straight-backed chairs tidied, the table newly scrubbed, and the day's dishes and pots and pans washed and laid by, there was a feeling in there like that of a sunset – a beautiful, still, sad sunset when the birch and pine trees, even the brackens, are so very, very still it is as if they have been bewitched . . . Just such a feeling was over the chairs, the dewy table, the neatly stacked dishes and the shining pots and pans that hung in a row from the same shelf.

'Peggy?' I would say as I came in. 'Peggy? – Peggy draw me a face.'

She might be seated in front of the big kitchen range which, being now closed and banked-up for the evening, was – in this indoor sunset – the equivalent of that faraway, bright rosy band above the woods. Or else she might be seated, hands propping her chin, at the table, bent over a love-story magazine, a weekly magazine printed on a coarse, off-white sort of paper and with illustrations in black line.

Almost certainly she would agree to draw me a face. And, in practice, that meant several faces, copied either from the illustrations to the love-stories in the magazine or from those to the advertisements (for corsets, cheap scent, and so on) that appeared on the pages towards the back. She would stand up, and crossing to the shelf beneath that for the dishes, she would fetch the writing-pad, the pencil and india rubber; then, having carefully sharpened the pencil to a fine point with the old kitchen-knife, she would begin to draw me a face . . .

How can I say how lovely it was? I would lean up close to her, my elbows on the table, scarcely breathing – breathing very slowly through my open mouth while I held my tongue curled up just as if there was some mysterious, radar connection between the carefulness of the moving pencil-point, and *its* . . . Then, after a while, a sort of painless pins-and-needles would start to creep up on me, beginning, I think, in about the knees; and after another while I was half-asleep . . . As for the face Peggy drew, it was one with long, literally shiny eyelashes, two dots for nostrils, smiling rosebud lips, and bobbed hair. (This I pictured as being of a brown colour.) And, as soon as one face was completed, 'Now draw me another, Peggy,' I would say. Because I couldn't bear that she should stop drawing and so break the magical spell . . .

One night I met my mother at the head of the stairs down to the basement. She said, 'You're not to go down to see Peggy tonight.'

'Oh, but Mummy,' I protested, 'why can't I?'

'Never mind! Why should you, a child, be told why you can't? You just aren't to go down; that's all.'

I turned and went into the drawing-room, but later, my mother having for some reason gone up to her bedroom, I did go downstairs.

Everything in the sunset kitchen was just as usual, except that an unfamiliar, grown-up young man was seated on a kitchen chair, opposite Peggy, to one side of the range. He was seated very upright and very silent; and he wore a blue suit and had a red face and hands which, spread out stiffly on his blue knees, were exactly the colour of Lifebuoy soap. What was *he* doing here? I thought. And as he, it seemed to me, was ignoring Peggy, I decided to ignore him, too.

'Peggy?' I said. 'Peggy? Peggy, draw me a face.'

Imagine my astonishment when she shook her head and said, 'No. No faces tonight. Just you be a good little boy and run away back upstairs.'

And the young man, suddenly taking his eyes, as it were, from that rosy band above the woods, said, 'Go on, sonny. Listen. There's your Mummy calling you. Now run along.'

That, of course, was untrue, but I went. I left the two of them alone there, silent, their straight-backed chairs like two separate rocks. I wondered if they really were as bored as they seemed.

And after that the young man came into the kitchen in the evening quite often. Harry something was his name. Once he had a thick bandage across two fingers of his right hand. Peggy said he had hurt it at his work. He always sat very upright and very silent, and then he pretended to hear my mother calling me from somewhere upstairs. One night when he wasn't there I noticed that Peggy was wearing a new ring . . .

'What's that?' I asked her.

I spoke softly, but even so I broke the magical spell that lay on us as we sat drawing faces out of the love-story magazine.

'That?' said Peggy. 'That's a ring.'

'Yes, I know,' I said. 'But what's it for, that ring?'

'It's an engagement ring,' she said.

'An engagement ring – what's that?'

'It means I'm going to be married.'

'Now?'

'Soon.'

'To Harry?'

'Yes, to Harry.'

'Oh. Now draw me another face. You've spoiled that face,' I said.

And the young man, Harry, came more, and then still more often. So that we never drew faces. I have the impression that he was in the kitchen – Peggy's kitchen – every night. And a long time, maybe four or five whole weeks, passed. The bad time had an end one night when, as I came into the kitchen expecting to see Harry there, I found Peggy all alone and, as I thought, fast asleep. Her arms were folded across the love-story magazine, which wasn't open, and her head was laid on her arms.

'Peggy? Peggy?' I said shaking her by the shoulder. 'Peggy, draw me a face.'

After all, she wasn't asleep, but she didn't look up then – only shook her head once or twice.

'Oh go on,' I pleaded. 'Be a pal. Just one face.'

'No, please.' She shook her head again, several times. 'Please no faces tonight.'

'Oh *please*, Peggy. Please. Just one. If you do –,' I hesitated, '– if you do you'll be my best pal, for life.'

So Peggy stood up, and she went through the beautiful, still, sad sunset to fetch the drawing things from the shelf. Her eyes were swollen and red round the edges as though, maybe, she had been crying; and as she stood sharpening her pencil with the old kitchen knife I could see a red mark on her finger where she had had the ring. Then she opened the love-story magazine and began to draw me a face. I leaned up close to her, scarcely breathing; the painless pins-and-needles crept slowly up me. It was lovely! . . . Soon I was half-asleep.

From *The Sea-Bed and Other Stories*, 1958
Alna Press

ORKNEY LYRICS

One
Peedie Mary Considers the Sun

The peedie sun is not so tall
He walks on golden stilts
Across, across, across the water
But I have darker hair.

Two
The English Colonel Explains an Orkney Boat

The boat swims full of air.
You see, it has a point at both
Ends, sir, somewhat
As lemons. I'm explaining

The hollowness is amazing. That's
The way a boat
Floats.

Three
Mansie Considers Peedie Mary

Peedie Alice Mary is
My cousin, so we cannot kiss.
And yet I love my cousin fair:
She wears her seaboots with such an air.

Four
Wash Day

Rub-a-dub-dub, the moon in a tub
Till it shines like a seaboot stocking.
Rub-a-dub-dub, rub-a-dub-dub,
Then pop it back in its stocking.

Five
Mansie Considers the Sea
in the Manner of Hugh MacDiarmid

The sea, I think, is lazy,
It just obeys the moon
– All the same I remember what Engels said:
'Freedom is the consciousness of necessity'.

Six
Folk Song for Poor Peedie Mary

Peedie Mary
Bought a posh
Big machine
To do her wash.

Peedie Mary
Stands and greets

Where dost thoo
Put in the peats?

Silly peedie
Mary thoo
Puts the peats
Below, baloo.

Peedie Mary
Greets the more,
What did the posh paint
Come off for?

Seven
John Sharkey Is Pleased to Be in Sourin at Evening

How beautiful, how beautiful, the mill
–Wheel is not turning though the waters spill
Their single tress. The whole old mill
Leans to the West, the breast.

'Peedie' is the Orkney word for 'wee'. Many Orkney girls
have two Christian names, and many Orkney men are called
'Mansie', which is the diminutive of 'Magnus'.

OPTIMIST

My would-be father, old and slow,
Did buy himself a kind of tin-
Can for brewing proper, out-of-door tea in.
The bloody fire, though, it wouldn't go.

It was the bloody wet sticks, and everything.
Alone he kneeled on the out-of-door grass,
Blowing with love. I remember how, home again,
He brewed wild tea on the domestic gas.

THE WRITER AND BEAUTY

The best a writer writes is Beautiful.
He should ignore the Mad and Dutiful.

Meanwhile, of course, the Lie is there,
The posh Lie struts in the social air

And writers write it, and it is
Part of the analyst's neurosis.

Well, a writer should defy
It. A writer writes of sky

And other things quite sad and Beautiful.
He should ignore the Mad and Dutiful.

See how lame and blind he goes.
See how he dances on his toes!

From *The Dancers Inherit the Party*, 1960
Migrant Press

see me
wan time
ah wis a fox
an wis ah sleekit! ah
gaed slinkin
            heh
an snappin
            yeh
the blokes
aa sayed ah wis a GREAT fox
aw nae kiddin
ah wis pretty good
had a whole damn wood
in them days
hen

anither
time
ah wis a
minnie
aw
the pond
haw
the shoogly caur
gaun
see s
a frond
fir
ma wee jaur

an wance
ah wis a zebra
heh heh
crossin

From *Glasgow Beasts, An a Burd*, 1961

Metaphors and Metamorphoses

Reference has already been made to the short story from 1958, which opens this section, and to the 'poster-poem' from 1964 which closes it. At the centre of each is the same metaphor – the fishing-boat as pony – though the narrative form of the story and the visual immediacy of the poster ensure that we read the two works in very different ways. All of the other pieces here, whether they date from before or after Finlay's abandonment of traditional prosody, encapsulate a metaphor. Or perhaps it would be more accurate to say that they enact a metamorphosis. The lobster becomes a helicopter (a process which was once enacted in reverse when aerial television cameras sidled up to Stonypath along the Dunsyre valley!). The track along which the ship steers becomes (in Edward Wright's typographical version from 1967) a dense array of rigging in which the guiding 'star' is caught.

Tugs and Barges

The tug has a more ambiguous persona than the fishing-boat. Identified first of all by his cheery sound (toot), he plays at being a circus-pony, then simulates the roaring of a bull (toro). Associated with a near-homonym in Gothic type (Der Tag), he parodies the masthead of a German newspaper. The barges which he brings behind him are less self-assured in their nomenclature. Their names suggest spinsters and songbirds, parrots in cages and afternoon tea.

Found Poems

Four of the preceding barge names were invented (Names for Barges), and three of them taken from actual boats (Names of Barges). Finlay was able to find in nautical almanacs and newspapers a range of specific and suggestive names which opened up miniature worlds of congenial symbolism. But the interpretation of these names, for and by the reader, depends upon the degree of success with which they are presented, graphically and typographically, upon the page. Rough stencilled capitals evoke the fishing-boat name in its original, functional expression. Eloquent drawings form a backdrop, conjuring up perhaps those adventitious sheep by means of which the mythic Odysseus escaped from the Cyclops' cave!

The Boy and the Guess

It was a fine, sunny, summer day. I suddenly decided I would go for a walk to the end of the rocks. They ran in parallel rows, like railway platforms, from the foot of the blue-shadowed cliffs right into the middle of the bay. On the top of the cliffs was the old town with its grey, ruined spires and bright red roofs, all shining in the sun. The tide was full-out.

I kept on to the very end of the row of rocks, and there a boy was already seated, dangling his bare toes over the calm water. He was one of those immemorial young boys with a thick, blue, hand-knitted jersey and bare, thin, brown legs caked with the white salt from the sea. As I came up, he turned his head, and he glanced at me lazily out of half-open eyes, as though the eyelashes, too, were caked with salt and were too sore to open wider.

'When I came down these rocks,' he said in a slow, thin, drawling voice, 'I had brown hair, but now it's been turned yellow by the sun.'

I looked at his hair but, of course, it was still brown. Then I looked out over the water to where a fishing-boat with a rough, red-brown canvas sail, and with glass net-floats as green as grasshoppers' eyes stacked by the wheel-house, was drifting very slowly around the point of the long rocks next to our own. Then, all at once, there came a puff of wind; the boat's sail filled out, and, with two sort of hops and a glide, it was gone. It was hidden by the rocks. A puff of black smoke from the helmsman's clay-pipe came drifting back towards us across the bay.

'Do you know any riddles?' I asked the boy, as I took a seat on the rock.

He gazed down past his toes to where, on the bottom of the sea, amid the mysterious, dark seaweed, beyond the ledge of our own rock, there was a patch of bright yellow sand.

'No,' he answered after a moment, shaking his toes in a sleepy negative way so that the salt or perhaps the sand-grains between them cracked a little. 'I don't think I do. But do you know any?' he asked.

'I just thought of one,' I said. 'At least, it's maybe not a real riddle that rhymes. It's more, I think, what you'd call a guess – a thing that you've to guess from my hints.'

'Give it to me, then,' said the boy. And, nodding his toes rather doubtfully, he added: – 'But you'll have to give me big hints.'

'Then here's a big hint to start with,' I said. 'This thing – that you've to guess – it's like a pony in this way, it is tied up with a rope when it is not in use. In fact, you often see several of them tied up together, in a certain quiet place, and then they are like a string of sturdy little hill ponies hobbled there, tied together nose-to-tail, and all, as it were, nibbling at the grass below a high dyke.'

As I ended the hint, another puff of wind brought the faint tinkling of the sand-donkeys' harness-bells and the shouts of the children who were having rides. They were hidden from us behind the curve of the cliffs.

'Well, did you get it yet?' I asked him.

His toes made polite, thoughtful movements. Half of his mind was on the guess, and half was still on the sand-patch, which was about a yard square, while the water was at least a dozen feet deep. The tide, by then, was on the turn, too. At any moment a big, bearded codfish might cross the sand, like a tiger a clearing in the jungle.

'No,' he said, 'I didn't get it yet. I think you'll have to give me a bigger hint.'

'Then this thing is like a pony in another way,' I went on. 'I don't mean in its moral character, though they may have that in common as well. No, it's like a pony in this way, that if you were standing on a high rock and then this thing came slowly ambling underneath the rock, like a pony might, you would get an awful itch in your toes. You would start to wiggle your toes and then, suddenly, with a yell like that of a cossack or of a wild, drunken tinker, you would take a flying jump down. Down, you see, onto this thing. Now have you got it?' I asked.

'No, I still haven't got it,' said the boy. 'You might see a big fish down there,' he added, pointing with one big-toe at the sand-patch.

'Then think of a caravan instead,' I said. 'Not one of those horrible, streamlined, modern caravans, but one of the old kind with a door made in two halves, so you can keep the bottom half shut, to lean your elbows on, while the top half is still open and you can gaze out . . .'

'What would you see?' he asked me.

I scratched the salt-grains in my yellow hair. 'What would you see? Well, you'd see the sad, blue smoke from your own chimney, and . . . and then some thin little trees . . . crooked trees with the loch behind. And then, of course, you'd see your horse. Your poor old horse tied up to a tree with a long bit of rope that would rustle in the grass when he shook his head.'

'Got it!' exclaimed the boy, his toes twitching with excitement, 'it's a horse!'

'Silly,' I said, 'it is not a horse.'

'But it was you yourself said it was tied up with a rope,' he protested.

'All the same, it isn't a horse,' I said. 'And besides, the horse is irrelevant. It's the old caravan we're concerned with. For this thing – that you haven't guessed yet – is like a caravan in this way, it is very exciting to go inside. Just as it's nicer in a caravan than in a house, so this is more exciting than a caravan. Only you go down into it instead of up.'

'Has it wheels?' asked the boy.

'No,' I said, 'it hasn't wheels. It has – oh, better than wheels.'

'Wings?'

'No, better. Better even than wings. And you would probably have to bend down while you were inside, and you might be offered a big mug of tea. Boiling hot, black tea with condensed milk.'

'No,' said the boy, now shaking his toes quite despondently, – 'no, I'll never get it. It's too hard. But then,' he added, 'I'm only thirteen.'

And just with that, the same fishing-boat came drifting slowly back around the point of the next rocks. There was a sudden puff of wind, and the rough, red-brown canvas sail filled out. Then the boat came gliding smoothly right under the lee of our own rock.

The boy was on his feet in an instant. He began to wiggle his toes and then, suddenly, with a wild, delirious, ringing yell, he leaped down on the deck. There came a second puff of wind, and the boat skipped away out to the open sea. I sat on there, watching the sand-patch, wondering if a big, bearded cod-fish would swim in with the tide. Sometimes I could hear the sand-donkeys' bells.

From *The Sea-Bed and Other Stories*, 1958
Alna Press

CASTLES

One man is chosen king of every castle
Whose bricks are soft as snow or crumbling clay.
Embedded in them here and there's a thistle.
The game is for a June or July day.

The others have to stay below the castle.
Like servants or like slaves they never say
It's their turn to be kings. Can they not wrestle?
They should have shots at each, alternately.

The kings, however, also build the castle.
The work is slow and serious – and gay.
Whole hordes of castles harden as they settle.
The kings leap down and land in moats of hay.

CATCH

There once was a fisherman of Scrabster
Caught in his pot a gey queer lapster.

Thought he, this lapster's a sure seller,
A tail it has, and a wee propellor,

In fact, it's no ordinary lapster felly,
It looks far more like a peedie heli –

You know yon kind of hoverlapster,
A what do you call it, helicapster.

Aye, aye, it's a peedie helicapster:
There's lots are caught in the sea off Scrabster.

From *The Dancers Inherit the Party*, 1960
Migrant Press

ring of waves

row of nets

string of lights

row of fish

ring of nets

row of roofs

string of fish

ring of light

netnetnetnet
netnetnetnear
netnet
netnear
netnetnetnetnetnetnetnet
netnetnetnetnetnetnetnear
net
near
netnetnetnetnetnetnetnetnetnetnetnet
netnetnetnetnetnetnetnetnetnetnetnear
netnetnetnetnetnetnetnetnetnetnetneat

'Ring of Waves', 1968

From *Poor. Old. Tired. Horse.* 13

star
star
star
s t a r
star
star
star
star
star
star
star
star
steer

le circus!!

on the right, a red blinker

smack

K47

and crew

they
leap
BARE-BACK
through
the
rainbow's

also

corks

nets

etc.

hoop

on the left, a green blinker

'Star/Steer', 1966
screen print, with Edward Wright
Tarasque Press
'. . . The wise is one, knowing the plan by which it steers all things through all.' Heraclitus.

Poster Poem, 1964
screen print
A pastiche which treats both early dada and the Scottish fishing-boat K47 with cheerful affection

THE TUG

Tug at Bay

Where the fishers wait for bites
Toots the little tug – in tights!

Round each river bend and loop
TOOT! – like through a circus-hoop.

The Towns say Tut, that boat's not black,
It's far more like a Union Jack!

The Steadings never even peep
Because they are all fast asleep!

So on and on, for hours and hours . . .
The sky is blue, each bank's all flowers.

And when for Tea the Captain whistles
The crew sit down to spangled rissoles!

roar
rora
oaro
atro
roat
taor
rota
toro
orot
otro
toto
otot
toot

From *Poor. Old. Tired. Horse.* 13

From *Tea-leaves and Fishes*, 1966
booklet

'Der Tag', 1972
card, with Ron Costley

3 Names of Barges, 1969
card, with Margot Sandeman

GREEN WATERS
BLUE SPRAY
GRAYFISH

ANNA T
KAREN B
NETTA CROAN

CONSTANT STAR
DAYSTAR
STARWOOD

STARLIT WATERS
MOONLIT WATERS
DRIFT

'Green Waters', from *The Blue and the Brown Poems*, 1968
Jargon Press, USA

SAVED BY HELICOPTER

Two fishermen were plucked from certain death after their lobster boat, the *Morning Star*, ran aground at Needles Eye.

The plight of the *Morning Star* was seen by another boat, the *Twilight*, which raced to raise the alarm.

A helicopter then arrived on the scene and winched the fishermen to safety.

Attempts to salvage the *Morning Star* began on Thursday morning.

From *A Sailor's Calendar*, 1971
with Gordon Huntley
Something Else Press, USA

ML   METHIL.

From *The Olsen Excerpts*, 1971
Verlag Udo Breger, West Germany

DE   DUNDEE.
  38 Constance (am)
  65 Shelagh Ann (m)

GN   GRANTON.
16 Granton Falcon (m)
18 Lothian Leader (m)
19 Granton Osprey (am)

72 Granton Merlin (m)
73 Schiehallion (m)
77 Granton Harrier
                    (m)

One-Wo

An Inlan

K   KIRKWALL.
  259 Amber Queen (m)
  680 Radiant Queen (am)
  742 Laurel (am)
  827 Smiling Morn (m)
  867 Lilac (m)
  880 Enterprise (m)
  885 Evelyn (m)
  892 Silver Fern II (m)
  896 Achilles (am)
  914 Flourish (m)
  916 Ocean's Gift (m)
  919 Girl Mina (am)

THE BOAT'S BLUEPRINT

water

WAVE

a v ē

RING

net

DOVE

THE CLOUD'S ANCHOR

swallow

From *Peter*
booklet, wit

From *Stonechats*, 1967

One-Word Poems

In the mid-1960s, Finlay was a notable participant in the international movement of concrete poetry, and one of his contributions was the propagation of the 'one-word poem', a mode which he anthologised in his magazine Poor.Old.Tired.Horse. No.25. Although it owed something to the reductive forms of concrete poetry, and no doubt to the contemporary cult of the Japanese haiku, the one-word poem had other connotations as well. Apollinaire had written one-line poems at the height of the Modern Movement, but, a millenium before Apollinaire, Carolingian scholar-poets had polished up their Latinity through poetic riddles (Q. 'What is Autumn?' A. 'The Barn of the Year.'). The unvarnished simplicity of the one-word poem – formed from a word and a title – puts us in mind of the didactic examples of rhetoric and grammar in the Classical tradition. 'The Cloud's Anchor / swallow', with its formal alignment of the worlds of the sea and the sky, suggests the Aristotelian definition of a metaphor of proportion. Although Finlay originally expressed his one-word poems on the printed page, he was to identify their 'classical' feeling by using them for some of his first ventures into epigraphy – the practice of inscription of stone.

An Inland Garden

Little Sparta, the garden at Stonypath, is not (in William Morris' term) 'A Garden by the Sea'. But it is an inland garden where reminiscences and evocations of the Sea are omnipresent. This small group of cards and prints takes as its basis the invitation to envisage the garden – with its inland lakes and its abundant vegetation – as a microcosm of the faraway Ocean. Like sea-shells placed to the ear, trees will conjure up the sounds of adjacent water. Home – in this case, perhaps, the cottage of Stonypath, perched above the steeply rising track – is to be compared to the final port, which the boat evokes in its receding wake.

Elegy

At Stonypath, the Ocean is one absent domain. Another is the classical world, to which its inscriptions and citations repeatedly return. The elegiac is the note of feeling which pervades all of these fragmentary references to a lost order.

THE BOAT'S BLUEPRINT

water

WAVE

a v ē

RING

net

DOVE

THE CLOUD'S ANCHOR

s w a l l o w

From *Stonechats*, 1967

DEEP-V HULL
geese

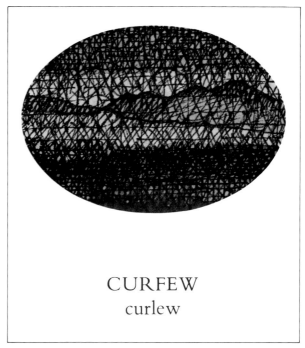

CURFEW
curlew

MOORLAND
marquetry

OSIRIS
osiers

From '*35 One-Word Poems*', 1983/4
with Ian Gardner

TREE-SHELLS

Instructions: Apply ear to Tree-shell.
Listen for Lakes.

They returned home tired
but happy.   The End.

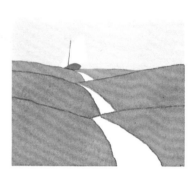

Tree-shells, 1971
card, with Ian Gardner

'They returned home tired but happy', 1972
card, with Ian Gardner

Penny Browns, 1982
print, with Ian Gardner

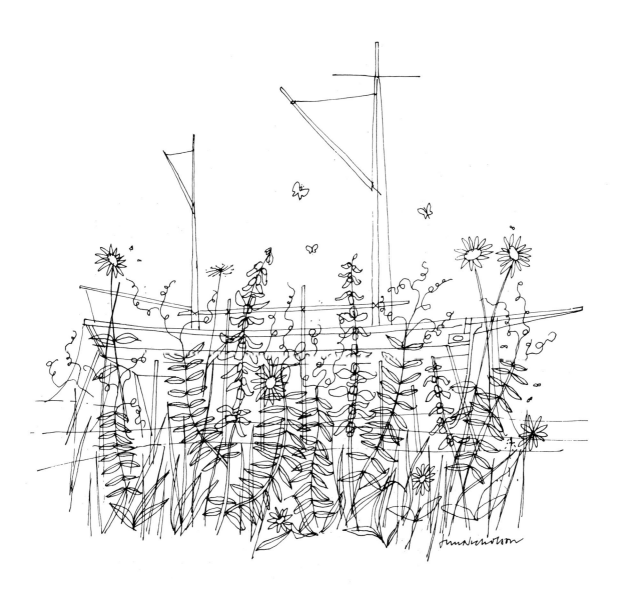

A Memory of Summer
In Trelew Creek, During
Mr Thomas Gray's Building of the Hobah[1]

A ketch

∗ ∗ ∗ ∗

in vetch

[1] *1878.'When she was finished the little yard was abandoned, the*
hut dismantled, the sawpit filled in by the slow tides;
and for generations it has been forgotten locally that there
was ever a ship built in Trelew Creek...'
Basil Greenhill, The Merchant Schooners, *Vol. II*

A Memory of Summer, 1971
folding card, with Jim Nicholson

Horloge de Flore, 1975
folding card, with Laurie Clark

FLOTTE
DE FLUTE OF
PÊCHE THE
PEACH

'Flotte de Pêche', 1974
card, with Ron Costley

Les Hirondelles, 1970
card, with Ron Costley

COME ALL YE HANKIES

Come all ye hankies now ashore,
In dim shirt-drawers, or under pillows,
New masts we'll raise, new rigs explore
—And sail to islands on the billows.

THE HANKY SAILS

White sails shake like Maytime blossom,
Grey sails gleam like misted leaves,
Red sails burn like leaves in autumn,
Sun-bleached brown sails stand like sheaves.

THE STOPPED SAILBOAT

This little boat won't put to sea.
—Whatever is the matter?
The clouds have lost the wind's white key
—Or else it's in the water.

THE HARBOUR

When from the Nor' Nor' West it blows
And sudden showers make waters chilly
I wrap my sails about my nose
And anchor by the water-lily.

From *A Mast of Hankies*, 1975
with David Paterson
The idiom is that of R. L. Stevenson's 'A Child's Garden of
Verses'. The little boats were made from crate-wood and the
sails from coloured handkerchiefs.

Henry Vaughan Walk, 1984
stone and lead, with Nicholas Sloan

The text is extracted from 'The Mount of Olives, or Solitary Devotions', by the English seventeenth-century poet Henry Vaughan. Following the sense of Vaughan's words, the informal brick pathway leads the reader from darkness to light.

'Small is Quite Beautiful', 1976
card, with Ron Costley

3   NEOCLASSICAL

Heroic Emblems

*Mario Praz once put the question: 'are emblems really such dead things?'
Of course, the point of asking the question is to answer it in the negative.
Emblems can be resuscitated by anyone who thinks deeply about the visual
and poetic sensibility of Renaissance Europe, which did not view them as
mere eccentricities, but set great store by them and credited them with a real
philosophical importance. Since 1964, when Praz asked his question, this
point has been readily taken by the community of historians of art and
culture. But it has perhaps been seized only too readily, with the effect that
the emblem books – rich storehouses of examples – tend to be treated as the
secret code-books of post-Renaissance art. No wonder that a distinguished
painter and historian took the opportunity of a recent conference on Dutch
seventeenth-century painting to declare a six-month moratorium on emblem
books!*

*Ian Hamilton Finlay is not using emblems for their archaistic charm.
He is not trying to unlock a store of hermetic knowledge buried deep in the
treasure-house of the post-Renaissance tradition. For him, the form of the
emblem generates, in Gombrich's words, 'a free-floating metaphor', formed
from the conjunction of motto and image, setting it apart from more
conventional methods of establishing meaning. Turner certainly understood
this capacity, and in a painting like* The Sun of Venice going to sea
*(1843), he brought together the motto-like title and the striking image;
his own verses were the supplement to this conjuncture of words and image,
turning their combined message into a meditation on the decline and death of
great civilizations, and on human life itself.*

*These 'heroic emblems' are also intended to provoke meditation. Finlay
sets before us a cultural tissue in which the Classical, the Renaissance and
the Modern are indissolubly linked. Out of the mysterious aptness of the
combination of terse motto and striking image comes the resonant metaphor.
The commentary is a movement away from this metaphor, which begins the
process of interpretation but necessarily never completes it since it is endless.*

Among the favourite subjects for the original *imprese* were the various machines of contemporary warfare: siege-engines, flint-lock guns and numerous types of cannon. Here is a modern equivalent for these citations from the technology of war. But the motto which is added casts the device back into an entirely classical context. The three words employed, which are a fragment of the work of the pre-Socratic philosopher Heraclitus, imply that the tank's 'fire-power' holds two symbolic meanings: as an index of its dominant role in modern field warfare, and also as a metaphor of fire as the governing principle of the universe. The tank is the modern equivalent of Heraclitus' thunderbolt, in that it represents not only the supreme natural force of destruction, but also the dynamic element which regulates the cosmos.

It may be added that this fragment from Heraclitus has attracted numerous different interpretations. Part of its ambiguity lies in the fact that the 'thunderbolt' is both a conventional personification of Zeus by synecdoche (substitution of the part for the whole) and a metaphor illustrating the philosopher's own cosmology. The new *impresa* retains and builds upon this ambiguity. The tank's equivocal status suggests a conjecture of traditional Epic form, in which the divine guarantee of order is always present, and the demythologised forms of Modernism.

G. S. Kirk (ed.), *Heraclitus – The Cosmic Fragments*; Burnet, *Early Greek Philosophy*; Walter Pater, *Plato and Platonism*; Karl Jaspers, *The Great Philosophers*, Vol. II; Robert J. Icks, *Famous Tank Battles*; Richard M. Ogorkiewicz, *Armoured Forces*; Chamberlain and Ellis, *Tanks of the World 1914–45*; General Heinz Guderian, *Panzer Leader*.

One of Panofsky's most justly celebrated essays in iconology (the term he takes directly from Cesare Ripa) is concerned with Poussin's painting *Et in Arcadia Ego*. Contemporary disputes about the significance of this enigmatic work lead him back to Greek pastoral poetry and the progressive formation of the cultural concept of 'Arcady', with its almost infinite tissue of poetic references converging upon the point that even here, in the ideal pastoral world, death is present. But Panofsky has not checked the speculation about the inner meaning of Poussin's picture, which may indeed be bound up with a hermetic interpretation of the golden section and might even lead (it has been suggested) to the rediscovery of the lost treasure of the Albigensian heretics in a particular part of southwestern France.

The metaphorical presentation of the tank *as* Poussin's inscribed monument, within the Arcadian setting, offers us not so much an emblem as an enigma. Estienne describes the role of Enigma as that of serving 'as a Rind or Bark to conserve all the mysteries of our Ancestors wisdome'. We are not immediately tempted to generalise or extend the implications that we see, as in the 'moral' emblem. The treasure, such as it is, is necessarily remote from us, and we have no foolproof method of lifting the hermetic seal (an oblique comment on the fact that here, particularly, Finlay's adoption of a pre-existent motif has proved a stumbling-block to those who would deny the relevance of wide-ranging cultural reference, Estienne's 'ignoramusses').

Virgil, *Eclogues*; John Sparrow, *Visible Words*; E. Panofsky, *Meaning in the Visual Arts*; Walter Friedlaender, *Nicolas Poussin*; Elizabeth Wheeler Manwaring, *Italian Landscape in Eighteenth Century England*; F. M. von Senger und Etterlin, *Die deutschen Panzer 1926–45*; *Wenn alle Brüder Schweigen* (foreword by Colonel-General Paul Hausser).

From *Heroic Emblems*, 1977
with Ron Costley and Stephen Bann
Z Press, USA

In this emblem, the seemingly innocent pun which allows us to shift from 'Paros' to 'Paras' (and from singular to plural) mobilises a whole series of cultural references which are, so to speak, encapsulated in the image. The original motto is a one-line poem by the French poet Emmanuel Lochac, published in the 1930s and doubtless a reflection of the influence of Apollinaire. Yet in its content it is a strong evocation of the Neo-classic tradition, perhaps of Winckelmann's lyrical passages on Graeco-Roman sculpture where the 'eternal action' of the marble and its 'immobility' are equally stressed. The substitution of 'Paras' for 'Paros' (the island specially associated with the production of Greek marble) allows a new, hyperbolic image to supplant the old: the descent of parachutes against the blue sky having the same quality of 'eternal action' as the immobile, classic art. At this point, where the conjunction could clearly have been made by an image of descending parachutes, meaning has been displaced once again through a return to the cherished garden imagery of the emblem books. We have not simply parachutes as classic art, but roses as parachutes as classic art (the supplementary meaning being made possible, of course, by an image which allows the rosebush to assume this metaphor, as well as by the Spanish custom of calling the parachute the 'rose of death').

Would it be appropriate to suggest yet another displacement? To the poet's own garden, Stonypath, where such a white rose-bush, sedulously trained over its parachute-like frame, will undoubtedly appear one of these days.

Emmanuel Lochac, *Monostiches*; Winckelmann, *Von der Nachahmung der griechischen Werke in der Malerei und Bildhauerkunst*; Charles Whiting, *Hunters From the Sky*; Graham Stuart Thomas, *Climbing Roses Old and New*.

The motto is the closing part of a hexameter from Virgil's *Eclogues*, a borrowing which recalls Estienne's precept that quotations from classical poets fall outside the general rule of concision in mottoes (and a normal restriction to three words). We move from the tank, camouflaged or as a monument, to another term of modern warfare: in this case the American heavy cruiser *Minneapolis* is shown in her leafy camouflage, against a woodland setting (the device is based on an actual photograph). The line from Virgil is re-animated by the substitution of new 'Gods' for old, the modern fighting ship for the pagan deities whose manifestation in the sylvan setting might have been taken as equally marvellous, or anomalous, in the classical period.

Minneapolis seems, in addition, a curiously apt point of reference for this emblem. Not only does it recall, in its apparently Greek etymology, the profusion of cities named with the same suffix ('polis' = city) dotted over Asia in the wake of Alexander's conquests – a fair analogy for America's imperial might. It also suggests a kind of homage to the present-day American artist Charles Biederman, an inhabitant of the woodlands of the state of which Minneapolis is capital, a translator of Cézanne's painting into the terms of the 'structurist relief' and the author of an issue of Finlay's magazine *Poor. Old. Tired. Horse.*, in which his 'Artistic Credo' was illustrated exclusively by photographs of woodland.

Virgil, *Eclogues*; Plutarch, *Isis and Osiris*; Proclus, *The Elements of Theology*; *Encyclopaedia of Sea Warfare*; Silverstone, *U.S. Warships of World War II*; Charles Biederman, *Art as the Revolution of Visual Knowledge*.

Through that pure virgin-shrine,
That sacred veil drawn o'er thy glorious noon,
That men might look and live, as glow-worms shine
    And face the moon;
  Wise Nicodemus saw such light
  As made him know his God by night.

Henry Vaughan's poem, 'The Night', invokes Nicodemus, the wise man who came to seek out Jesus by night in order to learn the secret of salvation. For Vaughan, the night is a 'shrine', in which the mysteries of the true light are veiled from view, and the searcher after truth, who would otherwise be dazzled by its brilliance, has the task of training his own miniature apparatus of perception upon the occluded prospect. That he is able to see in the night is, of course, a result of the fact that God has planted all creation with the 'seeds' of external light: even the flint-stone – which gives its title to Vaughan's *Silex Scintillans* – reveals by its flashes of mica the destiny of all sublunary matter to act as a theophany, leading men towards the eternal unclouded being. The radar screen serves in this way as an image of the hermetic pursuit, of the task of the skilled operator who locates the material object beyond normal vision and registers it as pure intelligibility – the moving dot of light upon the opaque screen. But the hermetic pursuit – the destiny of the mystic – involves not only the discipline of proceeding from the visible to the intelligible world. It is also a transformation of the person, a humility beyond wisdom, a darkness beyond brightness – in Vaughan's words:

  There is in God (some say)
A deep, but dazzling darkness; as men here
Say it is late and dusky, because they
    See not all clear.
  O for that night! where I in him
  Might live invisible and dim.

Plotinus, *The Enneads*; Kathleen Raine and George Mills Harper, *Thomas Taylor the Platonist*; Henry Vaughan, *Silex Scintillans*; E. H. Gombrich, *Symbolic Images*.

Like the 'Thunderbolt' motto, this is in origin a pre-Socratic fragment. Its author, Empedokles, may have intended an explicitly sexual reference, as to the 'cleft' meadows of the 'Mons Veneris'. But the adjective could as well be taken as 'divided', an interpretation which here lends itself both to the 'divided meadow' of the aircraft carrier's flight deck, and to the sea itself, split between warring fleets (the Greek word for 'divided' is the one from which we take the term 'schism'). Just as Empedokles sought to embody the cosmological categories of Love and Strife in the mythological guise of the Olympian deities, so the carrier suggests a contemporary equivalent in our own culture for the ultimate ideas of power and beauty. But it is an identification which passes through, and is enriched by, the element of 'Pagan Mystery' in the art and literature of the Renaissance – the Renaissance which shows us Aphrodite rising newborn from the waves with her attendant Zephyrs.

Burnet, *Early Greek Philosophy*; Kirk and Raven, *The Presocratic Philosophers*; Werner Jaeger, *The Theology of the Early Greek Philosophers*; Edgar Wind, *Pagan Mysteries of the Renaissance*; Donald Macintyre, *Aircraft Carrier – The Majestic Weapon*.

The USS *Enterprise* appears by name as the final, evolved exemplar of the modern warship. It also unites in itself the different elements of the cosmology of Heraclitus: earth being represented in the landing ground offered by the carrier deck, air by the element in which its aircraft move, fire by the dynamic and destructive character of its nuclear capacity and water by the surrounding ocean. Modern physics has set up a progressively more accurate picture of the material world which is analogous in imaginative terms to the world of the pre-Socratics. In the same way, the nuclear-powered carrier embodies in intimate and terrifying conjunction the power released by the splitting of the atom, and the poetic message of union of the elements.

One may well wish to meditate further upon the purpose of this invocation of Heraclitean cosmology in relation to modern nuclear warfare. It is as if this vicarious presence in the age which immediately preceded the establishment of the Western aesthetic codex, with Plato, were a method of gaining priority over the Platonic system. As if, on the other hand, the references to the modern fighting fleet were intended to bracket off the codes of warfare – the epic, the chivalric and indeed the romantic view of sea-faring being radically fore-closed in the elemental heroism of the nuclear confrontation. In a sense, the operation of these two brackets (the first anticipating Platonic and Aristotelian aesthetics, and the second demarcating the codes of the past) places the Western cultural tradition in parenthesis. And the self-contained form of the medallion seems to be the precise correlative to this poetic act.

Furley and Allen (eds.), *Studies in Presocratic Philosophy*, Vol. 1; Plato, *Timaeus*; R. D. Hicks, *Stoic & Epicurean*; Sandbach, *The Stoics*; Edward Hussey, *The Presocratics*; G. S. Kirk and J. E. Raven, *The Presocratic Philosophers*; F. Nietzsche, *The Birth of Tragedy*; Simone Weil, *Gateway to God*; Gareth L. Pawlowski, *Flat-Tops and Fledglings*; Commander W. H. Cracknell, *USS Enterprise (CVAN 65)*.

An argument about the persistence of the emblem in everyday usage might well take as its example the trademark of Tate & Lyle, who use the motto above in combination with the image of a dead lion on their tins of syrup. The original reference is to the story of Samson in the Book of Judges, and relates to a riddle which the strong man is obliged to solve. The verbal formula is explained by reference to a lion's carcase, in which the bees have started to make honey. Here the terms of reference are altered to include HMS *Lion*, one of the largest of British warships, and the helicopters which swarm like bees above her improvised helicopter deck. The contrast obtained in the original between strength and sweetness works on this new level, but in an unexpected way. Not only does the warship provision the helicopters, storing their (honey) fuel for them. But it may be called upon to contradict its usual warlike role and supply relief in times of famine and flood: in this case the stored 'honey' is of the most direct benefit.

As with the 'Semper festina lente' emblem, this works through a kind of oxymoron – the juxtaposition of opposed terms. But here the terms are slightly displaced: the direct antitheses would be strong/weak, sour/sweet, and the conjunction strong/sweet plays on the vestigial sense that the other terms have been suppressed. The figure used in the motto is a synecdoche, 'sweetness' being conceived as a 'part' of the 'whole' which is strength. But there is also the metonymic substitution of 'sweetness' for 'bees' (the contained for the container), which parallels on the verbal level the visual antithesis between the one and the many (ship/lion and helicopter/bees). The apparent simplicity of the emblem therefore belies a complex rhetorical structure: this is the underpinning which allows the immediate message to be retained as a text for meditation.

Judges 14; W. G. D. Blundell, *Ships of the Modern Royal Navy*.

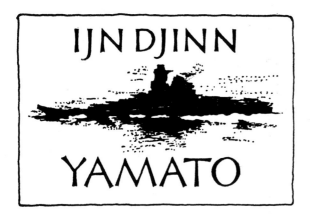

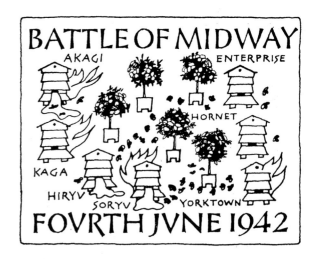

This particular emblem, and the one which follows, both take as their point of reference the Pacific War between the United States and Japan. The *Yamato*, at the time the world's largest battleship and a remarkable tour de force of construction, was designed to dominate the Ocean with its presence. It finally succumbed to American attack only as late as April 1945. 'IJN' – the contracted form of 'Imperial Japanese Navy' – is here used to summon up an unexpected connotation: that of the 'Djinn' or 'Djinnie' raised by the rubbing of Aladdin's Lamp. The *Yamato* is seen as an equally powerful and magical manifestation of the small (lamp-shaped?) islands of Japan.

The form of the emblem is not simply a means of sketching out an extended metaphor. Here, as in almost every case, reference is made to a specific cultural code, which is both cited and placed in suspension. Aladdin and the stories of the *Thousand and One Nights* are the very archetype of story-telling; they weave a continuous web of fiction in which the fantastic is a constant resource to be drawn upon. By contrast, the magic of the *Yamato* is short-lived, and the story within which it makes an appearance stops brutally short just after its own demise.

The Thousand and One Nights; Masataka Chihaya, *IJN Yamato: The Japanese Navy in World War II* (introd. Dr Raymond O'Connor); Andrieu D'Albas, *Death of a Navy.*

The crucial events which were to determine the outcome of the Pacific War are celebrated in this image. Under the emblematic cover of a Renaissance pastoral, we see enacted the conflict of 4 June 1942, when the four ships of Admiral Naguno's I Carrier Striking Force were destroyed by dive-bombers from their American counterparts, *Enterprise* and *Hornet* (*Yorktown* being the major American casualty). The dramatic success of this action depended on the fact that the American planes were able to engage the Japanese fleet at its most vulnerable – whilst each of the carriers bore a full deckload of armed and fuelled aircraft. The effect of American bombing was therefore to ignite petrol tanks, bombs and torpedoes, causing unquenchable conflagration. The analogy of the Renaissance garden shows us the carriers as hives, the American attack planes as swarming bees and the conflagration of overspilling honey. Formal trees in tubs fill out the pastoral conception, while signifying at the same time the ocean, in whose lush distances the opposing carriers were concealed from each other.

At Stonypath, Ian Hamilton Finlay's home in Lanarkshire, there is an interaction and interpenetration of the Garden and the Ocean. A series of stretches of water of greater and less magnitude is juxtaposed with the enclosed (the 'inland') garden. But even within the garden, poem inscriptions pick up the distant murmur of the sea. The axis of this opposition, which can hardly be explained more fully in this context, has perhaps become the base structure of Finlay's poetics.

Virgil, *Georgics*; Mitsuo Fuchida and Masatake Okumiya, *Midway*; Samuel Eliot Morison, *History of United States Naval Operations in World War II*, Vol. IV; Derek Clifford, *A History of Garden Design*; Barbara Jones, *Follies and Grottoes*; Julia S. Berrall, *The Garden*; Sir Christopher Andrewes, *The Lives of Bees and Wasps.*

Deliberate Forms

Finlay has often taken a satirical or polemical stance towards the styles and sensibilities of modernist art. His 'Unnatural Pebbles' relates unmistakably to the modern cult of the pebble, perhaps originating at St Ives, where sculptors like Moore and Gabo picked up and adopted what they found on the beach, and certainly still celebrated in the accoutrements of the Kettle's Yard Gallery, at Cambridge. For Finlay, the natural pebble is devoid of meaning. It must therefore be reclaimed for culture. Each unnatural pebble is, as it were, a parody of the real thing; but it is also a work of art, because its inscription carries an idea. Extending the same line of thought, the 'Talismans and Signifiers' may at first appear like miniaturized examples of American minimal sculpture. But they are lying in ambush for the unsuspecting visitor, not only smooth and aesthetically pleasing talismans of stone, but signifiers communicating a telegraphic message of didactic classicism.

'Piranesi', 1980
wood, metal and stone, with Nicholas Sloan

'The mathematics of picture-making lead me to the physics of representation.'

Juan Gris, *Notes On My Painting*

(Cf. *Playing-cards and Fruit-Bowl*, 1918; *Guitar and Fruit-Bowl on a Table*, 1918; *Siphon and Fruit-Bowl*, 1920; *Le Carnigou*, 1921; *Pitcher and Carafe*, 1925; *The Red Book*, 1925; *Fruit-Bowl with Blue Grapes*, 1926; *Book and Fruit-Bowl*, 1927)

'If a flying arrow occupies at each point of time a determinate point of space, its motion becomes nothing but a sum of rests.'

William James, cited in *Studies in Presocratic Philosophy*

'Unnatural Pebbles', 1981
slate, with Richard Grasby
(see catalogue of same title – Graeme Murray Gallery,
Edinburgh)

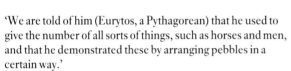

'We are told of him (Eurytos, a Pythagorean) that he used to give the number of all sorts of things, such as horses and men, and that he demonstrated these by arranging pebbles in a certain way.'

J. Burnet, *Early Greek Philosophy*

'The mighty sea is father of clouds and of winds and of rivers.'

Xenophanes

  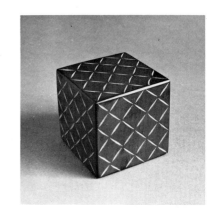

'Now we observe that physical beauty exists only when form prevails over matter; for matter is ugly and devoid of beauty, and form when overpowered by it is filled with ugliness and shapelessness and becomes as it were formless, being assimilated to the underlying nature.'
Proclus, *Alcibiades Commentary*

'Form has beauty – the artificial form more than the natural form.' Vitulio, *Teorema Della Bellezza*

'We must proceed to distribute the figures whose origins we have described between fire, earth, water and air. Let us assign the cube to earth; for it is the most immobile of the four bodies and the most retentive of shape, and these are characteristics that must belong to the figure with the most stable faces.' Plato, *Timaeus*

The cube represents the conceptual earth (quality), the circle the sphere (present in the cube), the circle as mirror the immediate or material sphere (the world), the circle as a mark on a die, an enlarged dot or one.

'What distinguishes the Philosophy of Nature from physics is, more precisely, the kind of metaphysics used by them both; for metaphysics is nothing else but the entire range of the universal determinations of thought, as it were, the diamond net into which everything is brought and thereby first made intelligible.'
Hegel, *Philosophy of Nature*

Net, n. an intelligible articulation. – See also Wittgenstein, *Tractatus Logico-Philosophicus*, Proposition 6.341.

'Talismans and Signifiers', 1984
with Richard Grasby
(see catalogue of same title – Graeme Murray Gallery, Edinburgh)

'Each order, including the lowest order of bodies with which all division is terminated, can be said in a remarkable way to have and not to have being. What is stated affirmatively of the lower is stated negatively of the higher. Likewise what is stated negatively of the lower is stated affirmatively of the higher. In the same way, what is stated affirmatively of the higher is stated negatively of the lower; and what is stated negatively of the higher will be stated affirmatively of the lower.'
Erigena, *Periphyseon*

Erigena adds: 'Every order of rational and intellectual creature is said to have and not to have being. It has being insofar as it is known by higher creatures or by itself; it lacks being insofar as it does not allow itself to be comprehended by its inferiors.'

'The entire universe is like a lyre tuned by some excellent artificer, whose strings are separate species of the universal whole. Anyone who knew how to touch these dextrously and make them vibrate would draw forth marvellous harmonies.'
John Dee, *Propaedeumata Aphoristica*

'Mufike' is Dee's usual spelling of 'music', fortuitously supplying one letter for each face of the cube. The cube/sphere now suggests the stable (cube) and spherical (the letters being a re-placement for the dots or diamonds), heliocentric universe (as understood by Dee).

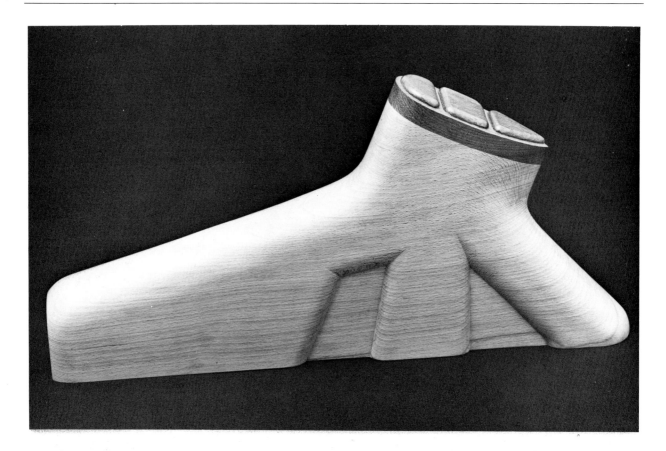

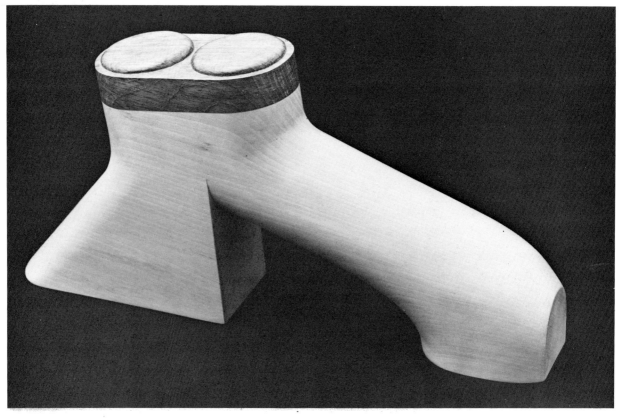

Japanese Stacks, 1979
wood, with John R. Thorpe

Here 'stack' means 'funnel'. The stacks are based on models derived from scale drawings of World War II Japanese destroyers, cruisers, and aircraft carriers

Into the Forest, 1989
stone, with Gwyn Watkins

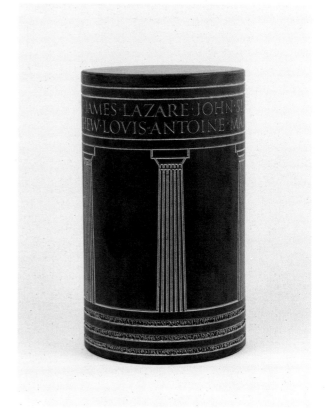

Beautiful, Fanatical . . ., 1988
slate, with Annet Stirling

l'Ombra Medita Sulla Luce, 1988
slate, with Annet Stirling

'Angel of the Terror', 1990
slate, with Annet Stirling

'Now the Names of the Twelve are these . . .', 1989
slate, with Annet Stirling

'Neoclassicism builds . . .', 1988
slate, with Annet Stirling

'Temple, n.', 1989
marble, with Annet Stirling

Corday, Lux, 1989
slate, with Annet Stirling

'Arch, n.', 1989
slate, with Annet Stirling

Events Are a Discourse, 1988
slate, with Annet Stirling

Landscape Improvements

The eighteenth-century English garden designer Humphry Repton produced 'Red Books' in which he proposed 'improvements' to the country estates of his clients. Finlay has published numerous proposals of this kind, which exist first of all as booklets or prints, but often result in large-scale landscape features that reflect a more integral approach than the mere placing of a sculpture in a natural setting. Early schemes, like the 'Wave Wall' and the Peterhead plan, are really 'townscape improvements', and anticipate his most grandiose transformation of the urban scene through an elemental text in the Glasgow Bridge Pillars of 1990. Others are conceived as strategic interpolations in the secular spaces of modern sculpture parks, like the Sacred Grove at the heart of the Kröller-Müller, Otterlo, or the Virgilian Olive Grove which keeps its distance from the avant-garde objects at Villa Celle, Pistoia. The recently completed neo-classical garden at Stockwood Park, Luton, is however a self-contained achievement, which revives the 'spirit of the place'.

From *Peterhead Power Station Projects*, 1978
with Ian Appleton
Printed by Robert Matthew, Johnson-Marshall and Partners

Wave Wall, 1976
with Denis Barns and Ron Costley
Livingston New Town, Scotland

A BRONZE OVAL PLAQUE
fixed to an olive tree. The bronze has
a dull, rusticated finish and is inscribed
with the words (rustic Roman letters),
Il flauto d'argento | La scorza rozza
La scorza d'argento | Il flauto rozzo

A PLOUGH of the Roman sort,
but made in bronze; on the shaft is
the inscription *The Day Is Old By Noon*

A BASKET OF LEMONS,
but made in bronze. Bronze bands
around the top and bottom of the
basket, with the words (top band),
Silence After Chatter and (lower band)
The Astringent Is Sweet

A SMALL CIRCULAR TEMPLE,
or tempietto; on the frieze the
inscription *L'Ombra Medita Sulla Luce*

From *A Celebration of the Grove*, 1984
a proposal for the Villa Celle, Tuscany, Italy
with Nicholas Sloan

FLUTED COLUMNS

A series of fluted stone columns will be placed in the area of the pool. These will be slender columns, carefully sited in the vicinity of bushes & birch trees, the trunks of the birches rather than (say) of the beeches providing the 'key' or the scale. In effect, the columns will constitute a small anthology of possible flutings — spiral flutings, vertical flutings, square flutings on rectangular columns etc. The scale however will be (in comparison to the larger trees) miniature.

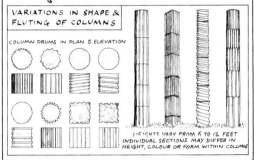

VARIATIONS IN SHAPE & FLUTING OF COLUMNS

COLUMN DRUMS IN PLAN & ELEVATION

HEIGHTS VARY FROM 6 TO 12 FEET
INDIVIDUAL SECTIONS MAY DIFFER IN
HEIGHT, COLOUR OR FORM WITHIN COLUMN

Instead of Roman grandeur, there will be a kind of chamber music of columns of all sorts, all in pale stone and arranged not in colonnades but singly, wistfully, in the glades around the pool. The types of fluting will be referred to in the general documentation of the area available in the Visitor Centre. Plants (roses, ivy, honeysuckle) can be grown up selected columns, as suits their particular siting. The occasional erudite visitor might be reminded of Pater — "listening to music ... to the sound of water, to time as it flies..." (Walter Pater, The School of Giorgione)

LOGS AS BENCHES IN PICNIC AREAS

These resting areas will be placed in the general vicinity of the tracks, but a little back from it, & with a screened, seemingly haphazard air which makes them seem more like discovered glades than official picnic sites. Seats will take the form of large logs.

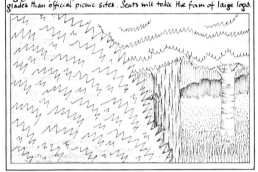

PROPOSED INSCRIPTIONS FOR TREE-SEATS

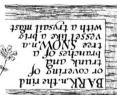

of flutes & wildroses

Writing in the catalogue of the Victoria & Albert Museum exhibition 'The Open and Closed Book', Robert Kennedy explained that Ian Hamilton Finlay 'creates poetry by providing words with a rigorously controlled & potently significant environment.' Clearly this inscription is not a 'poem' as we know it, but equally short fragments appear in recent translations of Archilocus, Alkmann, Sappho. In that case, time (as it were) provides the context for the fragment. Here, the words exist in relation to their surroundings — the wild roses, the fluted columns, the Pan-pipe flutes... & the sound of the breeze.

SNOW, n. atmospheric vapour frozen in crystalline form
BARK, n. formerly any small sailing ship

This 'poem' was discovered in the dictionary. With a slight pruning of the original, the definitions, juxtaposed, present an evocation of woodland elements — or merely useful information. As in the technique of 'collage', real elements both retain their integrity & can function in another way.

CARVEL-BUILT
Whitbeam·Willow
Beech·Yew
Laburnum·Sycamore
Hazel·Spindle
Lime·Alder·Plane

CLINKER-BUILT
Chestnut·Cypress
Pine·Oak·Aspen
Buckthorn·Poplar
Hawthorn·Elm
Redwood·Box

'Clinker' & 'Carvel' are of course nautical terms, 'clinkerbuilt' meaning that the planks of the ship's hull overlap, where a carvel hull is flush. Here, the terms designate trees with rough bark & with smooth bark. As well as allowing us to take pleasure in the carved lettering, the distinction again reminds us that bark may signify either the kind of the tree, or a small boat, poetically conceived.

Flûtes
Roses

JULIE

The notes spell JULIE — the heroine of Rousseau's La Nouvelle Héloïse, with her famous paradise garden. Composers have traditionally paid homage with coded notes, and in this case the notes which spell 'Julie' have been used as a theme for a little composition by Wilma Paterson. The completed music is scored for Flutes and Roses (the Roses however playing only rests).

greenness, leaf or bark

The phrase 'greenness, leaf or bark' occurs in Henry Vaughan's poem 'The Timber' (Silex Scintillans). In the variation, where barque (the type of sailing-ship) is substituted for bark, it is as if the resurrection which is the theme of Vaughan's poem is translated into a parallel, nautical portrait, recalling Watteau's Isle of Cytharea, by means of a one-word clue. Either version is of course appropriate to the location (on a felled tree, in a wood).

Ces nymphes,
je les veux perpétuer

This inscription is the first line of Mallarmé's L'Après-Midi D'un Faune. Here (though not in Mallarmé) the nymphs are to be understood as the trees, and the need to 'perpetuate them' is explained by the setting of the inscription — on a felled & fallen tree. Coincidentally, all the Montviot 'motifs' occur in this famous but obscure poem by the French Symbolist: woods, roses, flutes, wind, marshes, springs.

From *The Montviot Proposal*, 1981
with Nicholas Sloan

Sacred Grove, 1982
with Nicholas Sloan
Kröller-Müller Rijksmuseum, Otterlo, Holland

Plaques on trees, 1984
with Nicholas Sloan
Bruglingen Gardens, Basel, Switzerland
Five oval plaques are inscribed with the names of classical
lovers, and five rectangular plaques identify particular species
of trees

Performance of Wilma Paterson's Bruglingen Suite, 1984
Bruglingen Gardens, Basel, Switzerland

white	weiss
&	&
bark	leicht
black	schwarz
&	&
light	licht
bark	leicht
&	&
light	licht
white	weiss
&	&
dark	dunkel
black	schwarz
&	&
white	weiss

Black and White, 1985
stone, bronze, birch trees, paving slabs; with Nicholas Sloan
Schweizergarten, Vienna

The plaques contain two rows of texts on bronze plates; that
on the left is by Finlay, that on the right is a free translation
by the Austrian poet Ernst Jandl.

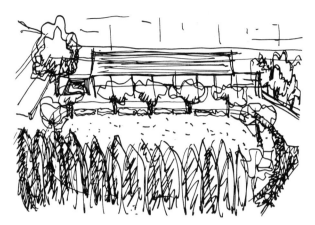

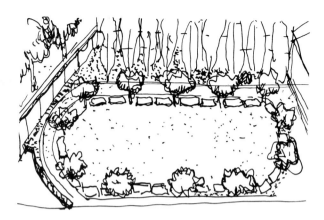

The Bicentenary Garden occupies the site of the demolished Assembly Hall and so may be said to stand on the birthplace of the French Revolution. It was here that the King summoned the Estates General in 1789.

The grass lawn fills exactly the area of the seating once used by the Deputies. Likewise, the exposed wooden timbers of the restored building (left) duplicate the placing of a row of columns once part of the Hall. This building now provides space for a number of studios and, at the far end, a small museum.

A sentence from Michelet's *History of The French Revolution* is inscribed on huge, unworked blocks of stone selected at the quarry face. Vigorous, inspiring, the sentence sums up the spirit of *The Rights of Man And of The Citizen*, the complete text of which will be displayed within the museum. Everyone will understand that it is not

simply Michelet who is speaking from the stones but the whole French nation.
The sentence is inscribed in the Roman manner, without punctuation, continuing uninterruptedly from stone to stone.

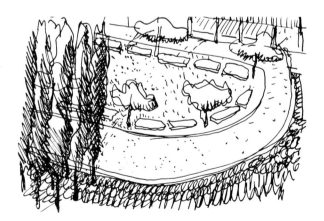

Between the stones are planted small wild cherry trees. Stones and trees together allegorise the two main aspects of the Revolution, the titanic and the pastoral.

Previous pages: Inscribed Stone, 1987
Furka Pass, Switzerland
The stone, set in a characteristically Hodleresque scene, carries an enlarged representation of the Swiss artist's signature

In spring the blossom from the cherry trees will fall on the stones while in summer the ripe fruit can be picked by the visitors.

From *Un Jardin Révolutionnaire*, 1988
booklet, with Alexander Chemetov, Sue Finlay and Nicholas Sloan, 1988

Pear trees are planted in the triangular area formed by the museum and the boundary wall. A Tree of Liberty, the triangular orchard area, and the area of poplar trees, are intended to allegorise the theme of Liberty, Equality and Fraternity. The triangle has equal sides, while the *poplar* tree suggests a play on the word *people* – all historians agreeing on the vital role played by The People in the French Revolution.

The poplar trees have the additional and practical purpose of helping to screen the tall tenement to one side of the site.

At the entrance from the Avenue des Etats Generaux the gateposts are restored and now include two stone plaques inscribed with the dates 1789 and 1989. The plaques are not merely added to the gateposts but are part of their structure. Lime trees are planted outside the wall, in the street, to increase the garden's seclusion.

The square pool provides a deliberate contrast with the triangular shape of the orchard. Placed in the area adjacent to the building which houses the studios, it will gather and store the rainwater from the roof, for the purpose of watering the lawn.

It is intended that the House of Little Pleasures will be restored and used as an art college where special attention will be paid to questions of landscape design. Students will use the garden as an

informal meeting place. The inscribed stones placed around the edge of the lawn can also be treated as seats.
The tree of Liberty is adjacent to the pool.

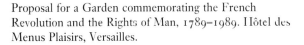

Proposal for a Garden commemorating the French Revolution and the Rights of Man, 1789–1989. Hôtel des Menus Plaisirs, Versailles.

The marble urn is formed as a void and thus encloses[1] a portion of the landscape. While the unenclosed portion stands for nature with a small 'n', the urn and the enclosed landscape together signify the idealizing and classicizing appreciation of nature – Nature with a capital 'N' – characteristic of Rousseau. 'The idea of nature was for Rousseau what it had been for the Greeks, a way of maintaining an ideal of human nature . . . He it was who made the idea of nature the ethical, political and critical inspiration of a whole generation.'[2]

[1] 'Contains'.   [2] Alfred Cobban, *Rousseau and the Modern State*.

Proposal for a Monument to Jean-Jacques Rousseau, 1986 lithographic folding print, with Gary Hincks

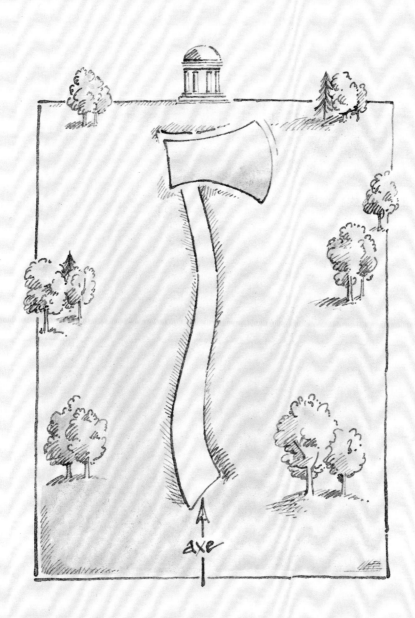

Projet pour un parc républicain

Ian Hamilton Finlay and Gary Hincks. Wild Hawthorn Press

Projet pour un Parc Républicain, 1988
proposal, with Gary Hincks

From Six Proposals for the *improvement* of Stockwood Park
Nurseries in the Borough of Luton, 1986 (completed 1991)
prints with Gary Hincks; garden installations with Bob
Burgoyne

Tree Plaque, 1988
print, with Gary Hincks
stone, with Nicholas Sloan

Capital, 1991
print, with Gary Hincks
stone, with John Sellman

Proposal for a landscape with stones.
Ian Hamilton Finlay and Gary Hincks, after
Claude Lorrain (*Pastoral Landscape*, pen, wash,
and chalk, 1645). The largest of the stones
carries the inscription: **FLOCK, n. a number
of a kind, an amplitude. The Pythagoreans
regarded men as the property of the gods,
as a sort of FLOCK, which may not leave
its fold without the consent of the gods. –
Zeller.** Compositionally, the stones replace the
sheep in the original Claude. Published by the
Wild Hawthorn Press, in an edition of 250
copies, 1985.

Flock, 1988
print, with Gary Hincks
stone, with Nicholas Sloan

'A group of stones suggestive of a flock; on the largest stone
is some lettering; the grass is neatly clipped around the
stones.'

Aphrodite Herm, 1991
print, with Gary Hincks
stone; head traditional, lettering by Nicholas Sloan
'A woodland grove with a herm of Aphrodite (Venus).'

Bridge Pillars, River Clyde, Glasgow, 1990
stone, with Annet Stirling and Brenda Berman
Commissioned for TSWA-Four Cities Project in
collaboration with the British Railways Board and Glasgow
District Council

The Third Reich Revisited

'The Third Reich Revisited' was The Little Spartan War in an earlier form. It was – is – an attempt to raise (in a necessarily round-about way) the questions which our culture does not want to put in idea-form. The exhibition consists of drawings and commentaries. Most of the drawings are of buildings, some imaginary, some real (or some which were real in Hitler's time). Likewise, the commentaries include invented and actual history, used in such a way that one can't be sure what is 'true' and what is not . . . This mixture of the real and invented is important because it gives a kind of pressing quality to the projects; they are not mere mythology (far less whimsies); and they are therefore related to events – things which happened, or might happen.

Ian Hamilton Finlay. Studio International, April 1984.

Apollo/Saint-Just (after Bernini), 1985
plaster, with Alexander Stoddart

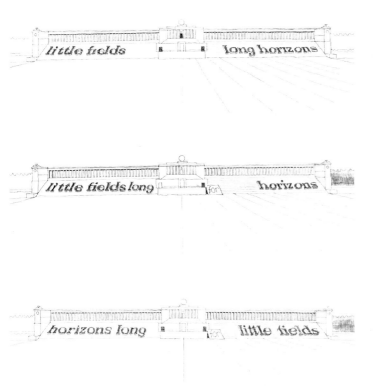

'LITTLE FIELDS' AT NUREMBERG

Speer's Zeppelinfeld (now an artificial ruin: see Reichskanzlei) is known to the world through Leni Riefenstahl's film, 'Triumph of the Will'. It is the perfect setting for the three-part concrete poem 'Little Fields', the words of which were formed by the Arbeitsdienst (Reich Labour Corps) while the additional, smaller 'For' (inscribed on a banner) was borne from the far end of the field by volunteer members of the SA – to tumultuous cheering. As each man remained with his letter, the interludes/crossings over between sequences involved a temporary mêlée – immediately in front of Hitler. The contrasting orderly accomplishment of each sequence was greeted with deafening applause.

The employment of the actual Arbeitsdienst personnel – each man with his spade strapped across his back – was obviously helpful to the effect of the poem. (Imagine if the medium had been massed Boy Scouts!) Suspending questions of blood and soil and Reich expansionism, it is interesting to relate the performance to a passage from Duns Scotus (*circa* 850): 'Surely place does not long to be in anything, but all things in it rightly long for the boundary and limit in which they are naturally contained and without which they seem to flow on to infinity . . .' (The Russian Steppe?)

HITLER'S COLUMN

A monumental neoclassical 'totem-pole'. Erected as an element in the reconstructed North-South Berlin Axis, it was popularly known as 'Hitler's Column', after Hadrian's Column. Being *German* neoclassical the column was cuboid rather than cylindrical; in place of the relief scenes on the Roman monument there is a barbaric semi-abstract 'concrete' poem – reminiscent of the 'sound poems' of the 1960s – composed from abbreviated elements of the German technological/military vocabulary. Jagd. is short for Jagdpanzer (Tank Hunter), Pak. for Panzer-abwehrkanone (Anti-tank gun) . . . etc. Compare this monument with the virtually meaningless neo-primitive 'Aztec' (etc.) cast concrete totem-like structures in the new towns of Britain in the post-war period.

From *The Third Reich Revisited*, 1982
with Ian Appleton

APOLLO IN GEORGE STREET

The statue is stone, the sub-machine gun is only plaster. It was added by disillusioned Abstractionists, as a protest, but *looked* so acceptable that it remained unnoticed till the plaster was damaged by frost and the addition fell off. Apollo's emblems are the bow-and-arrow, and lyre; the gun is only the former, appropriately up-dated (though unlikely to be approved of by present fashion).

One of the enigmas of the 70s and 80s is the failure of pluralist democracy to produce a public art for itself. Where (except possibly in the new Sculpture Parks) is there any public celebration of radical secularism? Of ecological utilitarianism? Of caution-at-all-costs free conformism? Of Benthamite pacifism?

EHRENTEMPEL, MUNICH

Hitler's first architect, Paul Ludwig Troost, designed the Ehrentempel (twin-Temples of Honour) as a memorial to the martyrs of the NSDAP 1923 *putsch*. Troost's widow wrote, 'No damp vault enclosed the coffins of the fallen. Surrounded by pillars they rest under the open sky of the homeland . . .' In 1947, at the end of the War, the Americans decided to blow up these examples of heroic classicism. But an alternative was proposed: the interior frieze, framing the 'open sky', was used for a deNazifying inscription (this was the period of the De-Nazification Tribunals). A high-principled but barbaric vandalism was avoided by retaining the *architecture* while altering the *sense*.

The 'Suprematist' inscription acknowledges the sky (The Beyond, The Infinite, The Immeasurable) as the climax of the Ehrentempel. It preserves the transcendental aspect of the original architecture while managing to avoid both the old militarist/heroic and the new democratic/secular. The subject of the inscription is *invoked* rather than *evoked*, and remains enigmatically mid-way between the set of words qualified by questionmarks (minus) and the identical set (in a slightly altered order) with the exclamationmarks (plus). It is not in fact neoclassical like the architecture but neopresocratic.

SUNDIALS AT THE ZEPPELINFELD

This wing of the Zeppelinfeld (scene of the major NSDAP rallies) does not face south. However, its architect Speer considered this a possible advantage (letter to Ian Hamilton Finlay) – no doubt because of the dramatic and allegorical possibilities of a pair of sundials sited in shadow. Practically, there is no difficulty in constructing a dial for other than a North–South axis (shades of the abandoned Berlin plan!) – though unlike those depicted it would be asymmetrical.

The dials are based on sun-trajectories drawn up for architects designing glass-fronted buildings. The vertical lines show the hours, the horizontal the length of the shadow cast by the gnomon at points through the year. (This seems to echo the classical sense of the year as a coherent round.) The motto adds a further dimension by allegorising the lines, the horizontal now standing also for Sea, and the vertical for Land. Together, they form the emblem of the globe (the world is a network of lands and oceans). At the same time, the setting gives rise to an additional hermetic (and ironic) reference to German geopolitical ambitions, Germany Over All.

REDEMPTION (RENOVATION) SCHEME, CHARLOTTE SQUARE, EDINBURGH

The Square (gardens, roadway and buildings) is converted into a pine forest. The adjacent Edinburgh New Town functions as a rigidly formal, horizontal 'plinth' for this planned 'natural' wilderness, reminiscent of the paintings of Caspar David Friedrich and symbolic of 'Desecularisation'.

Initially, only the gardens and roadway were planted. Natural imperialism of the forest (foxgloves, willowherb, etc.) soon annexed the neoclassical architecture of the surrounding Square. Buildings are carefully maintained in the new form of romantic semi-ruins, establishing the boundaries of the Scheme (excluding the New Town 'plinth').

Prior to Desecularisation, the Square was synonymous with the Scottish Arts Council. Before work on the Scheme had commenced, the SAC HQ (the infamous 'Number 19') was attacked by the so-called 'Saint-Just Vigilantes' and 'Ayatollah Aesthetes'. The art-files, artist case-histories and reports of the Censoring Committees, were burned, and the facade was hung with extremist slogans (some of them misspelt).

Idylls

Webster's Dictionary defines the idyll *as 'a short pictorial poem, chiefly on pastoral subjects: a story, episode, or scene of happy innocence or rusticity: a work of art of like character in any medium'. Such a definition perfectly encompasses the range of works included here: the poem remains short, and its guiding idea simple, but the range of media employed extends from the basic resource of typography, through the poem-print, to the colourfulness and brilliance of the neon works.* Cythera, *commissioned for the 1991* Metropolis *show in Berlin, and probably Finlay's most ambitious indoor work to date, began its career as a poem-booklet and design for a landscape feature in the 1960s.*

Sometimes the idyll is made more poignant by its implied context. Finlay is mindful of Rousseau's 'Idyll of the cherries', an autobiographical passage whose happy tone contrasts with the sombre catalogue of the philosopher's misfortunes. The works which refer to the simple life led by Robespierre, as a boarder in the house of the carpenter Duplay, intimate a similar contrast between blithe pastoral imagery and the cares of political office: 'His bed/ a meadow, /his brow/ in shadow'.

Poverty pitted with larks, 1991
screen print, with Julie Farthing

Diamond-studded fish-net, 1991
screen print, with Julie Farthing

AUTUMN

The woods
milestones

The mountains
signposts

Autumn, 1991
Poem in folder

On the Path of Language, 1990
stone, with Keith Bailey

Sea Coast, after Claude Lorrain, 1985
lithographic print, with Gary Hincks
proposal for the Campus of the University of California at
San Diego

A grove of gean or wild cherry trees. On a small fluted column among the trees is a bronze or stone basket of cherries with the words *l'idylle des cerises*.

'I climbed into a cherry tree, and threw bunches of cherries down to the girls, who then returned the cherry-stones through the branches.
Seeing one of the girls holding out her apron and tilting her head, I took such good aim that I dropped a bunch into her bosom. "Why are my lips not cherries?" I thought. "How gladly would I throw them there too!"'

Jean-Jacques Rousseau, *Confessions*. For a sympathetic account of the famous 'idyll of the cherries' see Renato Poggioli, *The Oaten Flute*.

From *L'Idylle des Cerises*, 1986
booklet, with Michael Harvey

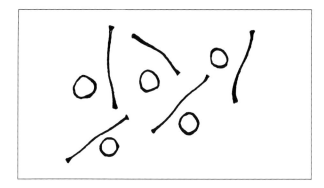

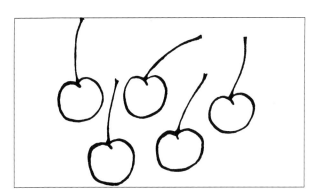

L'Idylle des Cerises, 1987
with David Ballantyne

The Orgy of The Cherries / L'Idylle des Cerises
from *Little Sermons Series: Cherries*, 1982, booklet,
with Ian Gardner

The chamber of the deputy of Arras contained only a wooden bedstead, covered with blue damask ornamented with white flowers, a table, and four straw-bottomed chairs.

Matisse chez Duplay, 1989
neon, with Julie Farthing

Matisse chez Duplay, 1990
ceramic and wood, with Julie Farthing

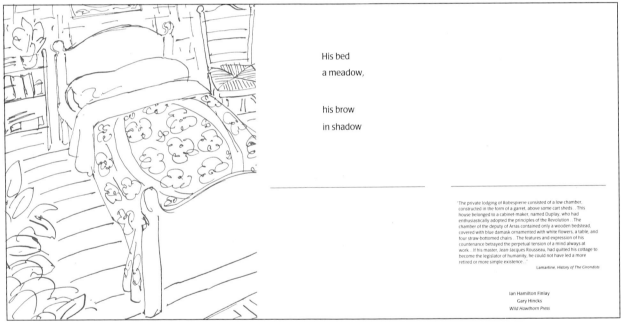

His bed
a meadow,

his brow
in shadow

'The private lodging of Robespierre consisted of a low chamber,
constructed in the form of a garret, above some cart sheds... This
house belonged to a cabinet-maker, named Duplay, who had
enthusiastically adopted the principles of the Revolution... The
chamber of the deputy of Arras contained only a wooden bedstead,
covered with blue damask ornamented with white flowers, a table, and
four straw-bottomed chairs... The features and expression of his
countenance betrayed the perpetual tension of a mind always at
work... If his master, Jean-Jacques Rousseau, had quitted his cottage to
become the legislator of humanity, he could not have led a more
retired or more simple existence...'

Lamartine, *History of The Girondists*

Ian Hamilton Finlay
Gary Hincks
Wild Hawthorn Press

His bed a meadow, 1990
lithograph folding card, with Gary Hincks

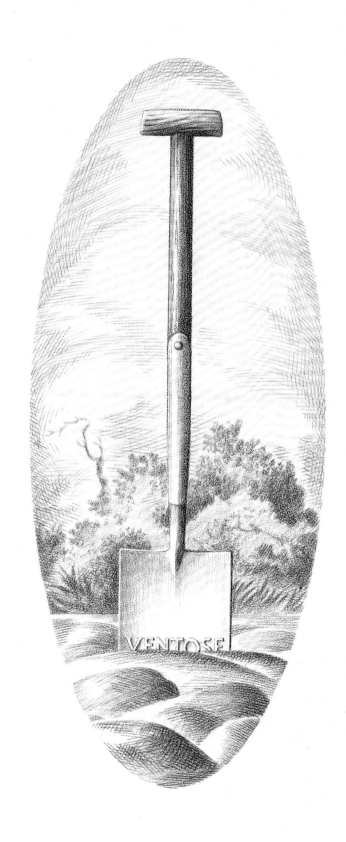

Ventôse, 1991
print, with Gary Hincks

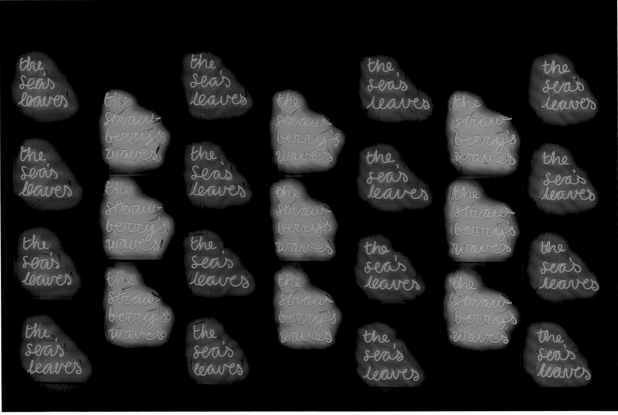

Dove, dead in its snows . . ., 1989
neon, with Julie Farthing

The Sea's Leaves, The Strawberry's Waves, 1990
neon, with Julie Farthing

Swallows Little Matelots, 1989
neon, with Michael Harvey

Cythera, 1991
neon, concrete, polished granite; with Michael Harvey and
Neil MacLeish
Installation in Metropolis, Berlin, 1991

PART II

1 WHAT'S IN A NAME?

'I hate autobiography and biography (both), because it seems to me that *much* of one's life is only nominally related to oneself, yet the telling of it seems to assume that it is telling about the person in a "true" sort of way.'[1] This rejection of the idea that one's activities can or should be related directly to an obvious notion of self is a common gesture of Finlay's. For him, art and poetry must satisfy other criteria. He insists that they must first and foremost be beautiful.[2] This is more important to him than his overt participation in the twentieth-century movement towards ever more diverse art forms, materials and media. Finlay's Gris series, spanning some twenty years, gives a good indication of the way in which his work develops: by dissemination along various axes, but also by a concentration which repeatedly returns to the same motifs and preoccupations.

Rapel (1963), Finlay's first collection of concrete poetry, contained poems referring to cubism. The initial impact of this movement, in the years preceding World War I, had been violent. Nevertheless, one might fear that the transposition of its techniques into the sphere of poetry half a century later would turn out to be little more than a mannerist exercise. Not so in Finlay's case. In 'A Peach an Apple' (p. 160), he gives the cubist idiom a semantic function, celebrating the still life represented in the poem: 'eatable table apple'. While the fragmentation of words into sounds duplicates the voracious force innate in early cubism, the fragments themselves become simple structural units for the composition of the text.

Finlay associates this sort of transformation of the energies of cubism with the name of Juan Gris, a painter who reduced the components of his art to flat coloured shapes producing visual rhymes. It was after the publication of his first Gris poem – 'To the Painter, Juan Gris' (p. 161), a punning homage to his excellent still lifes[3] – that Finlay read Daniel-Henry Kahnweiler's *Juan Gris: His Life and Works*. This monograph in fact constitutes a survey of the theory and history of painting, in which Gris features as an exemplary instance. Finlay commented in 1970 that it needed a concluding chapter on concrete poetry.[4] His own *Homage to Kahnweiler* (p. 162) once again highlights the almost tactile quality which Finlay described as fauvist (rather than cubist),

while a page from his later *Improved Classical Dictionary* (p. 163) assimilates Juan Gris to the classical impulse. The pebble talisman *Peras* (p. 112) explicates the link between fauvism and classicism. Stephen Scobie has insisted that it is the classical sense of clarity in Gris' work which has always fascinated Finlay.[5] This is underlined in the note appended to the pebble. Here, Finlay recalls that 'Peras' or 'the Limited' is the Pythagorean ideal of the Good, as opposed to 'Apeiron', 'the Unlimited' or Bad. The pear, which appears in a number of paintings by Gris, Finlay considers to be 'the ideal fruit, on the cubist tree (or table), suggest[ing] a perfect limited form'.

The later works in Finlay's Gris series thus suggest that the cubist artist represents an incarnation of the spirit of classical art, a recent incarnation of Apollo.[6] At the same time, the *Peras* pebble shows how the move towards a renewed classicism underlines the ethical dimension which was always implicit in Finlay's aesthetic. As for the 'Pierrot' sub-series, this seeks to gauge manifestations of the classical spirit in different fields: sculpture, the circus, toymaking, technology (p. 164).[7] The list is typically heteroclite, for Finlay has always been intent on a comprehensive investigation of all types of cultural activities, whether mainstream or more marginal.

For Finlay, then, the name of Juan Gris does not so much denote an individuality, however strong or attractive, as it connotes a cultural effect. This is typical of all his evocations and homages. And it is with an effect of a similar nature that Ian Hamilton Finlay's own name is also to be associated.

a peach
    an apple

                a table

an eatable
    peach

        an apple

                an eatable
                table
                apple

            an apple
            a peach

From *Rapel*, 1963

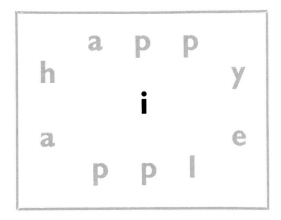

to the painter, Juan Gris

From *Rapel*, 1963

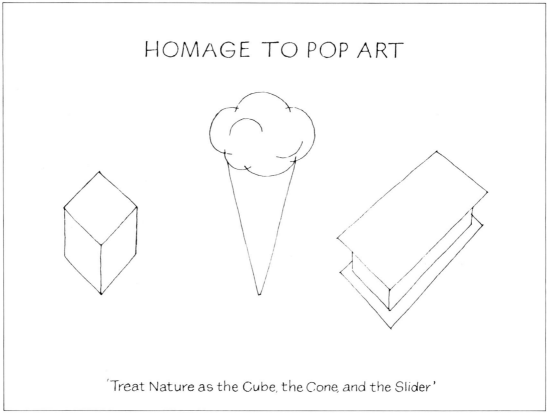

Homage to Kahnweiler, 1972
card, with Stuart Barrie

Homage to Pop Art, 1973
card, with Sydney McK. Glen, Graphic Partners, Edinburgh
The card is a play on Cézanne's famous observation: 'Treat nature as the cube, the cone, and the cylinder.' Here we have the Oxo (or similar) cube, the ice-cream cone, and the ice-cream slider (Scottish for wafer).

Analytical Cubist Portrait

Daniel-Henry Snowman

MANDOLIN, *n.* **a painter's instrument.** Rather like rhymes in a poem, two forms, generally of different sizes, are repeated. In 1920 these metaphors are fairly evident and are based on the simplest objects (playing cards, glasses etc.). Then a bunch of grapes is compared to a MANDOLIN.

Daniel-Henry Kahnweiler, *Juan Gris*

From *The Mailed Pinkie*, 1982
booklet, with Gary Hincks
Verlaggalerie Leaman, West Germany

From *An Improved Classical Dictionary*, 1981
booklet, with Nicholas Sloan

Pierrot, 1975
balsa wood
A small balsa glider becomes a 'sculpture' in the idiom of Juan
Gris. The glider's tail puns on the angle of the pierrot's feet.

2 NEAR AND FAR

The title piece of Finlay's first published book – a collection of short stories that appeared in 1958: *The Sea-Bed and Other Stories* – revolves round a strange experience. It tells the tale of two boys on a fishing expedition, a 'wholesome and mysterious' occupation but, on this particular occasion, unfruitful. Then:

> Suddenly, about an hour later, one of the boys felt that his skin no longer fitted him. His heart stopped beating for a second as he watched the great cod.
>
> He knew it was certainly a cod because of the dark tuft that sprouted from its chin. He knew, also, that the tuft was not really dark, but was only dark like the rest of the fish above the yellow sand, with the light coming down on it from above.
>
> The boy let out his breath and stared at the sea-bed. It was just the same as before, but now it had an air of silence and emptiness which was not like Sunday. It had been changed by the cod.
>
> The boy found himself shivering, and his hand was making bites at the end of the line, so that the sunk mussel was twitching and shivering too. His excitement ran down his fingers and down the line, to the bait like lightning running down a wire and into the ground. It was several minutes before he stopped shivering violently.
>
> The fact was, he could scarcely believe in the cod which had come like a herald from the sea-depths, for such a short space of time. He stared downwards, rubbing his finger on his lip, thinking, wondering. Then suddenly the sea-bed down there became real to him, and he could feel it going out and out, below the sea, further down than even it was there, and frightening to think of. He looked inland towards the cliffs.[1]

This is an instance of the paradigmatic Finlay moment: a shock seemingly in excess of its immediate pretext, feelings almost religious in their strangeness and intensity. Walter Benjamin would have said that the great cod had aura – 'the unique phenomenon of distance, however close it may be'.[2] It leaves behind it an atmosphere that is uncanny, and an impression of distance quite explicitly in excess of reality.

Finlay's short stories are full of comparable experiences.

'A Broken Engagement' (p. 72) provides an example on another scale and in a different tone. The narrator is remembering the kitchen in his childhood home:

> there was a feeling in there like that of a sunset – a beautiful, still, sad sunset when the birch and pine trees, even the brackens, are so very, very still it is as if they have been bewitched . . . Just such a feeling was over the chairs, the dewy table, the neatly stacked dishes and the shining pots and pans that hung in a row from the same shelf.

Here, the kitchen range

> was – in this indoor sunset – the equivalent of that faraway, bright rosy band above the woods.

It is important not to underestimate the difference in accent between the two instances of aura which have been cited. The second example, nostalgic and pastoral in its imagery, is easily enough assented to. However, one might well regard the tone of 'The Sea-Bed' as problematical, were its protagonist not a twelve-year-old. The phenomenon is specific neither to this story nor even to Finlay's work taken as a whole. An important analogue is provided by Geoffrey Hartman, who warns that it is sometimes difficult to value Wordsworth's emotions, and who quotes Coleridge as saying that these emotions 'may be disproportionate to such knowledge and value of objects described, as can fairly be anticipated of men in general, even of the most cultivated classes'.[3] An interesting instance of this problem is the (now widely appreciated) 'daffodils' lyric ('I wandered lonely as a cloud . . . '). Coleridge found its last stanza excessive in its stated emotion, while Anna Seward, another contemporary and also a poet, reacted to it with contemptuous astonishment and disgust, regarding it as a proof that Wordsworth was mad. Such reactions to the poet's imaginative and emotive power are at odds with the picture of the simple pastoral Wordsworth, popularized by Matthew Arnold and handed down by generations of British schoolmasters. However, another Victorian critic, A. C. Bradley, recognized Wordsworth's sublimity, as opposed to his simplicity.

Finlay's work is vulnerable to a similar misunderstanding. The earlier stories and much of the subsequent work certainly appear simple, and are not infrequently pastoral. However, if the strength of the emotions expressed in 'The Sea-Bed' seems problematical, the difficulty is accentuated in much of his work from the early 1970s onwards, where military motifs are frequently to be found in bucolic contexts (p. 169). Finlay himself recognizes the dual impact of his work, and uses categories drawn from the history of modern art movements to express this, employing the term 'fauve' when formal rigour implies the virtue of simple goodness and 'suprematist' when the question of power becomes more obvious. In the early 1970s, the name of Malevich, the quintessential suprematist artist, became expressly associated with aerial warfare in Finlay's work (p. 208).

The notion of aura accommodates both the comforting and the disturbing aspects of Finlay's work. Once again, Geoffrey Hartman gives a useful summary of what is involved: 'The aura is something like an intimation of immortality, but with a contradictory aspect: it flashes up from within ordinary life, like an epiphanic gleam or cathected desire, and it also defends against this shock by evoking a *"pays natal"* or *déjà vu* that is deeply if abstractly fulfilling'.[4] The ambivalence is manifest in Walter Benjamin's account of aura. In theoretical passages he denounces aura as a reactionary religious mystique. However, history and Marxist sociology fail to emancipate art from its magical power. For Benjamin, the aura of a work of art is its unique presence – an authenticity incorporating its authority as an object of veneration and implying a ritual function, together with its inscription within a tradition. To the extent that such a presence still makes itself felt, our modern secular societies continue to be haunted by an awareness of the religious dimension. The concept of aura focuses on the conjunction of religion, power and art, and also on the problematical way this constellation of motifs remains active in the contemporary world. Finlay's work constitutes a further and increasingly sophisticated reactivation of the problem, as illustrated both by his reformulation over the years of texts dealing with the aura conveyed by 'distance, however close it may be', and by the garden poetics he has evolved at Stonypath.

An early poem, 'Catch 23' is a reworking of 'The Sea-Bed'. It strives to come to terms directly with what is most inexpressible in the story – the impact of the great bearded cod. The result – a play on 'oddfish' and 'codfish', with a cedilla being used to represent the beard – is perhaps disappointing.[5] 'Catch 23' nevertheless shows Finlay's concrete poetry seeking to articulate the experience of aura, which the poetics of the modern short story, as instanced in *The Sea-Bed and Other Stories*, communicates only as a private and tenuous epiphany. The poem is not simply a typical example of modernistic reduction, making use of minimal verbal materials and the restrictive medium of typescript. It is also an attempt to invest a vein of experimentation associated with the concrete poetry movement with a concern for a traditional cultural experience.[6] It is thus symptomatic of Finlay's stance towards the avant-garde throughout the period of his connections with concrete poetry.

A more successful typescript poem articulates directly the evocative theme of proximity and distance. 'Fir/far' (p. 173) constructs a notional canvas, using as a model classical perspective, and not the cubism of 'A Peach an Apple'. The poem creates distance out of a minimal verbal change and plays on memories its reader will have retained of landscape paintings or nature poems with auratic fir trees. It was subsequently recast in several forms – as a supercool minimalist drawing executed by Jud Fine, as an element in Finlay's *Third Reich Revisited*, and as a tree in the poet's garden, pierced with an arrow (p. 176). The reiteration of a traditional subject in different idioms and media is an instance of the way in which Finlay's work confronts different aspects of culture and has serious implications, which are not merely aesthetic, but can also be political and ethical.[7]

The *Third Reich Revisited* is a set of sketches, either after existing edifices or else wholly imaginary; the commentaries are a pastiche of those in architectural journals. The *Ehrentempel, Munich* drawing from the series (p. 143) is also a reworking of an earlier poem – Finlay's 'First Suprematist Standing Poem'. The modulation from exclamation to interrogation in this work (p. 177) indicates the artist's early questioning of the value of aura, to which a letter on suprematism also testifies:

I approve of Malevich's statement, 'Man distinguished himself as a thinking being and removed himself from the perfection of God's creation. Having left the non-thinking state, he strives by means of his perfected objects, to be again embodied in the perfection of absolute, non-thinking life . . .' That is, this seems to me, to describe, approximately, my own need to make poems . . .

though I don't know what is meant by 'God'. And it also raises the question that, though the objects might 'make it', possibly, into a state of perfection, the poet and painter will not [. . .] and one does not want a *glittering* perfection which forgets that the world is, after all, also to be made by man into his *home*. I should say – however hard I should find it to justify this in theory – that 'concrete' by its very limitations offers a tangible image of goodness and sanity [. . .] It is a model, of order, even if set in a space which is full of doubt.[8]

Far from reiterating the often crass confidence of post-war denazification programmes in Germany, the *Ehrentempel, Munich* drawing restates the doubt high-lighted in Finlay's letter on a historical and ethical plane, inviting the beholder to ponder on the forces which animate Western civilization.

The bridging of Finlay's concrete and neoclassical periods can also be illustrated by the successive avatars of *Canal Stripe Series 4*. This was originally a booklet poem – a mode which represents one of Finlay's most distinctive contributions to concrete poetry. It, too, meditates on the phenomenon of proximity and distance:

LITTLE FIELDS   LONG HORIZONS
LITTLE FIELDS LONG for HORIZONS
HORIZONS LONG   for LITTLE FIELDS

Mimetically deriving its constructive energies from landscape (the limited variations suggested by canals) and meditating on the significance of landscape itself, the poem occupies a position on the frontier between art and nature. It can help explain what lay behind Finlay's decision to place poems in a natural environment: not a desire to merge his art with the forces of nature, but rather the need to put its rhetorical energies severely to the test. So it is that *Canal Stripe 4* became one of Finlay's first constructions specifically designed for a garden or park.[9] It also later found a place in the *Third Reich Revisited* series. This time, the force with which the energies of 'Little Fields' are confronted is altogether more sinister (p. 142). The drawing and text form an impressive reflection on the aesthetics of power in the modern world – and also on the power of aesthetics, a chiasmus which has increasingly come to preoccupy Finlay. It is significant that the ideal point for viewing the 'Little Fields' ballet – the place of the artist or viewer – is that reserved for the Führer.

The interplay between proximity and distance has ani-mated Finlay's work on his garden at Stonypath from the start. This is clear from the way in which the sea and sea-going vessels are omnipresent in the poet's domain – for what is more distant from the enclosed spaces of an inland garden than the far-flung world of the oceans? Yet Finlay immediately brought the sea into the Southern Uplands of Scotland, in works involving minimal lingu-istic elements and based on metaphorical play. These culminate in the appropriately entitled *From 'An Inland Garden'*, a booklet of poems invoking the sea, which were executed as garden pieces at Stonypath. One of the works returns to the aura of fir trees (p. 176), just as the earlier 'Column Poem' (p. 174) subtly introduces a seascape into a woodland context. Embarking on the theme of warships, Finlay subsequently commissioned a series of stone carvings intended to make the dimensions of his garden 'immeasurable'.[10] Miniature vessels can be seen emerging from foliage, or else acting as bird-tables which transform hungry birds into aircraft landing on and taking off from their carrier (p. 178, p. 10).

The introduction of sculpted warships at Stonypath is interesting, not only for the way in which it connotes the traumatic aspect of aura (in contrast to the earlier use of fishing vessels), but also for its overt cultural implications. The bird-table/aircraft carrier forms part of a series of works in stone entitled *Homage to the Villa d'Este*, as a deliberate invocation of the classical tradition, while *Nuclear Sail* (p. 179), simulating the conning tower of a modern submarine, is a fine example of Finlay's neo-classicism that, by the very quality of its execution, questions the energies and values of a whole school of modern sculpture in rounded polished stone.[11] The conjunction of modern warfare and an elegiac invocation of sailing ships in the title of *Nuclear Sail* shows how fine a balance Finlay maintains between the dark and sustain-ing aspects of aura. These elements had been present from the outset, as is wittily demonstrated by the earlier *Elegiac Inscription* calling for the restoration of the birch, to which the Finlays themselves responded by judicious planting (p. 175)!

In such works the distance invoked is as much tem-poral as geographical. In aesthetic terms, the neoclassical project still being carried out at Stonypath knowingly incorporates what Stephen Bann, quoting Erwin Panofsky, refers to as the northern artist's pathos of distance from the classical world. For Albrecht Dürer, 'antiquity was neither a garden where fruits and flowers still bloomed, nor a field of ruins the stones and columns of which could be re-used. It was a "lost kingdom" which had to be reconquered by a well-organized campaign.'[12] The observation is of obvious relevance to Finlay's gardening. However, his design is not so much to recover the immediacy of classical antiquity (aesthetics since the early German romantics are based on the realization that it is too late to do so), as to test the remnants of the classical tradition in a hostile environment. Hostile for climatic reasons: the inscription which was one of the first works to be installed at Stonypath, next to a pond dug by the Finlays themselves, is an obvious attempt to rise to the challenge. *Pond Inscription* (p. 44) is a work whose defiance of its originally barren surroundings served to shape the development of the garden in its vicinity. One of the most striking avatars of Finlay's systematic transplanting of the classical is undoubtedly to be found in the 'views' he prepared for the exhibition *Nature Over Again After Poussin* in 1979. The views are signed with the monographs of artists from Dürer to Fragonard (p. 180, p. 181). They draw upon the tradition of the eighteenth-century landscape garden, at the inception of which painting – that of Poussin and Claude in particular – was all important, and show Finlay once again operating on the borderline between art and nature, in order to induce a meditation on the complexities of the auratic glimmer.

The garden at Stonypath frequently bridges cultural chasms in a manner that may appear perplexing to the visitor. Does Finlay's neoclassicism produce a forced conjunction of terms (the ancient and the modern), demonstrating by the very violence of its procedures that the last threads of a tapestry going back to ancient Greece have been broken? Or does it imply structural continuity between the terms it unites?[13] Romantic and post-romantic irony depend on the fact that such questions cannot be finally settled. What is significant is that Finlay's response to this situation is not to compose one more melancholy variation on the theme of the death of art, but to come up with a strategy which, in a radically conflictual cultural context, can appropriately be called polemological.

The most contentious modification to Finlay's garden in recent years was the transformation of an outhouse formerly used as a gallery into a Garden Temple. This gesture must be understood in terms of the hostile environment in which Stonypath finds itself. Only this time the hostility is not so much climatic as cultural – the modern secularized bureaucratic state. The reactions, not only of various British authorities but also of other artists, testify to this. The implantation of the Temple, considered in geopolitical terms, challenges the state of Western culture in a north-westerly outpost of contemporary Europe. One might feel that this is to overstate the case. Ultimately, however, Finlay's enterprise demands to be judged on such terms. Only time will tell if the imaginative and rhetorical force he has developed will prevail. Let it at least be noted that the inscription on the Temple – 'To Apollo his music his missiles his muses' (p. 67) – not only demonstrates that Finlay labours under no illusion regarding the magnitude of the task, but also indicates yet again the unresolvable duality of the energies animating the entire enterprise.

Betula Pendula
(*Silver Birch*)

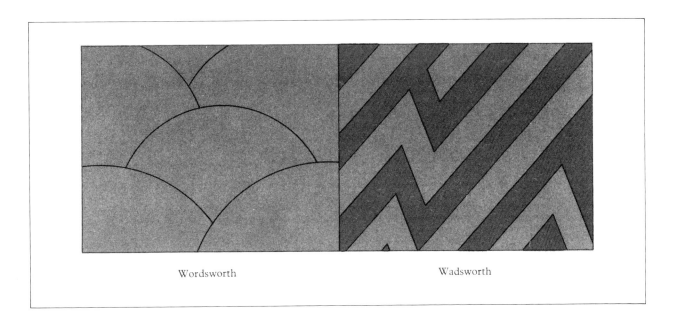

Wordsworth   Wadsworth

Betula Pendula, 1977
card, with Gary Hincks

Wordsworth/Wadsworth, 1977
card, with Jim Downie
Art deco circles and zigzags are particularized in the identification
of the former with Wordsworth the pastoral poet, and the latter
with Wadsworth the English twentieth-century Vorticist; in the
case of Wordsworth we read the design as Lakeland hills and in
that of Wadsworth as World War I naval camouflage (of the
dazzle variety).

Camouflage Sentences

To camouflage a tank is to add what Shenstone calls 'the amiable to the
severe' – the beautiful to the sublime, flutes to drums.

———

Camoufleurs are Monday painters.

———

It is the bufineff of dazzle camouflage to caufe an s to appear an f, and an f an s.

———

Psychologists discover everything to be camouflage. It is then made clear
how very little these experts know of tanks.

———

Realism is a style which purports to be, and is at first often taken to be,
without camouflage.

———

Every style in art is a camouflage through which, by our own
reconstruction, we think we see 'real' nature.

———

Nature loves to hide – said Heraclitus.

———

Classification of German Panzer Camouflage:
Primitive (1939)   overall dark grey
Classical (1943)   dark yellow, olive green, red-brown
(Cf. N. Poussin's *Funeral of Phocion*)
Plein Air (1944)   'the hedgerow campaign' – real foliage, grasses, etc.,
over a dark yellow ground.

———

The Presocratic philosophers regarded the apparent world as a camouflage;
they differed as to whether the thing confused, was Fire (Heraclitus),
or Water (Thales), or Air (Anaximenes), or The Boundless (Anaximander).

———

AFV crews who applied camouflage colours to their vehicles, staked their
lives on their art.

THE MONTHS
Receipts for the Working of Samplers

JANUARY
An obsolete Tank, painted White; the Numeral on the Turret
hand-painted in Black and White; some old Evergreen
Branches tied around the Gun.
Divisional Sign a Water-Bearer.

FEBRUARY
A cruiser Tank with a Mottled Finish; some Bare Branches protruding
from the Storage Bin; daubs of White on the Side Skirt,
with fresh streaks of Mud.
Divisional Sign a Fish.

MARCH
A fast, amphibious Tank; an Ambush Scheme applied to the Side Skirt;
some Snowdrops and Violets tied on the Gun.
Divisional Sign a Ram.

APRIL
A Bergepanzer (recovery tank), with a surprising new White Finish;
on the Superstructure, Daffodils; on the Tow-hook, a Daisy-chain.
Divisional Sign a Bull.

MAY
A small, light Tank decked with Blossom, a twist
of Blossom on the Radio Antenna.
Divisional Sign a Pair of Twins.

JUNE
A light Tank, the dark grey base completely concealed with a
Yellow Spray-coat; on the Cupola and protruding from the
Smoke Bomb Discharger, some short Leafy Boughs.
Divisional Sign a Crab.

JULY
A heavy Tank; an all-over Green with the outlines obscured by piled-
up Foliage; even the Road-wheels sprayed with Green, and
with a Darker Green on the Side Skirt.
Divisional Sign a Lion.

AUGUST
A flame-throwing Tank, with a layer of Dust over a Red-brown
Base-coat; some ripened Wheat-ears dangling from the Idler
Wheel, and some Poppies from the Gun.
Divisional Sign a Virgin.

SEPTEMBER
A slow, broad Tank, well thatched with Straw, the Engine Louvres
strewn with Apple Boughs; the Gun traversed, the Hull and
Storage Bin heaped with Plums and Cucumbers.
Divisional Sign a Pair of Scales.

OCTOBER
A medium Tank with a Dark-yellow Finish, some Yellowing Boughs
thrown on the Glacis Plate; a Lighter Colour on the Turret-sides;
the Headlamps bound with Straw.
Divisional Sign a Scorpion.

NOVEMBER
A heavy Tank with an Olive Green Undercoat and some Branches of
Evergreen arranged on the Superstructure; the Turret topped with
a small Wreath of Evergreen; a Swede in the Gun-muzzle.
Divisional Sign an Archer.

DECEMBER
A medium Tank in a Dark Grey Finish; with Sprays of Holly on the
Saukopf Mantlet; the Commander's Cupola standing open;
the Machine-gun wound with Mistletoe.
Divisional Sign a Goat.

Ian Hamilton Finlay, Wild Hawthorn Press · Printed by Nicholas Sloan, Parrett Press

The Months, 1981
print, with Nicholas Sloan

SOME VERSIONS OF PASTORAL

Homage to William Empson

Some Versions of Pastoral, 1978
card, with Gary Hincks

SCENE

The fir tree stands quite still and angles
On the hill, for green Triangles.

Stewing in its billy there
The tea is strong, and brown, and Square.

The rain is Slant. Soaked fishers sup
Sad Ellipses from a cup.

fir tree   rock root rocketrocketrocketrocketrocketrocketrocketrocket

count-down of a fir tree

```
        10
         9
         8
         7
         6
         5
         4
         3
         2
         1           fir                           fir
         2           fir fir                   fir fir
                     fir fir fir           fir fir fir
         3           fir fir fir far fir fir fir
         4           fir fir fir           fir fir fir
         5           fir fir                   fir fir
         6           fir                           fir
         7
         8
         9
        10
```

From *The Dancers Inherit the Party*, 1960
Migrant Press   From *Tea-leaves and Fishes*, 1966

wind
wind

wave
wave

bough
bow

star
star

Column Poem, from *The Blue and the Brown Poems*, 1968
Jargon Press, USA

Elegiac inscription, 1971
stone, with Michael Harvey

Arrow, 1984
bronze, with David Ballantyne

A Pinnate Evergreen
metal

how blue ?	how blue !
how sad ?	how far !
how small ?	how sad !
how white ?	how small !
how far ?	how white !

First Suprematist / Standing Poem, 1965
folding card

Aircraft carrier Fountain, 1972
bronze

USS *Nautilus*, 1979
stone, with John Andrew

Nuclear sail, 1974
slate, with John Andrew

From 'Nature Over Again After Poussin', 1980
with Nicholas Sloan and David Paterson
Collins Exhibition Hall, Glasgow
Corot, Salvator Rosa, Guercino, Gaspard Duguet or Poussin

3 THE WORD

'Words, too, have an aura of their own', Walter Benjamin declares, quoting Karl Kraus to the effect that 'the closer the look one takes at a word, the greater the distance from which it looks back'; and Stephen Bann suggests that concrete poetry provides specific occasions for 'fathoming' words.[1] Aura intervenes here, not as a theme, but rather as an essential aspect of poetics. In Finlay's case, one comes across a striking manifestation of this phenomenon in a series of concrete poems whose visual aspect is not directly representational. Each of the poems takes the form of a block of words. In 'Acrobats', which was conceived for a playground (p. 184), the letters play the part of circus performers in motion,[2] while of 'Tendresse' (p. 183) Stephen Bann observes that it has 'a shimmer and dazzle that is purely optical', even if – as was the case in 'A Peach an Apple' (p. 160) – the verbal play also has a thematic import. M. L. Rosenthal suggests that 'Tendresse' produces a 'gently erotic texture',[3] a sensual fauvist pleasure. However, *Homage to Malevich* (p. 183) has suprematist connotations. Its wordplay indicates the dimension of doubt, as opposed to 'glittering perfection', which Finlay stresses in his letter to Pierre Garnier.

A single word can condense an entire descriptive sequence without losing the element of aura the corresponding prose passage would seek to convey. This can be seen in the *Homage to Vuillard*, which may usefully be considered in connection with the description of a kitchen in the short story 'A Broken Engagement' (p. 185). Stephen Bann notes that the conjunction of the *intimiste* painter and the name of the Singer sewing-machine company creates an enclosed domestic space. 'Singer' evokes both the machine and its song, while the Roman lettering suggests 'a kind of classical personification of the machine, which becomes, as it were, the Siren of the machine age'.[4]

In a striking paraphrase of Aquinas, Joyce suggests that the auratic epiphany fuses 'whatness' and 'radiance': '*Claritas* is *quidditas*'.[5] Can Finlay's neon poems not be seen as a variation on this theological theme? There was a room of neon poems at Finlay's Serpentine exhibition in 1977. The catalogue rightly points out that these are the successors of the fauve poems in *Rapel*, with the intense luminosity of neon light replacing the earlier use of coloured inks. Once again, Finlay is conflating traditional qualities and modernist manner. Working with neon is not an idiosyncratic gesture, but inscribes a section of Finlay's production in a corner of a minor but well-established trend of art works in neon. Finlay avoids all suggestion of modernist reduction (painting reduced to pure colour without substance). A poem like 'L'étoile' (p. 186) – a reworking in expressive calligraphy of a typescript poem from *Telegrams from my Windmill* – can usefully be referred back to Joyce's sacred and aesthetic epiphany. In *Strawberry Camouflage* (p. 186), the very bold fauvist impact introduces the element of force more typically associated with Finlay's suprematism. Finlay explains in his *Detached Sentences on Camouflage*[6] that 'The domestic strawberry disguises certain of its leaves as the ripe fruit; this is the principle of dazzle camouflage.' Shimmer, glitter, dazzle – it is worth risking a generalization and suggesting that the common ground linking natural and verbal aura in Finlay's work may be understood in terms of a quality of light. Just as light, however immediate its impact, implies distance as a non-objectal phenomenon, so a single word with its eddies of connotations is never simply there, never just a desacralized tool.

Alternatively, the aura of a word can emerge from stone and – seemingly, at least – from the distant past. One of Finlay's collaborations with Jud Fine was subsequently re-cast as a stone inscription reminiscent of the panels one associates with archaeological sites (p. 188). Such a work seeks to gauge how the modern artist's 'epic quality' stands up to the ancient context, and then – in so far as the quality of the execution forces the viewer to assent to the assimilation – to imply that the 'secret' reaching a great distance across the ages is both formal and hermeneutic: a hieroglyphic force.[7]

The sculpture/poem *Starlit Waters* (p. 187) is in a more modernistic vein and was the object of a minor press campaign when first put on view at the Tate Gallery in 1976. This can doubtless be explained by the fact that it challenges the observer to ponder on its status. Like other similar works by Finlay, it stands between art and non-art, ready-made sculpture and poetry (Finlay preferring the latter denomination), but also between designation (fishing boat names) and description ('starlit waters'). As such, the hostile journalists' assimilation of *Starlit Waters* and Carl Andre's notorious bricks is understandable. The American artist deliberately deflates the convention whereby sculpture is erectile, inducing a hesitation – sculpture/not sculpture? – which interrogates the fetishistic dimension of art. As the controversial bricks also suggest an all-over painting displaced to floor level, they furthermore question the nature of painting and its conventions. Finlay's procedure in *Starlit Waters* has a somewhat different impact. The colours – letters/base/net – introduce an element of fauvist aura, and the figurative play induced by the words prolongs this. The deflationary disappearance of sculpture effected by Andre becomes here the dissemination of the presence of the work into an involuted network of correspondences, which do not so much question the status of *Starlit Waters* as establish its value. Finlay is 'civilizing' non-art, 'upgrading' what he considered to be suspect in the wrapping procedures of Christo. He thinks of *Starlit Waters* as 'a "wrapped object", with the net replacing the opaque wrappings, and the whole thing as a kind of purified vision of the profane (as it were) . . . a "good" instead of an "unpleasant" mystery . . .'.[8] Words have an aura of their own, and if this is not always of the assuaging order Finlay defines as fauve, it is never, in his productions, either mere religiosity or plain mystification.

```
lackblockblackb
lockblackblockb
lackblockblackb
lockblackblockb
lackblockblackb
lockblackblockb
lackblockblackb
lockblackblockb
lackblockblackb
lockblackblockb
lackblockblackb
lockblackblockb
lackblockblackb
```

```
tendressetendressetendressetendressetend
erdresstenderdresstenderdresstenderdress
tenderdresstenderdresstenderdresstenderd
ressetendressetendressetendressetendress
etenderdresstenderdresstenderdresstender
dressetendressetendressetendressetendres
setendressetendressetendressetendressete
nderdresstenderdresstenderdresstenderdre
ssetendressetendressetendressetendresset
enderdresstenderdresstenderdresstenderdr
essetendressetendressetendressetendresse
```

From *Telegrams from my Windmill*, 1964   Homage to Malevich, from *Rapel*, 1963

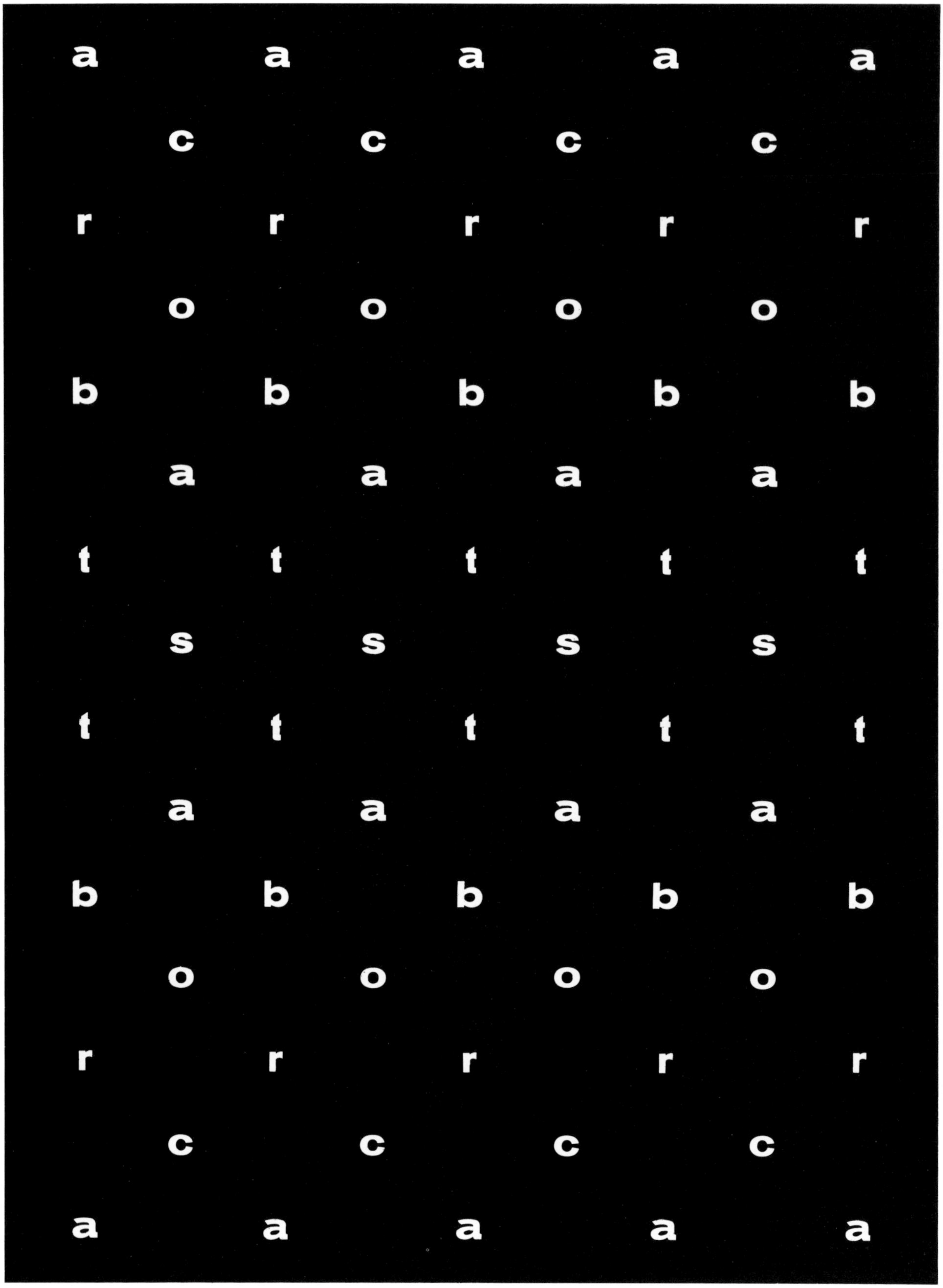

'Acrobats', 1966
screen print
Tarasque Press

Homage to Vuillard, 1971
print in folder, with Michael Harvey

L'étoile . . ., 1976
neon, with J. B. Anderstrem & Co

Strawberry Camouflage, 1977
neon, with Ron Costley and Merson Signs

Starlit Waters, Boat names and numbers series, 1968
wood and net, with Peter Grant

Drift, Boat names and numbers series, 1968
wood and net, with Peter Grant

Secret, 1976
stone, with Christopher Haysom
based on the drawing done with Jud Fine

4 METAPHOR, RHYME, CITATION

As its etymology suggests, metaphor is transference. The distance it incorporates by transporting words or meaning into a context where they do not literally fit explains its aura, hanging between its verbal and semantic levels (between what semioticians refer to as signifier and signified). Finlay pays close attention to metaphor. In 1966, he suggested that the simplicity achieved by some concrete poets would only remain possible if there could be found a way back to metaphor, and further stressed that the sum of any poem must be greater than its parts merely added together. This meant a new understanding of metaphor.[1] Finlay's own way with metaphor can readily be discerned in a thematic series of works, most of which were produced in the immediate aftermath of his pure concrete phase, but which had been anticipated in an earlier and more traditional poem The series was brought to a remarkable conclusion in the early 1980s. A purely formal analysis of the various works composing it would be inadequate, for these put the reader/observer in a position where he must always be ready to perform diverse figurative, generic and semantic operations.

The set can perhaps best be named after one of its central elements, the folding card *Rhymes for Lemons* published in 1970 (p. 194). The 'rhymes' are, in the first place, rhyming shapes or forms, such as have been encountered in connection with Gris and Kahnweiler. On this basis, the rhyme can be characterized as a metaphor which is essentially phenomenological in nature. It corresponds to Aristotle's notion of metaphor, as expounded in the *Poetics*. This states that a good metaphor implies an intuitive perception of the similarity in dissimilars.[2] Aristotle also argues that one cannot learn from others how to become a master of metaphor, as this is a sign of genius. If this is the case, then the genius to whom Finlay's entire 'Rhymes' sequence is indebted is an anonymous and presumably fictitious English colonel. Such, at least, is the claim put forward in the second of the Orkney Lyrics from *The Dancers Inherit the Party*:

The English Colonel Explains an Orkney Boat

The boat swims full of air.
You see, it has a point at both
Ends, sir, somewhat
As lemons. I'm explaining

The hollowness is amazing. That's
The way a boat
Floats.

One might wonder why a southern Briton on a Scottish isle should think of a Mediterranean fruit. The full cultural significance of the simile will only emerge as the 'lemons' series develops. With respect to this inaugural poem, Finlay explains that 'the world is obvious' and that 'one takes pleasure in, and finds one's content in, what *is*'.[3] The English colonel thus represents 'an objective, ironic, distanced look, at an actual boat'. The prosody deftly underlines the persona's hesitations and the effort required to find the right word or image, so that 'stops (pauses) and beginnings become actual things'. This seemingly naive quality is to be found in Finlay's other Orkney Lyrics, and is used to great effect in the delightful parody of Hugh MacDiarmid (p. 75).

The texture of such poems obviously constitutes a deliberate stylistic gesture. Both their rhymes and their imagery are (to adopt Finlay's own terminology) fauvist. To appreciate the significance of this, it may be useful to recall an earlier, historically important, exercise in a similar vein – the *Lyrical Ballads* of 1798. Wordsworth's Preface (added in 1802) pits poetry against rhetoric, seeking to justify the poet's own figurative energies by referring to the emotional power of 'the real language of men'. Now even so sympathetic a critic as Coleridge expressed reservations about the language of some of the Lyrical Ballads.[4] Wordsworth's idiom does indeed provide evidence of a degree of rhetorical discomfiture. The prose rhythms and persona of Finlay's rhyming poems deliberately heighten this phenomenon. It is doubtless the panache with which they are carried off that provoked the hostility of his Scottish contemporaries – and the admiration of American poets.

An enduring embarrassment concerning rhetoric is one aspect of our post-romantic heritage. Another, derived from the romantics' promotion of the more spontaneous values of imagination and feeling, is the notion of the image. A purely empirical commonplace, this concept provides the context in which much of Finlay's concrete and immediately post-concrete work can best be understood. 'So you want images . . .', Finlay seems to be saying as he shapes words iconically or juxtaposes word and image in his poem/cards and poem/prints. There is, however, a difference with respect to the vague ideology of the image which marks much Anglo-American modernism, and this is due, not so much to Finlay's mingling of modes and media, as to an uncommonly clear idea of the structure and potentialities of metaphor.

It is not only the shape of the boats which 'rhyme' in *Rhymes for Lemons*. On each of the pages, as they unfold, one also comes across the names of fishing vessels: Dulsie, Blenda, Nimrod, Yellowfin, Patty, etc. It is impossible to avoid the suggestion that this series of names also provides 'rhymes' which are, in a wide sense, metaphorical. They turn the boats into notional characters, male and female, some with names which are common enough, others with more unusual-sounding ones. These have a ring of suggested fable (Nimrod, Argo, Mizpah), pastoral (Amaryllis) or allegory (Ira). The series evokes classical poetic modes not unassociated with the region where the lemon tree grows. The suggestion is that the actual fishing-boats bearing these names fancifully re-enact such poems, in northern waters and in modern times. The programmatic 'rhymes' thus serve to capture and hold in suspension echoes – however faint and fleeting – of earlier ages of our civilization. They weave new variations from the last tenuous threads of classical culture. In the early nineteenth century, Heinrich Heine observed that the advent of Christianity had driven the pagan gods underground, and that they emerged from hiding only as elves and demons in the popular imagination – apparitions stripped of much of their power. In the second half of the twentieth century, Finlay finds less romantic traces of the past: not in legend, but in the clumsy remnants of rhetorical tradition and in the apparently banal act of naming. Thus he avoids the solipsistic charms of the modern image, and challenges us to ponder on the survival of our classical heritage.

3 Blue Lemons (p. 197) had already suggested an improbable link between classical rhetorical doctrine and modernistic iconoclasm. The names of the vessels imply values anticipating the neoclassical *pears/peras*

pebble (p. 112). Significantly, the card also has the sobriety of Finlay's overtly neoclassical work. At first sight, the title has something extravagant about it. '3 blue lemons': how brashly modernistic. One would perhaps be led to think of a surrealistic fragment; or of fauvist painting, with its wilful misplacing of colours. The minimalist restraint of Finlay's poem/card checks any wild flights of fancy, however, with the result that one is encouraged to find a rationale for the formula in rhetorical, rather than phantasmagorical, terms. On closer consideration, title and footnote can be seen to provide instances of classical metaphorical procedures, such as are to be found in the *Poetics* of Aristotle. '3 blue lemons' is a qualified metaphor similar to Aristotle's example, 'old age of the day', for evening. If Finlay's metaphor seems more arbitrary, this is because blue is an accidental (rather than essential) aspect of the boats. The footnote, 'in a tidal bowl, Peterhead', shows the process of qualification in more normal circumstances, as 'tidal' is an essential quality of the maritime component of the metaphor. Moreover, title and footnote taken together constitute a fine example of the type of figure most favoured by Aristotle: metaphor from analogy – lemons : bowl : : ships : harbour. The surprising result is that the baroque process of extending the metaphor rationalizes the 'illogical' modernism of the title taken in isolation, so that the development is as exemplary in its logic as it is imaginative. The footnote can be considered a heuristic device, leading the reader to discover the subtleties of metaphorical procedures, as well as an imaginative programme – a text it would be a challenge to visualize.

3 Blue Lemons in fact invites visualization in two ways. The layout suggests not only a poem, but also a notional canvas, with the boats moored side by side and painted blue, so that the text represents as well as names them. The postcard format also implies an iconic, rather than poetic, work. The visual aspect is developed in later items from the 'lemons' series. *Marine* (p. 196) was one of the first of Finlay's works to depart from purely verbal material. The lemons in the bowl are represented, while the seascape is suggested both by the use of boat registration codes and by the inscribed title, which invites an act of interpretation.[5] In *Glossary* (p. 195), the punning 'rhyme' between 'lemon' and 'leman' suggests another way of looking at the 'sturdy, plump' vessels.[6]

Another work from the series appears to be more obviously analytic in the way it details the metaphor. The title itself – *Still Life With Lemon (Detail)* (p. 197) –

together with the fact that it is printed in the appropriate place on the reverse side (in English, French and German), underlines the postcard convention already referred to. To the stylized scene depicted in the photograph, a hand[7] has added in blue ink a colour code and a semiotic key. This verbal element is characteristically intricate. 'Yellow', 'green', 'yellow': these items in the colour code contribute to the formation of the formal rhyme. Furthermore, two other verbal units point to the boat. In these, the colour code is relegated to a parenthesis, while new visual analogies are explicitly expressed by the metaphorical semiotic key: 'pips (silver)' and 'stalk (brown)'. The distinction between the colour and the semiotic keys is thus far evident. Either can be employed or stressed as required for the boat/lemon analogy. It is Finlay's treatment of the background which complicates the picture. If 'blue' indicates the horizon, and therefore both sky and sea, 'azure blue' points firmly to the sea. And this time there is no parenthesis. Does one then read these terms together: 'azure blue', in other words 'sky blue'? Or does one read them as synonyms? Or, finally, does one silently insert a parenthesis, to make this particular indication identical to the others employing two words? That would involve reading 'azure' as a noun, and as an element of the semiotic key, while 'blue' alone would belong to the colour code. This third possibility heightens the paradoxical implications of the first two, for it suggests interpreting the sea as sky. The vacillation between the cosmic elements on either side of the horizon thus answers the metaphorical ambivalence of the figure in the foreground.

What is forced on to the attention is the poetic charge of 'azure' – a term favoured by nineteenth-century symbolist poets – so that the card comes to constitute yet another variation on the theme of proximity and distance, or the finite (lemon) and the infinite (azure). The cultural connotations of this variation are heavily coded. If 'azure', via symbolism, points to the birth of modern poetry, the apogee of still life as a genre was perhaps the period from Cézanne to the cubists, in which modern painting emerged. What is at issue is a break from straightforward representational content, the function of conveying this being taken over by photography (and the photograph in *Still Life With Lemon* is very obviously an old one from the early days of the medium). Such a network of allusions underlines the historical texture of Finlay's poem/card, suggesting an archaeology of the modern movement in poetry and painting. *Still Life with Lemon* may be held to imply that, in departing from discursive sense and mimetic content, modernism sought, not so much to achieve a reductive painterly or verbal formalism, as to preserve the essential component of aura. And in *Lemons, Netted* (p. 197), a work related to his series of fishing-boat names and registration codes in painted wood, but which is also a variation on *Marine*, Finlay reinjects aura into the idiom of late modernism.

The greater part of the 'Rhymes for Lemons' series is fauvist. In what he suggests might be the 'last lemon', Finlay evokes more strongly than ever the *'pays natal'* and the sense of *déjà vécu* associated with fauvist aura by Geoffrey Hartman.[8] Yet the tone is altogether more akin to Finlay's suprematist mode. The work is an addition to the series of Heroic Emblems published in 1977 (p. 193). Its motto is taken from the poems of Herman Hesse; the illustration is a German warship. The emblem does not yet have an authorized commentary along the lines of those provided by Stephen Bann for the 1977 volume, so it will be useful to quote at length Finlay's first, and avowedly tentative steps towards providing one. The gloss touches upon a number of issues central to Finlay's work (the limited, romantic attitudes towards the classic; religious, political and aesthetic power . . .):

> As you will appreciate, there is a comparison being made, between the small and perfect (aesthetically perfect) warship, and the Greek temple (Greek temples are usually small, too – of frigate-size, one might say, as opposed to Roman temple-cruisers or even battleships –); the ungiven, implicit text is Goethe's 'Kennst du das Land, wo die Zitronen blühn . . .' – Do you know the country where the lemon trees flower –: which I am taking as an invocation of the South-land of classical culture – German 'homesickness' for which has always had an ambiguity, allegorised by the ambiguities of German classical architecture (whose longings, notoriously, were not confined to flowering lemon trees, or rather, which notoriously did not present itself as an actualisation of a merely verdant ideal). (The period of German idealist philosophy is also the period of the birth of German nationalism.) What the warship and the temple share, is an absolute (neither is a secular construction). This is why they can be interchanged, or is why the 'aesthetic' parallel is not merely whimsical. Democracies are not at ease

with their weaponry, or with their art, since both involve (take their stand on) other values – those of the 'South-land'. Perhaps democracy should be homesick for its own unbuilt temples – alternatives to weaponry, a truly democratic pluralist art – or perhaps such alternatives, and such art, are just not possible. Classicism was at home with power; the modern democracies (whose secularism has produced extraordinary power) are not. The warship is an unrecognised, necessary temple. From the citizen armies of the post-Revolution period, there is a return to mercenary armies (the soldier as outsider). Pacifism, which should be the real 'creed' of democracy, is obviously no more than a form of the utilitarian (the convenient, the easy) (i.e. as presently understood and 'lived'). The homesickness for classical culture, was an impetus towards wholeness, and since this clearly included the gods, and power (for gods without power are a contradiction), it had an ambiguous aspect; it was in our terms *dangerous*.[9]

There is a risk that one might object to so much indirection and protest that Finlay's 'Rhymes for Lemons' series is idiosyncratic and obscure to an unjustifiable extreme. There is, however, an antecedent in the Renaissance emblem, whose conventions Finlay quite explicitly evokes in his 'last lemon'. If the attendant commentary was an essential part of the emblem in the Renaissance, the problematical nature of its procedures and its length (which could run to several pages) has frequently been remarked upon.[10] Equally, the enigmatic nature of emblems has always been recognized, and in certain circumstances vaunted. The effect produced can be described by comparing the composite entity constituted by emblems to the anamorphic play with perspective practised in Renaissance painting.[11] If one is to appreciate that the oblong object in the foreground of Holbein's *Ambassadors* is a dead man's skull, one must look at the painting from a different point of view, well to the left of the canvas. Seen from straight on, it is uncanny and obscure. Similarly, the strangeness of an emblem pushes the reader back. It forces him to perform an act of inventiveness, if he is to be able really to take possession of it. To discern the meaning requires a gymnastic exercise, a display of acrobatics. It is dependent on the discovery of the strategic point which puts the emblem into perspective. Finlay's 'Acrobats' (p. 184) and his Nuremberg *Little Fields* (p. 142) thematically

stress a similar effect. To favour such operations is indeed a characteristic trait of his work as a whole, so that his revival of the Renaissance emblem simply recalls a historically attested analogue.

Such historical justification is nevertheless not sufficient. Even if its procedures pervaded painting to a much greater extent than is commonly realized, the Renaissance emblem could still be held to represent a deviation from the classic norm. Indeed, Aristotle had observed the kinship between metaphor and riddle, and had deplored those metaphors that leaned too far in this direction. It remains necessary, then, to pinpoint the virtues of Finlay's procedure. The Renaissance emblem was narrowly coded. In Finlay's 'lemons' series, however, the rhetoric and traditions of different aspects of Western culture must be taken into consideration if the reader is to make sense either of individual pieces or of the set taken as a whole. One of the principal questions raised by Finlay's work is whether or not it achieves structural continuity with the tradition. The 'Rhymes for Lemons' series suggests that the answer lies in what Jonathan Culler, adapting Chomsky, calls the literary – or, in this case more generally cultural – competence of the reader or viewer.[12] Finlay's work is frequently enigmatic. However, this is not the modernistic art of being difficult, associated with abstruse metaphysics or the desire for perpetual renewal. The commentaries which have increasingly become part of Finlay's works themselves are not so much explication as documentation.[13] The bibliographical aspect which they often assume demonstrates that their chief purpose is to connect the reader with the tissue of tradition. They do not, however, do so in the spirit of an appeal to authority, in the manner of traditional rhetoric or contemporary academic prose. The procedure is citational. Hence the stylistic variations akin to pastiche in the 'lemons' series. As Finlay himself has observed, his approach 'depends on a system of references to other works of art, and other methods'.[14] Parallels are evoked neither as source nor as *auctoritas*, but for their consonance, however problematical. They echo or rhyme. Or again, Finlay's work seeks to ring a bell. The effect – rallying call, Angelus, knell of a passing culture – certainly depends on the energies of the work itself. But it is also dependent on the reader or viewer's desire and capacity to respond and, by so doing, to reconstruct the necessary rhetorical continuity.

Citation must in the present context be taken in a quasi-judicial sense. What is at stake is an evaluation of cultural codes and forces. It has been suggested that every citation is also a metaphor, in so far as it presents an idea 'in the guise of another more striking or better known idea, which is in any case linked to it by no more than a certain degree of conformity or analogy'.[15] This definition of metaphor, taken from an eighteenth-century rhetorical treatise, implies a tactical aim related to the *doxa* (common opinion), and indicates a displacement from the more neutral and essentially phenomenological definition of metaphor given in Aristotle's *Poetics*. Aristotle may well be correct in claiming that one cannot learn to become a masterly producer of metaphors. However, mastering the art of accommodating metaphor is by no means an idiosyncratic or a passive skill. The ideas, conformities and analogies involved do not only imply an acuteness of perception, but even more a community and a culture. The most striking aspects of the art of this century may well seem to go against such values. But even where he espouses spectacular modernistic disruption and reduction, Finlay uses the modern anti-art vulgate to present the now less familiar idea of rhetorical tradition.

Emblem, 1984
with Ron Costley

From *Rhymes for Lemons*, 1970
folding booklet, with Margot Sandeman

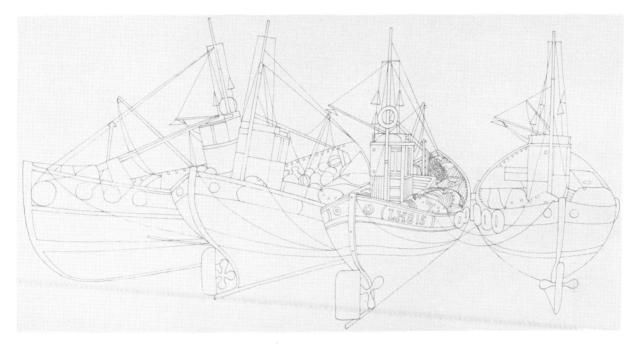

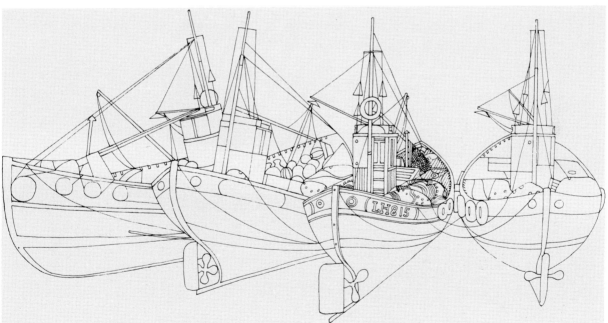

Glossary: Leman (Scots) – sweetheart

Glossary, 1971
print in folder, with Richard Demarco

Marine, 1968
screen print, with Patrick Caulfield

3 BLUE LEMONS *

ANCHOR OF HOPE

DAISY

GOOD DESIGN

* in a tidal bowl, Peterhead

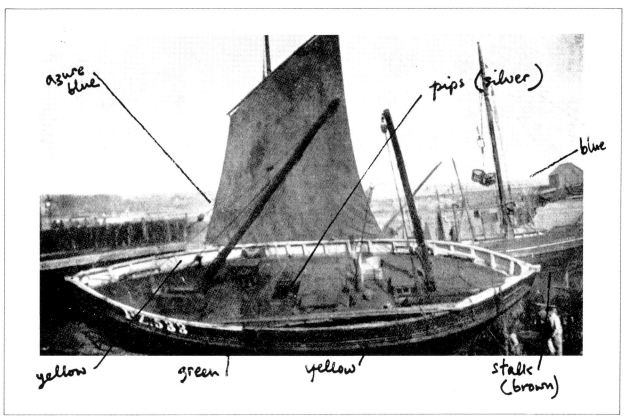

3 Blue Lemons, 1967 card

Lemons (netted), 1977
painted wood and net, with Peter Grant

Still Life with Lemon (Detail), 1970
card

5 CIVILIZING DADA

Letters of the alphabet and numbers, isolated or in groups, featured prominently in the work of the dadaists and constructivists of the heroic period of modern art. Their most aggressive role was doubtless the part they played in dadaist painting and poetry. It involved the eschewal of well-formed words and statements in poetry and the eruption of minimal linguistic elements into the visual arts. Letters and numbers can thus be taken as emblematic of the modernist refusal of rhetorical continuity. Their presence in works produced in the later twentieth century cannot avoid implying a reference to the break with tradition and the academy associated with early modernism. Numerous concrete poems could be evoked to illustrate the modern tradition of the new, which has paradoxically established a continuity in disruption by repeatedly referring back to – or merely reiterating – the more radical gestures of earlier modernists. Finlay espouses this *doxa* in appearance only. Letters and numbers in his work are but the sign of modernism, drawing the procedures of his predecessors into the field of his own citational practice.

'Arcady', produced in the mid-1960s, is as minimal a poem as one might wish for – a title plus the alphabet as text:

Arcady

ABCDEFGHIJKLMNOPQRSTUVWXYZ

'Arcady' can be taken to epitomize the one-word poem, the minimal, fragmentary mode devised by Finlay in the 1960s, which may be seen as symptomatic of the demise of traditional rhetorical energies in our post-romantic age. One should also note the phonetic play linking title and text in the poem – 'arcady': 'A[–]CD'; and also the suggestion of a mimetic relationship between the alphabet and an idyllic landscape.[1] These are typical of the formal processes most frequently found in Finlay's work. The artist frequently uses a fairly restricted set of mimetic or analogical (broadly speaking, metaphorical) figures based on wordplay: paranomasia (repetition of similar signifiers), antonoclasis (identical signifiers repeated) or syllepsis (one word, two functions or meanings), which were recognized by classical rhetoric; puns and portmanteau words, which are more often regarded as para-literary phenomena.[2] One is normally reluctant

to associate the latter with high art, and the very shock engendered by the coming together of the classical and the para-literary (in the case of 'Arcady', of paranomasia and a visual pun) illustrates yet again the displacement of the fragments of tradition outside the bounds of art as it is generally recognized.

In 1966 Finlay appended a series of questions to 'Arcady'. The last of these reads:

> The original Dada-ists of 1916 wrote a number of poems composed entirely of single letters. Do you think that *Arcady* is (a) a non-poem; (b) a neo-Dada poem; (c) a poem that tries to civilise a neo-Dada cliché by turning it into a light-hearted classical conceit?[3]

The question form indicates the role of the reader in pinpointing the problem with which Finlay's works based on letters and numbers are concerned: whether the idea of classical culture can be presented under the guise of the idiom of the modernists.[4]

In the case of 'Sea-poppy 1' (p. 199), the layout may suggest an aspect of suprematism as much as dada. However, for Finlay, the citation of dada remains essential here too. Commenting on versions of this work and its companion piece 'Sea-poppy 2' (p. 231), both later executed in sandblasted glass, he speaks of a deliberate intention on his part 'to produce a work which could not be confused with neo-Dada'.[5] This is further evidence of his intent to transcend the modernistic *doxa* and its futile repetitions. It is to be achieved, amongst other means, by a return to classical metaphor. The letters and numbers in 'Sea-poppy 1' are those of fishing-boats, and the title suggests that the pattern they form be taken as an Aristotelian metaphor from analogy – poppy : stamens : : sea : fishing-boats.

The sea-poppies seek to transcend neo-dadaism. *Ocean Stripe Series 5*, a booklet poem (p. 202), assumes an altogether more complex position with regard to the tradition of dada as a whole. The poem is a montage of visual and literary fragments.[6] The verbal elements are all from a single issue of *Form*, a magazine concerned with questioning the relationship between the early avant-garde and its later counterparts. Five of the fragments used in *Ocean Stripe Series 5* are from a manifesto by Kurt Schwitters, 'Logically Consistent Poetry', the rest being taken from statements by Jandl and de Vree, exponents of sound poetry who first claimed the attention of the public in the 1960s. These contextual details are important. Like *Form*, Finlay is engaged in a process of evaluation – in the present instance of 'sound' poetry. This, as Stephen Bann points out, is punningly appropriate. For *Ocean Stripe Series 5* is intent on gauging the soundness of the modernists. The visual material incorporated into the booklet (photographs of which were all taken from the periodical *Fishing News*) prolongs the play on 'sound', just as the obvious presence of fishing-boat registrations draws dada into the context of Finlay's own distinctive use of letters and numbers. The post-script, a poem by Schwitters, again invites a comparison between different moments of the art of the century, as it relates to Finlay's own use of letters.

Ocean Stripe Series 5 implies a radical revaluation of dada. It stresses, not the disruptive energies of the movement, but rather the way its forays into para-art or anti-art can be used in the cause of cultural continuity. '4 Sails' (p. 200) lies between the minimal questioning of 'Arcady' and the highly sophisticated interplay to be found in the *Ocean* booklet. At the time of writing this poem, Finlay observed that the sequence of capital letters (abbreviated names of fishing ports) reminded him of Schwitters.[7] The duality of Schwitters' work – of, say, his paintings in which 'a bus ticket may be an abstract area of colour'[8] – is here transferred into a play between 'found' letters and the suggestion of a traditional sea lyric.

The bucolic nature of 'Arcady' and the use of fishing-boat registrations in the other works cited here associate Finlay's project of civilizing dada with the fauvist component of his oeuvre. However, just as in the 1970s Finlay came to inject a polemological element into such works as 'Little Fields' or the 'First Suprematist Standing Poem',[9] so the same happened with regard both to the theme of Arcady and to his interest in sound poetry. If the word 'avant-garde' implies violence (it is a military metaphor and was deplored as such by Baudelaire), *Hitler's Column* from the *Third Reich Revisited* (p. 142) indicates the complexity of Finlay's attitude towards the forces of disruption and civilization in the modern era.

Sea-Poppy 1, 1968

Four Sails, 1967
sandblasted glass, with Edward Wright and T. and W. Ide

SOUND POEM KIT

Tamiya
Riko
Peco
Pyro
Trix
Hasegawa
Revell
Bandai
Fujimi
Veron
Wrenn
Frog
Aurora

LAND/SEA (2)

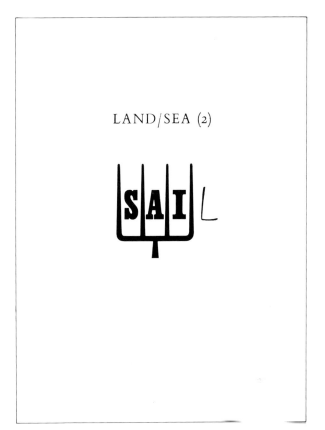

SKYLARKS

Skylarks are ground birds with aerial songs.

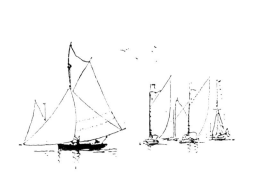

From *A Pretty Kettle of Fish*, 1974
booklet

From *A Pretty Kettle of Fish*, 1974
booklet
The agricultural implement with the letters SAI is the trademark of Scottish Agricultural Industries.

Skylarks, 1970
folding card

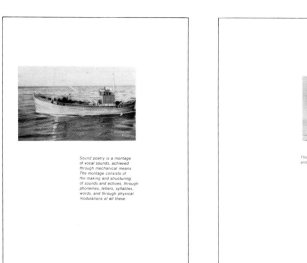

Sound poetry is a montage
of vocal sounds, achieved
through mechanical means.
The montage consists of
the making and structuring
of sounds and echoes, through
phonemes, letters, syllables,
words, and through physical
modulations of all these.

The sound poem concretises
and objectivises.

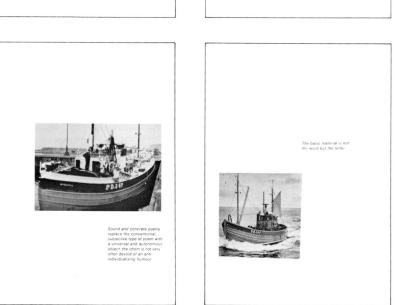

Sound and concrete poetry
replace the conventional,
subjective type of poem with
a universal and autonomous
object: the idiom is not very
often devoid of an anti-
individualising humour.

The basic material is not
the word but the letter.

Units of any size, from
sentence to single sound,
single letter, can be used in
experimental work.

Letters have no sound in
themselves, they only contain
possibilities of sounds, which
may be interpreted by the
performer.

From *Ocean Stripe Series 5,* 1967
booklet
Tarasque Press

Disregard of the conventions of language was rewarded by the discovery of new ways of producing.

Moreover, the experimental poem was willing to accomplish what its more conventional relative was only ready to describe. ("lechts und rinks kann man nicht velwechsern.")

Selection, transformation, amputation, transplantation would, however, only yield exhibits for an anatomical museum of language, if they were not occasionally followed by a kind of rehabilitation.

There must be an infinite number of methods of writing experimental poems.

A logically consistent poem evaluates letters and groups of letters against each other.

Poetic feeling is what the poet counts on.

It is impossible to explain the meaning of art, it is infinite.

Postscript.

W W
PBD
ZFM
RF RF
TZPF TZPF
MWT
RFMR
RKT PCT
SW SW
KPT
R Z
KPT
RZL
TZPF TZPF
HFTL

6 THE DESTRUCTIVE ELEMENT

In ancient times, rhetorical textbooks dealt with eloquence across a broad spectrum of public activities, the object of the doctrine being 'systematically to theorize the articulations of discourse and power, and to do so in the name of political practice: to enrich the political effectivity of signification'.[1] Aristotle lists three kinds of rhetoric, each with its own ends – political (deliberative), forensic (legal) and epideictic (the oratory of display, peculiar to ceremonial occasions where speeches of praise or blame were required).[2] The classification proved to be influential and engendered a long history. Now, even without going into the numerous reasons for its demise in modern times, it is obvious that classical rhetoric was co-substantial with structurally stable societies, in which the articulations it proposed were widely accepted, so that public utterance was freed from the need to insist upon the legitimacy of its procedures. However, in the unstable world we know today, in which discourse must itself light up the space in which it displays its energies, it becomes impossible to distinguish one type of eloquence from another, in the Aristotelian manner. So, as the contemporary rhetoretician C. Perelman has observed, 'for us, the epideictic genre is the central one, for its role is to intensify our adhesion to values without which speech aiming at action could not hope to find the means of moving and stirring its audience'.[3]

Ian Hamilton Finlay has long practised the epideictic mode of the homage[4] and in the early 1970s produced a series of militaristic homages to artists in the suprematist tradition. These constitute a forceful indication of the way in which Finlay's work has increasingly come to concern itself with matters which are not exclusively or reductively 'aesthetic'; as he himself says of one of the elements of his military iconography:

> The appearance of the warship in my work signifies the rejection of purity as inconsequentiality in favour of purity as commitment.[5]

The distance between the abstraction of Finlay's first 'Homage to Malevich' (p. 183) and the iconographical content of the second (p. 208) is emblematical of this shift.

The impact of the militaristic homages can perhaps best be judged by situating Finlay's procedures more closely within the tradition of romantic wit, and also by discussing the stance they assume towards the notion of the avant-garde. Let me begin, however, by setting aside a serious misapprehension concerning Finlay's use of militaristic themes. Critical reaction to this has been varied. Stephen Bann pinpoints the problem when he says of the artist's garden: 'Stonypath may have been renamed "Little Sparta", but it is still a Sparta in which watering-cans and tortoises can play a poetic part. It may celebrate the most potent images of power and destruction, but it does so always within the symbolic order that is the poet's province.'[6] The difficulty is that in the contemporary world there is no obvious consensus regarding order – symbolic or otherwise. One cannot, for example, accept the kind of distinction made by Paul Overy in an article reviewing both a display of political posters from May 1968 in France and an exhibition of Finlay's work. Overy argues that in Finlay's work images of modern warfare put into the context of traditional emblems are deprived of their power and violence. Finlay, he writes, 'is very far from being a political artist, but in his finest works the imagination is at least metaphorically seizing power'.[7] However, the incomprehension with which Finlay's *Third Reich Revisited* drawings were received shows that metaphor provides no such easy reassurance.[8] It is not so simple to render Finlay's thematics of violence toothless. Miles Orvell rightly suggests a more complex view of the matter: 'On the one hand, the domestication of armaments within an ordered space implicitly mocks their power over our lives. But the playful reduction does not remove the charge of violence from the objects. Rather, it is the special order imposed on instruments of violent disorder that creates the tensions and paradox in Finlay's armament works.'[9]

The series of drawings executed for Finlay by Jud Fine in the mid-1970s includes works that are fauvist (p. 24) and suprematist (p. 208). The latter are chiefly concerned with aerial combat. As Douglas Hall admits in his description of one of the drawings, warplanes are sinister and potent – but for the critic the sinister image is 'wittily neutralized'.[10]

Finlay's work is frequently witty or ironic. The question is whether the wit or irony can properly be regarded as neutralizing. This is certainly not the case in a work such as the *Homage to Max Bill* (p. 209). The problem can more appropriately be considered in connection with Finlay's notion of the Pure or the Absolute. There is historically a native British 'line of wit'. However, the Jacobean poets and the extraordinary 'preface' to *Tristram Shandy* notwithstanding, it is to the German romantics that one must turn for the fullest philosophical consideration of the faculty. This is how two French scholars define the status of wit in a study of the Atheneum group (poets and thinkers who laid the philosophical foundations of romanticism in the last years of the eighteenth century):

> From a tradition going back to the seventeenth century, Witz has received the fundamental qualification of being the reunion of the heterogeneous, which is to say, at the same time the substitute of genuine *conception* (taking place in and through the homogeneous), and the double of *judgement* (which links heterogeneous items together only under the control of the homogeneous). In fact, from its semantic origins (*Witz* is the double of *Wissen*, knowledge), and through its history in the form of French *esprit* and English *wit*, Witz has constituted, as it were, the other name and other 'concept' of knowledge, which is to say, knowledge other than the knowledge of analytic and predicational discursiveness. This is again to say that Witz, as received and ennobled by the Romantics, establishes itself extremely close to what Hegel was to call 'Absolute Knowledge', which is absolute, not so much by being unlimited knowledge, as by being knowledge which knows everything by knowing what it knows, and which thus forms the infinity of knowledge in action, and the *System* of knowledge.[11]

K. W. F. Solger, a minor figure in the German romantic movement, underlined the closeness of this notion of wit to the idea of the absolute provided by Hegelian dialectics, in a discussion relating to symbol and allegory.

The romantics insisted on the contrast between the synthesizing power of their own symbolic procedures and the supposedly limited, mechanical action of allegory. (The notion of the image inherited this distinction.) Solger's sense of estrangement from the classical absolute, however, leads him to transpose the historical argument and explicitly attribute the synthesizing power to wit:

> Just as in the spirit of classical art, the essence and the manifestation are always already symbolically unified in the activity itself, they are found here [in modern art] in an allegorical opposition, which can be mediated in no other way than by wit, which gathers together the isolated relations of things and thus suspends their isolation.[12]

Wit thus offers a means of relieving tension – of suspension (*Aufhebung*): it is a negation of the negation constituted by allegory.[13] The question of allegory is particularly relevant to Finlay's work. In the series of homages in a militaristic vein, for instance, *Homage to Agam* uses the names of the warships *Invincible*, *Inflexible* and *Indefatigable* (p. 210). However, it cannot be said that the wit, thanks to which Finlay here gathers together the heterogeneous forces of modern art and warfare,[14] is equivalent to a Hegelian *Aufhebung*, dissolving tensions.

A fragment from the *Atheneum*, attributed to Friedrich Schlegel, indicates what is involved in a much more satisfactory manner. There is, according to Schlegel,

> a species of wit which, because of its purity, precision and symmetry, we should like to name architectonic wit. In its satirical expressions, it produces real sarcasm. It must be as systematic as could be desired, and yet at the same time not be so; in spite of all completeness, something must seem to be missing, as if torn off . . .[15]

The highly finished aspect of Finlay's work, carefully balancing disparate forces, argues for an architectonic wit. And yet, in his treatment of military themes, it embodies a fierceness in excess of any formal purpose, and which is not subsumed by the perfected finish. Indeed, in the homages, the wit investigates the formal impulse of modern artists, in a gesture reminiscent of the Nietzschean 'philosophy with a hammer'.

Etymologically speaking, judgement is crisis.[16] Wit assumes responsibility for the critical moment of assertion implied by judgement, where philosophy more characteristically seeks the succour of the impersonal forces of logic. In Finlay's work, the emergence of military motifs represents a hyperbolical amplification of what is contained in the very notion of *krisis*. The German romantics, by making wit dialectical (and by doing so assimilating it to a form of historical irony), sought to bring the crisis of judgement to a close. For Friedrich Schlegel, it thus became the principle of universal philosophy. Finlay's wit is not philosophical in this sense. He is rather too suspicious of fusion with the Absolute for this to be possible.[17] The implications of his interest in 'suprematist' artists will allow us to define more precisely the originality of his stance. Malevich, Kandinsky and Mondrian, all of them heroic figures in the early phase of modernism, are by no means identical or interchangeable. Nevertheless, as champions of the suprematist (in Finlay's sense) avant-garde, they have striking similarities. It will therefore be enough to concentrate on one of Finlay's homages to these three artists.

In *Luftwaffe – after Mondrian* (p. 208) (done in collaboration with Jud Fine) the obvious clash between the overt values represented by the mystic artist, who fled from Europe in 1940, and those embodied by the (Nazi) German airforce, is accentuated by the fact that the drawing closely recalls a series of works completed by Mondrian in 1914–15. These are entitled *Jetty and Ocean* (a subject recalling preoccupations dear to Finlay himself). In Mondrian's own words, inspired by the grandeur of nature, he attempted in this series of drawings and paintings to represent 'the sea, the sky, the stars, by a multiplicity of crosses, and to express their vastness, repose, unity'.[18]

The transformation of Mondrian's quasi-abstract crosses into German military decorations is, on the face of it, an instance of cruel irony, even of sarcasm. The reality is more complex. In an article entitled 'Art Shows the Evil of Nazi and Soviet Oppressive Tendencies' (1941–2), Piet Mondrian argued that – by its negative action – oppression is creation: it reinforces its opposite and in the end produces freedom.[19] From such a perspective, life is always right. Finlay's Homage interacts with this optimism neither by assenting to it, nor yet by sarcastically rejecting it – but by wittily rephrasing it. To appreciate this, one must understand that, for all its overtly neoclassical idiom, Mondrian's art is engendered by a logic which is fundamentally romantic. Like the Atheneum group or – amongst his own contemporaries – artists such as Malevich, but also the dadaists, whom he admired, Mondrian considers art from the 'absolute' point of view of the end of art.

The conjunction of suprematism and dada underlines the ambivalence of such a notion. One cannot be sure whether the end of art involves an apotheosis or a catastrophe. The Fine drawing sombrely maintains this hesitation. For Mondrian himself, however, there is no such ambivalence. The end (or death) of art lies in its fusion with life. This motif is in harmony with the all-embracing principles of romanticism and with the assu-

aging notion of *Aufhebung*. The end of art is its death as a specific, separated form – the symptom, for Mondrian, of a tragic split between life and art. As the artist's reactions to contemporary tyranny underline, such a redemptive death is fated to come about, with the artistic avant-garde leading the way. Mondrian's theories are in the direct line of apocalyptic dialectics. For him, the apocalypse will be a joyous one. Here lies the significance of the theme of jazz and dancing in Mondrian's latest paintings. They constitute a premonition of a total art which would espouse the very rhythms of life. However, the joyousness does not prevent Piet Mondrian from sensing the violence inherent in his eschatological model of artistic development. It is significant that in 1943 he observed that the destructive element was too readily neglected in art. As for his own efforts tending towards the death of art, he believed that they put him on the very edge of an abyss.

Finlay can scarcely be accused of underestimating the destructive element. This is what is so impressive in his investigation of the logic – or the politics (the terms are interchangeable here) – of the avant-garde.[20] *Luftwaffe – after Mondrian* forces us to question the assertive forces lying behind the millennial fantasies of artistic avant-gardes and totalitarian ideologies. From about 1935, black lines began to proliferate in Mondrian's paintings, forming crosses and grills that have been interpreted as tragically prefiguring the approaching war. This does not really concord with the principles espoused in Mondrian's writings. Moreover, the black lines destroy the static wholeness of Mondrian's paintings and introduce a rhythmical element, so that the later works have also been described as representing 'an ever intensified attempt to realize in art the vitality of life'.[21] However, the Iron Crosses of the Jud Fine print (related, as has been seen, to works composed some twenty years earlier) do bring to the forefront the question of the 'destructive element' in art. In such a context, it is surely no exaggeration to see in Finlay's poem/card *Homage to Victor Sylvester* (p. 212) a re-working of Mondrian's last, unfinished painting – the *Victory Boogie-Woogie* of 1943–4, whose title incorporates both the historical and the aesthetic dimensions of the artist's theoretical writings. In Finlay's card, the destructive element is in no way denied or sublimated. It is foregrounded by the wit.

Wit in no way seeks to occult its polemological energies. In contrast to the Cartesian *cogito*, it does not establish truth in the bright light of intuition. Nor does it proceed by scientific deduction. It cultivates the sure glance, practises scheming and stratagems, and presents itself as a natural gift producing, not meditations, but aphorisms and sentences.[22] Its instantaneous flashes reproduce in an altogether fiercer mode a phenomenon which has characterized Finlay's poetics from the start: brevity. This, as Shakespeare insisted, is the soul of wit. Or, as the Germans say, *Witz ist ein Blitz* – a flash of lightning . . . but the word now has additional connotations. Such a saying is both a definition and an example of what it defines. So too, Finlay's military homages are what they proclaim themselves to be. They do not stand outside the artistic process, denouncing the covert violence which has animated art since it gained its autonomy with the romantics.[23] They partake of the spirit of conflict which they pinpoint. Only, they free it from the ruses of romantic and post-romantic dialectics, and thus meet up with the discursive energies of the presocratic philosophers. 'Thunderbolt steers all', Heraclitus declared. Quoting the philosopher, Finlay refuses to tone down the violence of the affirmation (p. 106). Or again, *Homage to Victor Sylvester* forces one to consider the critical nature of the Heraclitean notions of *polemos* (conflict) and dance (dance of the elements in his cosmology; but also dance of the signifiers in his poetics). As for the militaristic homages to two of Finlay's most appreciated companions in the international concrete poetry movement (p. 209, p. 211), they bring the lineage up to date. The association, in the Lax booklet, of a German fighter pilot from the heroic days of aerial combat and a post-Second World War American painter underlines the historical thread.

Homage to Malevich, 1974
print in folder, with Michael Harvey

Luftwaffe – after Mondrian, 1976
print, with Jud Fine

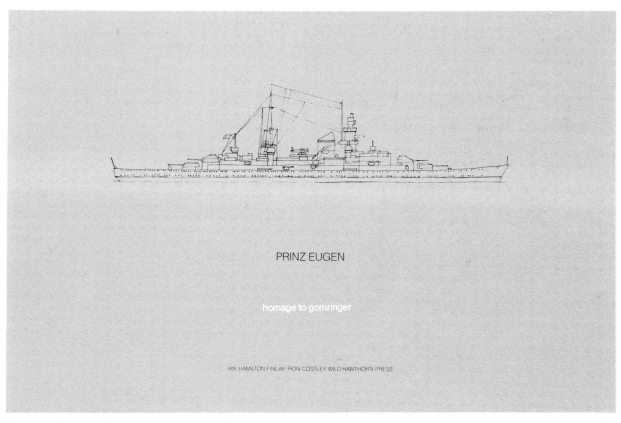

Homage to Max Bill, Wild Hawthorn Weapons Series 2, 1974
card

Homage to Gomringer, 1972
print, with Ron Costley

Homage to Kandinsky, 1972
card, with Ron Costley

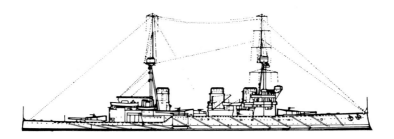

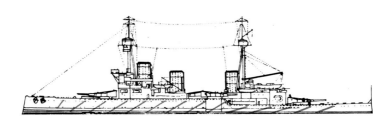

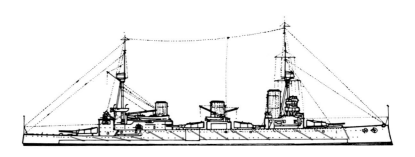

TRANSFORMABLE LINE SEGMENTS

INVINCIBLE · INFLEXIBLE · INDEFATIGABLE

HOMAGE TO AGAM

Homage to Agam, 1976
print in folder, with David Button

Richt-   Rein-
hofen   hardt

Richt-   Rein-
hofen   hardt

Richt-   Rein-
hofen   hardt

Richt-
hofen

Richt-   Rein-
hofen   hardt

Richt-   Rein-
hofen   hardt

Richt-   Rein-
hofen   hardt

Richt-
hofen

---

crim-   crim-
son   son

crim-   crim-
son   son

black   black

black

Richt-   crim-
hofen   son

Richt-   crim-
hofen   son

Rein-   black
hardt

Rein-
hardt

Homage to Robert Lax, 1974
booklet

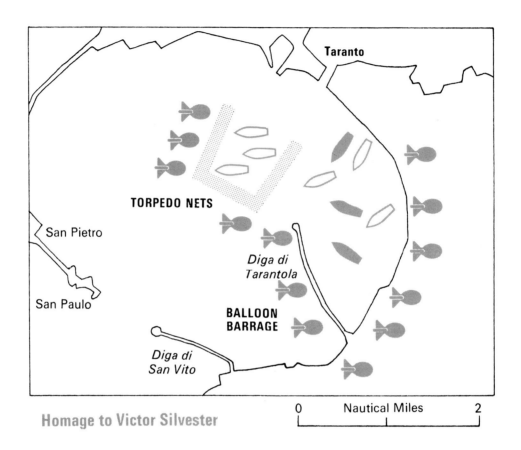

Taranto

TORPEDO NETS

San Pietro

San Paulo

*Diga di
Tarantola*

**BALLOON
BARRAGE**

*Diga di
San Vito*

Homage to Victor Silvester

0   Nautical Miles   2

Homage to Victor Sylvester, 1973
card, with Michael Harvey

7 HIEROGLYPH,
ALLEGORY, PORTRAIT

'Big E' (at Midway) (p. 215) is a potent hieroglyph commemorating a moment of extreme violence. For 'Big E' is the aircraft carrier USS *Enterprise* which played a prominent part in the Second World War Battle of the Pacific. It also refers back to the very origins of European culture: to the enigmatic inscription on a stone fragment near the shrine of Apollo at Delphi, which is the subject of a celebrated dialogue in Plutarch's *Moralia*.[1] When *'Big E'* was exhibited at the Serpentine Gallery in 1977, the text of Plutarch's 'On the E at Delphi' was placed next to it, in a gesture Finlay has repeated for more recent works. Finlay's purpose is again to intervene openly in the tissue of our culture. The Delphic inscription, mediated by Plutarch, has become a classic instance of the problem of interpretation. This can be linked to the classical question of Judgement by way of the Stoics, who defined *krisis* as the decision whereby a sign is associated with a thing. In both interpretation and battle, what is important is the conclusion, issue or decision. Such terms are equally at home in a philosophical or a military academy, and Finlay's work keeps alive the analogy between hermeneutics and warfare.

Because he considers modern forms of art as contributing to a historical process of demystification, Walter Benjamin deplores the fact that writers theorizing on photography or film should waste their time asking whether these are real art forms, instead of trying to understand how they transform the entire nature of art. He thus condemns the film director Abel Gance for suggesting that the film-maker's art is hieroglyphic.[2] For Benjamin, such an assertion is an example of mystification, seeking to reintroduce a ritualistic or sacred element into a medium which had already produced works free of these. Ian Hamilton Finlay occupies a position between Benjamin and Gance. In 'civilizing' dada or building a garden temple, he insists on classical and sacred values. But he does not utopically seek to come to rest in them. His wit and his hyperbolical transumptions focus on the very crisis others seek to resolve by archaic adhesion or modernistic demystification.

Finlay's series of *Heroic Emblems* demonstrates the complexity of the process. In his introduction to the collection published in 1977, Stephen Bann shows how

Finlay retrieves a tradition which had fallen into disrepute – which had perhaps never really been regarded with the seriousness it deserved, particularly so in Britain, where the emblem had long been associated with the insipid moralizing of Bunyan and was considered as nothing more than children's literature. With Finlay, a complex set of historical and cultural references comes into play: 'He mobilizes the gap between the modern period and that of the Renaissance, just as the emblematists themselves signified the gap between their own period and the Graeco-Roman world through the choice of classical tags and quotations. He sets before us a cultural tissue in which these various levels – the Classical, the Renaissance and the Modern – are indissolubly linked.'[3] It is the nature of this indissoluble bond which must be investigated.

The emblems of the Renaissance did not merely provoke interaction between cultural strata. The genre itself derives from an interest in hieroglyphs, associated with the rediscovery of a treatise dating back to the second or fourth century A.D., the *Hieroglyphica* of Horus Apollo. From this source, the emblem derives the prestigious aura of sacred antiquity. The Egyptian hieroglyphs were taken as an original, quasi-divine language, and Plotinus had attributed to them a status which anticipates that of the German romantic concept of wit. He saw in them 'science, wisdom, something seized at a single blow, and not an argument or a deliberation'. At the same time, the word 'emblem' (which was of Greek origin) in classical Latin meant marquetry, inlaid work, mosaics, incrustations, appliqué. It also had a figurative meaning: speech studded with citations used as rhetorical ornaments. From such artifice, it is but a short step to the tradition of allegory, which Friedhelm Kemp cites in a study of the emblem, suggesting that its origins lie both in the allegorical tradition of the Middle Ages and in a scholarly interest in hieroglyphs.[4] The ultimate effect, according to Gombrich's 'Icones Symbolicae', a study to which Finlay has frequently acknowledged his indebtedness, is that of 'free-floating metaphor', lying between allegory and hieroglyph.[5]

The dissociation and artifice associated with allegory are valuable concepts. Allegory necessitates a process of

deciphering, which foregrounds the problems of interpretation. History is not a transparent, self-realizing
text. According to Benjamin, it involves citation.[6]
Finlay's problem is to gauge whether the heroic past can
still be cited in the modern age, with its crisis of values.
Citation can perhaps best be taken here in its military
sense, and it is no accident that some of Finlay's
emblems have been made into medallions – the most
recent to commemorate significant moments in the
Little Spartan War (p. 244).

History is not a science but an art. Thus, for Paul
Veyne, the historian is not an anatomist striving to lay
bare hidden principles which would account for the
workings of the body of history. He does not have an
objective set of 'facts' to deal with. He is a physiog-
nomist, describing the complexion of historical objects
which are so many 'faces' that he must himself reconstruct. Like a portrait painter, one might say, prolonging
the analogy.[7]

A portrait has aura. This explains why Benjamin
regards portrait photography with the same disdain as
hieroglyphic theories of film.[8] As a mechanical medium
free of the trappings of craftsmanship or religion, photography should be a militantly modern medium, but
portrait photography is the 'ultimate retrenchment' of
aura. The purest Renaissance emblems, however, for-
went the representation of the human figure. Finlay
follows suit in his own emblems. But this is not to say
that the particular condensation of forces one finds in
portraits is absent from these. Finlay's emblems include
images of anthropomorphic deities – Zeus, Venus,
Muses (p. 106, p. 108) – and of an oriental Djinnie
(p. 110), all of which are reincarnated as modern war
machines. The visual element ('body', in Renaissance
terminology) of such emblems circumscribes the question of the figuration of historical forces – or of historical
forces as figuration. It implies a historiography referring
(as Veyne's explicitly does) to the Nietzschean concept
of a Will to Power which is also an artistic force.

A figure can also be a face. The militaristic homages[9]
can be taken as portraits. Their strength, and that of
Finlay's deistic emblems, can perhaps best be ascertained
by relating them to portraits crucial to the history of
twentieth-century art. One thinks of Rodchenko's Soviet
workers, heroic in stature and photographed in such a
way that they are transformed into colossi; or of the
sinister fascination of Leni Riefenstahl's Nubi tribesmen.
Also relevant are Mondrian's reflections on totalitarian
politics or Benjamin's strictures against portrait photog-

raphy. Finlay's muses and his Virgilian gods (p. 107)
recall de Kooning's women camouflaged in paint. His
two classic landscapes, a Watteau and a Veronese
(p. 217), focus on the question of the energies of colour
and the forces of figuration. They thus interrogate the
problematics of abstract painting, recalling the work of
Jackson Pollock, who went from violent Jungian hieroglyphs to the all-over mottled effect of dripping, and in
whose last paintings faces begin to emerge. The subject
of abstract painting is again alluded to in the drawing
Apollo in George Street from the *Third Reich
Revisited* (p. 143).

It is surely no coincidence that one of the more
dramatic episodes of the Little Spartan War concerned
the *dryads* (p. 7) housed in the Garden Temple at
Little Sparta. These are statuettes of classical divinities
in modern camouflage – the very incarnation of Finlay's
neoclassical rearmament. They had been placed under
summary arrest (*sic*) by the sheriff officer, but were
removed from the Temple and returned 'to the protection of the trees'[10] by the Saint-Just Vigilantes.

Making model aircraft is certainly a minor cultural
phenomenon. Yet Finlay has a way of humanizing such
models – in the 'Juan Gris' glider (p. 164) and also in
his *Marionette* (p. 217) – which introduces here too the
question of portraiture and the figuration of forces. The
Robin Redbreast which belongs to this series of modified
model planes incorporates a natural, rather than anthropomorphic, figuration of force (p. 216), while the *Watering-
can* which announced the re-opening of a 'regenerated'
garden and Temple a year after the Budget Day Raid
beautifully condenses both of these notions (p. 290).

Cherry Stones, 1975   'Big E' (at Midway), 1976/7
card   stone, with John Andrew

ROTKEHLCHEN

Rotkehlchen, 1975
card

From *The Boy's Alphabet Book*, 1977
with David Paterson
Coach House Press, Canada

Marionette II, 1978
card, with David Paterson

Classic Landscape, 1982
painted wood, with Ian Gardner and Fred Lyle

8 NEOPRESOCRATIC

Quotations and classical tags, together with an often lengthy commentary, formed an essential part of Renaissance emblems. The same is true of Finlay's. Indeed, the relationship between image and text in his emblems constitutes a useful introduction to a consideration of the verbal energies of Finlay's work over the past decade or so. The artist's neoclassicism is more than an idiosyncratic gesture. That this is the case is amply confirmed by the transformation in the discursive power of Finlay's production, which followed upon his elaboration of the idea of a neoclassical rearmament.

The Renaissance emblem was originally a personal thing, chosen by an individual, or else made to order for him. Thus, in the words of Cesare Ripa in the introduction to his *Iconologia* (1593), emblems 'affirm or deny something with respect to someone'.[1] This insistence on the discursive act of judgement (which would also have an incentive function, like all personal or family mottoes) is paramount, as becomes evident when Ripa contrasts emblems with a second type of image: the allegorical figuration of virtues and vices. Here the image is simply a definition. In either case, Ripa is dealing with 'images made to signify something different from what the eye sees' – a concept much more central to the history of art than is commonly appreciated, and which pinpoints the essential distinction between the description and the interpretation of images in art.[2]

The structure of the emblem was the subject of much speculation during the Renaissance. Robert Klein suggests that if the *impresa* or emblem is the indirect or metaphorical expression of a thought, then it is a logical entity. This would explain the kind of critical comments which were typically formulated with regard to emblems: 'the question of the quality or the aptness of the expression is never asked, but it is asked whether they [emblems] conform to the rules. It is enough for the *impresa*, like a syllogism, to answer exactly to its definition and to respect all the necessary material and formal conditions. A real syllogism is of necessity a true syllogism; a real *impresa* is necessarily "perfect".'[3] One could scarcely state more clearly the relevance of the emblem genre to Finlay's concern with breaking out of the enclave of the purely 'aesthetic'.[4] The difference between the Renaissance and the twentieth century is that there is no modern equivalent of the Aristotelian *Organon* or *Rhetoric*, laying down agreed rules for the formulation and expression of thought and judgement. If, however, as certain Renaissance theorists suggested, the relationship between image and motto in an emblem is to be assimilated to that between major and minor premises in a syllogism, how do the visual and verbal components interact in Finlay's work?

One might expect the image to serve as a focal point (grammatical subject), with the text commenting upon or interpreting it (predicate). If this were the case, then Finlay's mixed verbal/visual work would fit quite neatly into the age-old tradition of the epigraph and the epigram. However, even if Alistair Fowler has described Finlay as the finest epigraphist of the twentieth century,[5] it is not obvious that his work espouses a predicational movement of this order. A work which might well be taken to constitute a modernistic epigraph provides a good example.

Lessing suggested that the object which is an integral part of any epigraph should arouse curiosity. If this is so, then the appearance of a real piece of artillery in the context of a sculpture exhibition can undoubtedly be taken to satisfy the German critic's criterion. Is *Lyre* (p. 223) – an actual Swiss Oerlikon gun exhibited by Finlay in Battersea Park at the Silver Jubilee exhibition of modern British sculpture in 1977 – a classic example of the epigraph for all that? If this were to be the case, the accompanying inscription would – again according to Lessing – have to satisfy one's curiosity. On the base of Finlay's *Lyre* one can read:

> 'Applied to a lyre, harmonie might refer to the
> structure of the unstrung lyre whether tuned or not,
> or to that of the lyre tuned in a particular mode.'
> Edward Hussey, *The Presocratics*, Ch. 3, 'Heraclitus'.

The viewer's curiosity is scarcely satisfied in the manner to be expected in an epigraph. What gives an epigram or epigraph emphasis and pointedness has, as Fowler insists, much to do with its closure – with 'the final word, that makes it the last word'.[6] Now the *Lyre* remains somewhat enigmatic, so that it stimulates a desire for further thought and investigation. Its structure is open. It is a free-floating metaphor. In a letter to

Finlay, Edward Hussey (the philosopher quoted in the inscription) writes:

> You seem to have incorporated into your Lyre a point which occurred to me after the book was written: that an inner connection linking bow and lyre is given by the fact that both are instruments of the oracular god Apollo, who as "far-shooting" archer sends out messages of death, as lyre-player messages of music.[7]

Hussey thus pays tribute to the artist's decisive recognition of the fact that there is 'an area of culture' (Greek mythology) which assimilates the instruments of song and war – a citation which not only casts light on presocratic philosophy, but which must make us ponder on the deep structure of the lyric impulse. For Finlay, what is important is doubtless the particular way in which the instruments of art may be 'tuned'. However, the point more particularly to be retained here is that it is Finlay's image which proves to be the decisive element, 'commenting' on the text.

The same is true of the stone relief *Lyre (Mk 2)* (p. 222). Like the Battersea *Lyre*, this work has been published in the form of a poem/card featuring the photograph of a tiny model Oerlikon gun made by Finlay himself. In the card corresponding to the stone relief, the use of an orange colour and an oval format constitutes a deliberate reference to cubism. This is underlined by a contemporary quotation from Jean Cocteau (1921). Printed on the back of the card, it reads:

> With us, there is a house, a lamp, a plate of soup, a fire, wine and pipes at the back of every important work of art.

As in the *Homage to Vuillard* (p. 185), Finlay is concerned here with the *intimiste* tradition in art – which the image, inducing puns on 'pipes' and 'fire', contrasts with the heroic tradition. *Lyre (Mk 2)* invokes the neoclassical tradition as much as it does cubism (it was displayed in the neoclassical room at Finlay's 1977 Serpentine show). Finlay has stated that it is not necessary to show the Cocteau quotation alongside the stone relief. Nevertheless, like the images in emblems, the work constitutes an implicit statement 'affirming or denying something' with respect – not to someone, as in the Renaissance emblem as characterized by Cesare Ripa – but to the tissue of cultural referents it invokes.

It is this concentration on discursive force which distinguishes Finlay's emblems from those images that, in the words of E. H. Gombrich, reveal aspects of 'the structure of the world'.[8] Finlay is altogether more interested in the quality of an affirmation than he is in its referential values, even on a cosmological or a metaphysical plane. There is here an analogy with Nietzsche, and Finlay's reference to the presocratic philosophers can be understood in terms of the role they play in the Nietzschean revaluation of philosophical and cultural forces. There are a number of presocratic tags in the collection of Heroic Emblems. In his commentary to one of the emblems, Stephen Bann describes them as instances of an 'undifferentiated state' of language and of a 'poetic cosmology'.[9] The suggestion is that Finlay's particular way with free-floating metaphor provokes comparison with the concept of plurality which has become a commonplace of contemporary critical practice. However, although citation necessarily involves plurality, Finlay's way with language has a different impact. The equation of lyre, bow and Oerlikon gun in the Battersea poem/sculpture is not an example of sophisticated modernistic plurality. Nor is it plurality as such which one misses if one fails to see that 'pipes' and 'fire' are ambivalent. The question, once again, is one of evaluation – of the lyric impulse, of *intimisme*, or of some other cultural force. As for the Heroic Emblems, they evaluate the affirmations of presocratic philosophers, and of modern poetry (p. 107), biblical tags (p. 109) and classical and Renaissance aesthetics as such.

Finlay himself states antithetically what he is about when, alluding to modern sculpture, he writes in his *Detached Sentences on the Pebble*:

> Beside a true work of sculpture, the PEBBLE has the advantage (to the modern mind), that it is no sort of Test.[10]

The compilation of series of 'detached sentences' in the manner of the eighteenth-century poet and gardener William Shenstone's *Unconnected Thoughts on Gardening* (1764) is a mode which Finlay has adapted to a number of topics.[11] The move from 'thought' to 'sentence' is itself significant, since the oldest and broadest senses of the word 'sentence' incorporate the important notions of affirmation, citation, judgement and authority.[12]

Finlay's preoccupation with words, letters and numbers[13] followed upon a 'crisis of syntax'. This lay behind the poet's move to concrete poetry in the early 1960s, his break from the conventions of his short stories and rhyming poems stemming from the extraordinary (since wholly unexpected) sense that the syntax I had been using, *the movement of* language in me, at a physical level, was no longer there – so it had to be replaced with something else, with a syntax and movement that would be true to the new feeling (which existed in only the vaguest way, since I had, then, no form for it . . .).[14]

This crisis never implied a flight into the spheres of the irrational or the supposedly supra-rational, but engendered Finlay's new way with metaphor and his citational poetics. It provoked an exploration and a reawakening of the discursive energies which underpin reason and logic. This developed into a full-scale campaign, with a clearly designated adversary: the weak, insidious rationalizing which commonly passes for thought and will not accept that its claims to authority be examined, and even less contested. It is the language of the administrative and judicial establishment, both elected and bureaucratic,[15] but also of the literary and artistic establishment even (or especially) when it goes by the name of the avant-garde. Finlay is more than wary of the abrasive postures taken up by artists who 'are all such conventional wee people really'.[16] The Little Spartan War revolves around the definition of a building, its many painful episodes resulting from what might euphemistically be called linguistic misadventures, all illustrating the near impossibility of getting meaningful statements out of any number of British authorities (local or national, political, administrative or judicial) on a subject which challenges their understanding. So, as Finlay himself agrees, 'the bureaucratic battle is a language battle'.[17] The Greek word *syntagma* is not just a grammatical term; it also means 'constitution'. Finlay's artistic response to the behaviour of hostile authorities challenges the discursive and constitutional propriety of their actions (p. 28, p. 30).

Like Nietzsche's aphorisms, Finlay's sentences are instances of philosophizing 'with a hammer'. This explains his rejection of consecutive sentences.[18] It is important that the authority and vigour of affirmation be apparent and testable at every blow. Thus, if the appearance of the warship in Finlay's work signifies 'the rejection of purity as inconsequentiality in favour of purity as commitment',[19] modern war machines are his Nietzschean hammer. It does not follow that Finlay's sentences and works are blindly militant. If they test, they also offer themselves up for testing.

This is the case in the *Heroic Emblems*, with their citation of different philosophical, theological and poetic traditions. An emblem incorporating and transforming a one-line poem by Emmanuel Lochac published in the 1930s provides a good example (p. 107). Finlay uses the same process in a card which quotes and contests a statement by Herbert Read (p. 224). In both cases, it is the quality of the original affirmation that is being tested. With respect to the Read citation, the effect is overtly and polemically antithetical. The same is however not true of the confrontation of 'paros' (marble) and 'para' (paratrooper) in the emblem, which questions the related problems of purity and commitment, as raised by Finlay's own militaristic neoclassicism.

It is as an exemplary instance of discursive energy that the presocratic fragment intervenes as a stylistic reference in certain of Finlay's later one-line poems. *Epicurus at Chatou* (which raises the question of the dissemination and resurgence of cultural forces by way of its pastiche of Walter Pater) is a re-working of a poem inscribed on a post at Stonypath (p. 230) and also printed as a poem/card, over a photograph of water and the reflection of a tree. In both of these instances, what is suggested is an interchange of referents, and thus what Stephen Bann refers to as a poetic cosmology. But when, after Finlay's investigation of the emblem, with its discursive (rather than semiotic) energies, this same poem became a pseudo-presocratic fragment (p. 230), what came to the surface was not so much an aspect of a poetic universe, as a discursive force. Similarly, the fragment from Finlay's 1982 exhibition *A Pittenweem Fancy* (p. 230) recasts the artist's fishing-boat idiom in terms suggesting something more forceful than the assuaging auratic charm which characterized similar works in the 1960s.

It is this force – artistic, but also implying a process of evaluation; always aware of its polemological dimension – which can be characterized as neopresocratic. A barbarous sounding term, perhaps, but one coined by Finlay himself, in a context not devoid of irony. The neologism is, by way of pastiche, attributed to the jargon of scholarly architectural journals (p. 143), and perhaps bears the imprint of contemporary discomfiture in the evaluation of cultural forces. At the same time, in association with Finlay's neoclassicism, it usefully indicates a modification in Finlay's poetics in the early 1970s.

In the commentary to one of Finlay's Heroic Emblems, *A Celebration of Earth, Air, Fire, and Water*, Stephen Bann details the analogy the work implies between a modern aircraft carrier and the cosmology of Heraclitus: 'earth being represented in the landing ground offered by the carrier deck, air by the element in which the aircraft move, fire by the dynamic and destructive character of its nuclear capacity and water by the surrounding ocean' (p. 109). Representing the relationship between modernity and the philosophy of the dawn of our culture by means of a common world picture more usefully characterizes Finlay's earlier work. This suggests an interchange of elements by means of a metaphorical sign-system, as in 'Sea-poppy 1' (p. 199), or again in the more complex 'Sea-poppy 2' (p. 231), which brings an additional partner into the dance of the elements. Here as elsewhere, letters, syllables or words suggest a Heraclitean cosmology, which is also a model for modern plurality.

In some of Finlay's inscriptions from the 1960's, this type of poetics is particularly evident. Many of the works first installed in the poet's garden are reduced to a minimal combination of words and/or signs. These invoke absent terms (characteristically the sea and fishing-boats),[20] or else provoke an interchange of elements by means of 'Imitations, Variations, Reflections, Copies', to quote the title of a later booklet. The metaphorical flux thus achieved is well illustrated by the *Pond Board* completed in 1968. This consists of the single word 'cloud', together with conventional pointing hands indicating the sky and the little pool by which the board is set. The pond does not merely serve as a mirror for passing clouds, however, since Finlay extended the relationship metaphorically by planting. There are thus two types of aquatic plant in the water: a water-lily, like a billowing cloud in summer; and a starwort, with its small white flowers, for winter.[21]

The permutational poems also produced in the mid-to late 1960s further highlight Finlay's elemental metaphoricity, which is essentially fauvist and assuaging, producing a saturation of correspondences.[22] The garden at Stonypath has, however, since undergone a process of development, incorporating work which is more environmental than semiotic in nature. It is probably the series of works commissioned for the garden at the Max Planck Institute in Stuttgart that best retains the spirit of the earlier phase. Finlay started working on this project in 1974, but the inscriptions used in it antedate the militaristic mode he was then developing. The works are essentially reformulations of pieces already used at Stonypath, so that the Institute garden preserves the semiotic inspiration which had formerly presided over the poet's own domain – and does so in a context which challenges one to evaluate the cultural and philosophical seriousness of his earlier idiom (p. 228). Max Planck being one of the founding fathers of nuclear physics, Finlay may be taken to be quite deliberately invoking the analogy between the world picture of modern science and a poetic cosmology along presocratic lines. He thus achieves a significant triumph over the reductive formalism of much modernism.

The Max Planck inscriptions constitute a deliberate stylistic gesture, their pure lines openly invoking classicism, and this too provokes an evaluation of Finlay's earlier semiotic mode. The appropriate way of regarding such works is via the interplay of the cultural references they invoke. It is this citational aspect, going beyond the rendering of a poetic cosmology, which is essential to Finlay's neopresocratic mode.

The commentary attached to *A Celebration of Earth, Air, Fire, Water* (p. 109) in no way occults this dimension of Finlay's aesthetic, but suggests that the emblem participates in a conflict of discursive energies, of philosophical and/or artistic wills. Furthermore, the difference between Finlay's earlier and later permutational poems – between those based on words and those involving 'sentences' – is that, where the former may be taken to establish a poetic cosmology, the latter obviously evaluate polemological energies. The distinction is not absolute, and the artist's various reworkings of early pieces show that there was a potential there to be developed. The reformulations question types of artistic will embodied in the earlier versions. This is achieved chiefly by their adoption of a militaristic iconography. In the diverse 'dictionary' works produced by Finlay in the early 1980s (p. 28, p. 227), the artist's polemological energies are once again to the forefront, laying down a challenge to a culture which is perceived as lacking purity, commitment and rigour.

Lyre (Mk 2), 1977
stone, with John Andrew

Lyre, 1977
metal and inscribed slate, with John Andrew
Battersea Park, London
Accompanying the gun, a slate inscription reads: 'Applied to a lyre, harmonie might refer to the structure of the unstrung lyre, or to that of the strung lyre whether tuned or not, or to that of the lyre tuned in a particular mode.' Edward Hussey, *The Presocratics*, Ch. 3, 'Heraclitus'.

'In the back of every dying civilisation
sticks a bloody Doric column.'
Herbert Read, quoted by Charles Jencks

'In the foreground of every revolution,
invisible, it seems, to the academics,
stands a perfect classical column.'
Claude Chimérique, quoted by Ian Hamilton Finlay

Wild Hawthorn Press, Stonypath, Little Sparta, Dunsyre, Lanark, Scotland

'In the back of every dying civilization . . .', 1981
card

Plant trough, 1977
stone, with John Andrew

**Chant for a
Regional Occasion
2000 voices**

beast	**petal**	**lute**
brute	**peony**	**lyre**
bren	**pistol**	**luger**

azure	**fritillary**	**kettledrum**
aspen	**firefly**	**kultur**
asdic	**flamethrower**	**kristallnacht**

zither	**sos**	**nazarene**
zephyr	**sdkfz**	**nabis**
zimmerit	**ss**	**nazi**

(repeat)

Chant for a Regional Occasion, 1983
folding print

When he describes common bricks as *the brown bread of building*, or a Corinthian capital as *a republican crown*, or a volute as *a form subsisting in the tree-bark*, or a column as *a consonancy of drums and flutes*, or a pilaster as *a measure-bearing member*, or a peristyle as *a regular grove*, or the grove itself as *the string section*, or wood (the substance) as *a simple body* (this making a play on the Neoplatonic phrase), it is clear that his subject is not only architecture 'the art or science of building' (Johnson) but 'architecture a humanised pattern of the world' (Geoffrey Scott).

Lexical Diversions of Ian Hamilton Finlay. Drawing by Mark Stewart. The Wild Hawthorn Press.

Lexical Diversions, 1983
card, with Mark Stewart

TWO TRANSLATIONS

Ferme ornée

armoured farm

Arrosoir

evening arrow

Ian Hamilton Finlay
THE WILD HAWTHORN PRESS
for
THE COMMITTEE OF PUBLIC SAFETY
LITTLE SPARTA

Two Translations, 1983
card

Plinth (with inscription) for pool, 1976
marble, with Ron Costley

Wolke (Cloud), 1976
cast concrete and canvas, with Ron Costley

Architects: Brenner and Partner
Garden of the Max Planck Institute, Stuttgart, West Germany

Schiff, 1976
marble, with Ron Costley

Sails/Waves, 1976
steel, with Ron Costley

Unda/Wave, 1976
concrete and stainless steel, with Ron Costley

Architects: Brenner and Partner
Garden of the Max Planck Institute, Stuttgart, West Germany

DIAMOND·STUDDEDFISHNET

BLUEWATER'SBARK

Epicurus at Chatou, 1976
card, with Ron Costley

A Pittenweem Fancy, 1972
card, with Ron Costley

Blue Water's Bark, 1975
wood, with George L. Thomson

Sea-Poppy 2, 1968

STAR · DAY · STAR · STAR · MORNING · LIGHT · STAR · FAITHFUL · RADIANT · STAR · OF PEACE · NORRARD · FORTUNE · STAR · GUIDING · UNIVERSAL · STAR · OF · KINDRED · DIVINE · STAR · ONWARD · STAR · FREEDOM · STAR · WOOD · STAR

11 SUBLIMITY, TERROR, AWE

In one of his *Oxford Lectures on Poetry*, A. C. Bradley recalls an anecdote concerning a visit by Coleridge to the Falls of Clyde:

> After gazing at the Falls for some time, he began to consider what adjective would answer most precisely the impression he had received; and he came to the conclusion that the proper word was 'sublime'. Two other tourists arrived, and, standing by him, looked in silence at the spectacle. Then, to Coleridge's high satisfaction, the gentleman exclaimed, 'It is sublime.' To which the lady responded, 'Yes, it is the prettiest thing I ever saw.'[1]

Bradley regards the lady's remark as a sign of ludicrous incapacity: 'Sublimity and prettiness are qualities separated by so great a distance that our sudden attempt to unite them has a comically incongruous effect.' Perhaps so. It is nevertheless true that the lady's trivial superlative is doubtless closer to the modern vulgar usage than is the 'astonishment, rapture, awe, even self-abasement' which the Victorian critic cites as emotions evoked by sublimity. Here, then, is a striking expression of modern secularism.

This episode can cast light on the reduced scale and charm associated with much of Finlay's work. In such a context, however, it is worth recalling Hugh Kenner's early assessment of the poet: 'What would be whimsy from an Englishman, Finlay invests with a bleak and casual panic.'[2] Renaissance tradition or American virility may in some cases motivate the hyperbolical images of violence that abound in Finlay's later work. But this is no longer the case with respect to the tensions which are embodied in his homages to mystic modernists, or which infiltrate some of his toys. Finlay not infrequently appears to court accusations of slightness, or else – in sharp contrast – of extremism. Although his work is rarely overtly in the sublime mode, it often forces the observer to meditate on what the *vox populi* characterizes variously as sublimity, awe or terror. That these are ambivalent terms (they have, for example, not lost all their religious connotations) is suggested by the way in which Finlay's powerful *Third Reich Revisited* series was received when it first went on show.[3] One understands, of course, that the Third Reich, or even the French

Revolution, should provoke extremely hostile reactions. Yet the idea of revolution is a potent one, and in evolving the notion of the sublime, Edmund Burke repeatedly cited the great poet of England's own age of revolution. The particular force of Milton's verse has nevertheless itself been a perpetual source of anguish. It impinges, via T. S. Eliot, on the modernist movement in poetry. Finlay's own reaction to Milton, however, is much more forthright,[4] while his 'French' and 'German' works further develop his investigation of a power which will not be constrained by a purely aesthetic context.

'A well-timed stroke of sublimity scatters everything before it like a thunderbolt, and in a flash reveals the full power of the speaker,' writes Longinus in his treatise *On the Sublime*. This may be considered to link Heraclitus and Schlegel. In Britain, the question of power remains to the forefront in discussions of the sublime. Both Burke, in his *Philosophical Enquiry into the Origin of our Ideas of the Sublime and Beautiful* (1757), and Bradley, in his 1903 lecture on 'The Sublime', bear this out. In either case, the author finds himself forced to come to terms with the negative element which is central to the concept. Indeed, Burke places his entire discussion under the aegis of fear – but a fear which is sufficiently tempered for it to do no more than stimulate the gymnastics required to keep in trim the more delicate organs of our sensibility. For Bradley, fear in the limited sense is not a necessary ingredient of the sublime. The experience nevertheless consists of two stages. The first is negative. The overwhelming greatness of a sublime object 'for a moment checks, baffles, subdues, even repels us or makes us feel our littleness'. It is only then that, 'forcing its way into the imagination and emotions, [it] distends or uplifts them to its own dimensions. We burst our own limits, go out to the sublime thing, identify ourselves ideally with it, and share its immense greatness'.

For both Burke and Bradley, then, the threatening aspect of sublime power is subdued by a movement which is globally positive. Does this really account for the modern notion of the sublime at its strongest? It would seem, rather, that such a reassuring approach builds upon Socrates and ignores Satan – a procedure which Bradley himself explicitly deplores, saying that it

9 SUNDIALS

The designing of sundials and the theme of Arcady are two areas of interest which Finlay has explored over a number of years. The sundials demonstrate his concern to keep alive a tradition which has its roots in philosophical considerations, poetry and craftsmanship. Examples can be found in collections of poetry, on badges and cards, in the garden at Little Sparta, and also in public places – the town square at Biggar, near Finlay's home, the Universities of Kent and Liège, the Royal Botanic Garden, Edinburgh. They may offer a moment's respite from Finlay's militant concerns, but nonetheless refuse the status of rusticated delights. The incorporation of one of Finlay's most notable sundials into the context of the *Third Reich Revisited*, and the association with sundials of a leading figure from the French Revolution offer ample evidence of this fact.

Some of the earlier sundials accommodate both the fauvism of the fishing or sailing vessel, and the suprematism of the warship. The 'Four Seasons' series, which appeared both as poems (in *Honey by the Water*) and as real sundials in Finlay's garden, punningly interrelate the hours, the seasons and the oceans, by way of the names of types of boats, or indeed of actual vessels (p. 236). The conjunction/disjunction of 'harmonie' and *polemos* is graphically manifested in these essentially semiotic designs,[1] drawing once again upon popular culture (names and naming).

Three works from the booklet *Airs, Waters, Graces* demonstrate the importance to Finlay of the sundial as a fictional model. Here, the sacred, auratic moment of time arrested by the shadow of the gnomon, moves from the assuaging presence of Our Lady, via the more ambivalent charms of Venus (with an implicit reference to the Aphrodite of the *Heroic Emblems* [p. 108], who also figures in the booklet), to the polemological energies of a modified Heraclitean tag (p. 238).

The fictional dimension returns in sundials whose inscriptions are discursive, rather than semiotic. The sentence:

All Times on these sundials are Solar Time

figures on a poem/card entitled *Arcadian Sundials* (p. 240), while engraved on one of Finlay's finest sundials, in the Royal Botanic Garden, Edinburgh, is the inscription:

UMBRA SOLIS NON AERIS
The Shadow of the Sun and not of the Bronze

(p. 237). The first of these propositions would seem to be banal to the point of being tautological, while the second cannot, strictly speaking, be considered true. But then, its logic is not 'scientific'. The authorized commentary[2] states that:

> The motto refers, like many other sundial mottoes, to the mythic and philosophical associations of solar time. It is the 'golden' sun, rather than the bronze gnomon, that is the true origin of the shadow which indicates the hour. Similarly, in a tradition which goes back to Henry Vaughan's *Silex Scintillans*, Ficino's Neo-Platonism and the Augustan 'divine illumination of the intellect', it is the operation of the divine light in the universe that allows us to recognise and imitate the good. Wallace Stevens speaks of the poet coming 'out of the cavern', in a veiled allusion to Plato's myth of the cave. Here the form of the sundial is used to create a metaphor of this process: to indicate that turning from the shadow to the source of light which Plato portrayed as the mind's supreme activity.

It could be said that the Latin inscription is a disguised imperative, almost forcing the reader to turn his eyes from the beauty of the dial and up to the sun – unless it is to a sunless sky, which would seem to confirm the inscribed statement (there being in such a case no shadow whereby to read the hour). Similarly, *Arcadian Sundials* is an affirmation of value, anticipating the neoplatonism of *Umbra Solis . . .*, rather than a statement of fact so obvious as to be devoid of information value. In neither case is Finlay striving to convince us of a factual state of affairs. One is not expected to believe in the truth of such statements in the way one would accept the conclusions of a logician or a scientist. There is here a 'suspension of disbelief' of a radical sort, invoking the tradition to test the energies of artistic and philosophical forces.

In a booklet evaluating the evocative power of traditional genres and motifs, Finlay uses three captions referring to sundials:

A sundial by moonlight.

An enormous sundial in a shadowed gorge, the gnomon of the sundial encrusted with icicles.

A man bending over a sundial with his hand to his ear.[3]

In each case – as throughout the booklet – the 'illustration' is a blank page. As in the *3 Blue Lemons* (p. 197), we have here a challenge to 'visualize' the energies of the tradition – a 'civilized' variation upon the procedures of conceptual art. The fact that each of the situations suggested is obviously inoperative as regards the actual functioning of sundials is an implicit statement regarding the distance of modern pastoral or romantic sublimity from the 'divine' source of cultural energies.

Finlay has already been seen to cite different art forms or idioms in order to appraise both his own work and that of his contemporaries. This procedure is applied to sundials in a drawing from the *Third Reich Revisited* which makes use of a design which has known a number of avatars.[4] The poem/print 'Sea/Land' is not yet a sundial, simply a semiotic grid (p. 233). The dimension of time is added to that of space in the sundials in slate at the University of Kent at Canterbury (p. 235) and on a boulder at Stonypath (p. 235). The vertical lines tell the hour, while the horizontal curves indicate the tip of the shadow made by the gnomon at different times in the year. So the dial incorporates yearly as well as diurnal rhythms, and becomes a statement about the condition of the world.[5] Finlay used the same design for works in glass, giving it a more ambivalent status. For if the transparency of glass suggests a symbolic projection of the metaphorical lines on to the immediate environment, there remains also the at least hypothetical possibility of using the network to tell the time.

Finlay's sundials, in general, and 'Sea/Land' in particular, involve a meditation on the origins of art and on the grounding of the vocabulary and structures of art in reality. This is further developed in an embroidery done with Pamela Campion (p. 24), which associates the semiotic grid with a traditional craft, and finds its most strenuous formulation in the drawing of *Sundials at the Zeppelinfeld* (p. 144), with its conflation of the cosmological and the geopolitical. So potent is the meeting of art and reality in the *Third Reich Revisited* series, that certain viewers, unsettled by the mixture of truth and fiction in Finlay's commentary, actually thought that the artist had really created sundials for the Zeppelinfeld.

Finlay's powerful fiction can more appropriately be taken as the hyperbolical reformulation of a much earlier sundial – one that was actually installed both at Stonypath and in the neighbouring market town of Biggar (p. 239). This sundial is in the spirit of other works concerned with proximity and distance.[6] The interplay between the language of commerce:

AZURE & SON
ISLANDS LTD
OCEANS INC

and the tradition of the inscription (manifested in the quality of the lettering) implies tensions between proximity and estrangement, the sacred and the secular, purity and action (a form of commitment).[7] If the Biggar and Zeppelinfeld sundials can be considered to map out the context for Finlay's cosmological sundials as a whole, then the historical references which they establish overrun any metaphysical interpretation in terms of a presocratic 'word picture'.

The same is true of the sundial designs dedicated to Saint-Just. One of these is a badge worn by the Saint-Just Vigilantes (p. 239). What is at issue here is the myth of nature which in part engendered, and certainly served to legitimize, the French Revolution. This myth was Rousseauistic, rather than Platonizing or neopresocratic, in its inspiration. It went hand in hand with the neoclassicism that was the official idiom of the Revolution. By occupying a point at which natural, ethical and political philosophy meet up with aesthetics and metaphysics, Finlay's sundial designs and mottoes form an important strand in his ongoing evaluation of cultural forces.

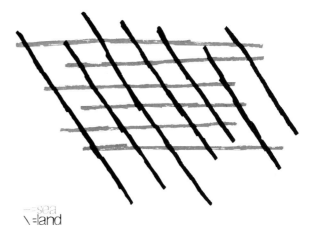

Sea/Land, 1967
print, with Herbert Rosenthal

Westward-facing sundial, 1971
wood, with John R. Thorpe

Terra/Mare, 1975
wood, with George L. Thomson

Sea/Land, 1972
slate, with Michael Harvey
University of Kent, Canterbury, England

Boulder, 1970
with Michael Harvey

Four Seasons sundial, 1970, enamelled metal,
with Michael Harvey

The Four Seasons as Fore-and-Afters, 1972, ceramic,
with Michael Harvey and Susan Goodricke

The Four Seasons in Sail, 1968, marble, with Maxwell Allen

Umbra Solis . . ., 1975
slate, with Michael Harvey
Royal Botanic Garden, Edinburgh

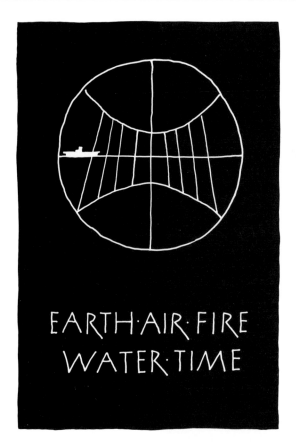

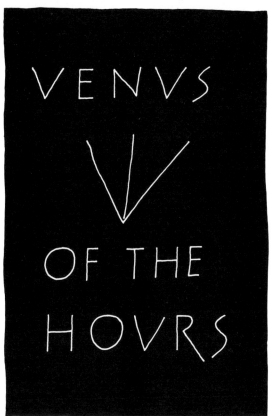

From *Airs, Waters, Graces*, 1975
booklet, with Ron Costley

From *A Sailor's Calendar*, 1971
with Gordon Huntley
Something Else Press, USA

Azure & Son, 1970
slate, with Michael Harvey
High Street, Biggar, Scotland

Badge, 1983 with Nicholas Sloan

ARCADIAN SUNDIALS

*All Times on these sundials
are Solar Time.*

Arcadian Sundials, 1970
folding card, with Margot Sandeman

10 ET IN ARCADIA EGO

The interaction of cultural forces with the destructive element is again at issue in Finlay's works on the theme of Arcady from the early 1970s onwards.[1] These constitute an important element of the artist's neo-classical rearmament. In his exploration of what is a significant strand of our cultural heritage he has since been joined by a group of artists from Yorkshire, the New Arcadians, constituted in the early 1980s.[2] Finlay's *Footnotes to an Essay*, published in 1977, represent his own most exhaustive exploitation of the theme to date.

The essay to which these *Footnotes* (p. 245) allude is Erwin Panofsky's '*Et in Arcadia Ego:* Poussin and the Elegiac Tradition' (1951), which is itself a reworking of an earlier text by the same author: '*Et in Arcadia Ego:* on the conception of transcience in Poussin and Watteau' (1935).[3] Both are relevant to an appreciation of Finlay's Arcadian pieces. The mythological domain of Pan, Arcady, was in reality a poor, bare, rocky and chilly country. Its inhabitants were famed in ancient times for their musical accomplishments, rugged virtue and rustic hospitality. Its geographical and climatic harshness scarcely made a suitable site for pastoral poetry, and the ancient Greeks in fact set their pastorals elsewhere. The scene of the *Idylls* of Theocritus is accordingly Sicily. Ovid and Virgil later transported pastoral poetry to a fictional Arcady, which was held by the latter to have all the charm of Sicily. It is also Virgil who introduced frustrated love and death – an acknowledgement of the discrepancy between supernatural perfection and the limitations of human life – into this idyllic setting. Panofsky's description of this recalls Finlay's accounts of suprematist 'perfection', as well as comments he made in a letter of praise addressed to Ad Reinhardt:

> There is a problem with concrete poetry, I mean my own – that they [Reinhardt's] are grave pictures. In Scotland there is a lot of heaviness that is something different from gravity, something quite unartistic and this made me feel that humour was a very important thing in so far as it makes a distance, a space, and art needs that sort of space . . . But I have started to feel that humour is not a way of doing things – that there ought to be evening poems as well as afternoon ones – and your pictures please me very much by having

this distance, they are absolutely *art* and not by being *funny*.[4]

Panofsky describes the Virgilian modulation of the Arcady theme in similar terms:

> In Virgil's ideal Arcady human suffering and super-humanly perfect surroundings create a dissonance. This dissonance, once felt, had to be resolved, and it was resolved in that vespertinal mixture of sadness and tranquillity which is perhaps Virgil's most personal contribution to poetry. With only slight exaggeration one might say that he 'discovered' the evening.

Virgil's evening poetry was elegiac, and the *Et in Arcadia Ego* motif which recurs in European literature, painting and gardening from the Renaissance on, is also predominantly elegiac.

The Latin tag *Et in Arcadia Ego*, probably devised by the future Pope Clement IX in the early 1620s, was originally a *memento mori* that should be translated: 'Even in Arcady, I, Death, hold sway'. Panofsky shows how a picture by Guercino painted between 1621 and 1623 incorporates Christian moral theology and the milieu of classicizing pastorals then in vogue. It took only two paintings by Poussin to transform the mode. In the Louvre version of *Et in Arcadia Ego* (late 1630s) in particular, the atmosphere is not at all that created by Guercino. There is no longer a dramatic encounter with death, but a contemplative absorption in the idea of mortality. The change, as Panofsky observes, is from moralism to elegy.

Poussin is much closer to Renaissance and modern notions of Arcady than was Guercino. The Renaissance had a very real nostalgia for the classical. The distance separating it from the classical world could be seen in terms which were either bitter or elegiac. There was even, at the Medici villa at Fiesole, an attempt to bridge the gap by means of a fictional identification of the court of Lorenzo the Magnificent with Arcadian shepherds.[5] The elegiac treatment of death in Arcady, as institutionalized in the wake of Poussin, is thus true to the Renaissance sense of Arcadian pastoral. Only in England, according to Panofsky, did the idea of the *memento mori* continue to be associated with the tag *Et in Arcadia Ego*. Examples of this 'insular' tradition, whose existence is of obvious interest to a consideration of Finlay's work, range from Joshua Reynolds to Augustus John and Evelyn Waugh.[6]

By renaming his garden Little Sparta, or by calling themselves New Arcadians, Finlay and his Yorkshire allies appear to be repeating the gesture of Lorenzo the Magnificent. The rigours of Sparta, however, serve as a reminder of the true nature of Arcady, as documented by Polybius, its most famous son. Just as the New Arcadians' documentation of the theme brings out what is harshly militaristic in Arcadia, so Finlay obviously remembers the Polybian and Ovidian ideal of rough, healthy frugality which we moderns are more apt to associate with Sparta, when he writes that:

Up at five and fold hammocks is the rule in Arcady.[7]

Thus we have the stirrings of a new and perhaps specifically northern British tradition, going back beyond the *memento mori* and the Renaissance or Roman Arcadies, to something which historians assure us to be true to fact.

Stephen Bann has already discerned in the *Footnotes to an Essay* an 'unexpected extension of the elegiac tradition' described by Panofsky – and one which, as the same commentator notes with reference to Finlay's variation on Guercino, casts elegiac musings into the background.[8] In many ways, the *Footnotes* continue the 'ironic iconoclasm' which Panofsky associates with twentieth-century contributions to the insular tradition of the Arcadian *memento mori*. They certainly react against the tranquillizing classicism epitomized by Poussin (in harmony, Panofsky notes, 'with the principles of Classical art theory, which rejected "les objets bizarres", especially such gruesome objects as a death's head'). Finlay's *Footnotes*, with their frequent references to the Waffen-SS, are hyperbolically gruesome. They reawaken the terror depicted by Guercino, but missing from the elegiac tradition. Is this to say that they emphasize the extremity of the contemporary cultural predicament?[9] Certainly – in the sense that such a predicament is not simply to be put down to that clichéd enemy of art, a hostile environment, but inhabits the very texture of the artistic process itself. In this case, it is the strength of Finlay's reworking of the Arcadian theme, rather than its overtly hyperbolical elements, which should claim the attention. The virtues – the *virtù* – of Finlay's treatment of death in Arcady can perhaps

best be demonstrated with reference to the neoclassical tag *Et in Arcadia Ego*.

The shift between Guercino and Poussin involves differing interpretations of the Latin phrase. 'Even in Arcady, I, Death, hold sway' – spoken by the death's head – is replaced by 'I, too, was born, or lived, in Arcady' – spoken by the person buried in Poussin's tomb. Now Panofsky shows quite clearly that the former is the only grammatically correct interpretation of *Et in Arcadia Ego*, even if he goes on to argue that Poussin's version, 'indefensible though it is from a philological point of view, yet did not come about from "pure ignorance" but, on the contrary, expressed and sanctioned, at the expense of grammar but in the interest of truth, a basic change in interpretation'. If the *Footnotes* or the Miltonic *Of Famous Arcady Ye Are*, in the context Finlay provides for it (p. 243), mark a return to the grammatically correct interpretation of *Et in Arcadia Ego*, this is a sign that what is really at stake in Finlay's reworking of the theme is the assertive value of the sentence. What Poussin does is to interiorize the impact of the Latin tag. The shock of the stark warning uttered by the death's head is replaced by an act of deciphering (underlined by the posture of Poussin's shepherds) which immerses the recipients in mellow meditation. This amounts to transforming what was an implicit imperative – 'Remember, in your moment of frolicsome joy, that death awaits you . . . and act accordingly' – into a pathetic plaint affecting the sensibility. Its force is now psychological. Is such a transformation not behind Poussin's assuaging cosmological metaphysics, as expounded by Panofsky?[10] Finlay counters such an approach by suggesting that

Cosmologies are the Arcadia's (Utopias?) of psychologies.[11]

If, then, Finlay reawakens the terror in the death-in-Arcady motif, the effect is not simply to foreground the immense pressures which contemporary life has brought to bear upon the tissue of European culture. Nor is it even just to underline the complicity which can exist between culture and violence (although the idea of a Reich can quite clearly be linked, as early as the eighteenth century, to a classical mythic ideal). By their very attachment to grammatical and philological rectitude, Finlay's variations on *Et in Arcadia Ego* exemplify the rigour which the artist himself calls for. They represent a radical transformation – with the Nietzschean hammer – of the elegiac tradition. Panofsky praises the misinterpretation of *Et in Arcadia Ego* provoked by Poussin on grounds of harmony. Despite its linguistic incorrectness, the reinterpretation 'reinstates the harmony between the text and the image'. And this image is itself 'in harmony with the principles of Classical art theory', which rejected whatever was gruesome. Finlay's position with regard to the aesthetic category of harmony is not neoclassical. If he himself puts the question, 'What is the value of harmony?',[12] his own Heraclitean *Lyre* (p. 223) provides the answer by implying that harmony includes an inseparable element of polemological energy. Let it also be recalled that the Arcadians, uncouth as they were, were celebrated for their musical accomplishments and rugged virtue. It is to these qualities that Finlay's use of a Virgilian tag in the monument commemorating the First Battle of Little Sparta (p. 244) in fact alludes. To quote the artist's own commentary:

> The machine-gun is a visual pun (or play!) on Virgil's flute, with the vents in the barrel-sleeve as the finger-stops. But – *Et in Arcadia Ego* – is the flute to begin, or the gun – or is the duet in fact to be a trio: does the singer (if he is to continue the pastoral) need both?[13]

In this way is the 'gravity' of the Virgilian evening transformed. Poussin performs the transformation of a *memento mori* into the revelation of a metaphysical principle. Finlay achieves a further displacement: from a neoclassical metaphysical cosmology which fails the genealogical test of the hammer, to the linguistic modulation which, adopting his own neologism, I have described as neopresocratic.

Et in Arcadia Ego, 1977
stone, with John Andrew

Of Famous Arcady Ye Are, 1977
poster, with Michael Harvey

FIRST BATTLE OF LITTLE SPARTA
FEBRUARY 4, 1983

THE MACHINE-GUN is a visual pun (or play!) on Virgil's flute, with the vents in the barrel-sleeve as the finger-stops. But – *Et in Arcadia ego* – is the flute to begin, or the gun – or is the duet in fact to be a trio: does the singer (if he is to continue in his pastoral) need *both*?

Bibl.: Virgil, *Eclogues*; Eyres, *Despatches From The Little Spartan War*; Hogg, *Encyclopedia of Infantry Weapons*.

MEDALS OF THE LITTLE SPARTAN WAR

Medal to commemorate the First Battle of Little Sparta, 1984
bronze, with Michael Burton

Monument to the First Battle of Little Sparta, 1984
bronze, brick, with John Andrew and Andrew Townsend

Footnotes to an essay[1]

1 The title suggests a number of different interpretations, some of them more appropriate than others. In the first place, and in the context of its original publication in 1977, it bears witness to the fact that these images and commentaries were appended to the end of my essay on the development of Ian Hamilton Finlay's work up to that point. In the second place, and with a continuing relevance to Finlay's artistic and cultural stance, it testifies to what Harold Bloom has called (partly with regard to Pater) the consciousness of 'belatedness'. The 'essay' is in this sense the 'text' of Western art and culture, upon which the modern or the Post-Romantic can do no more than place a final footnote (one which emphasises, through hyperbolic translation of a classical theme, the extremity of the cultural predicament). In the third place, and most precisely, this section takes as its point of departure Erwin Panofsky's famous essay 'Et in Arcadia Ego: Poussin and the Elegiac Tradition'. The five primary illustrations, drawn by Gary Hincks 'after' the crucial illustrations to Panofsky's text, are supplemented by five further versions, which incorporate Finlay's 'translation'. The exercise is both a homage to Panofsky, and an unexpected extension of the elegiac tradition which he has so brilliantly described.

And why Panofsky? No one demonstrates better (and no essay of Panofsky shows more clearly) the richness of a classical tradition in which poetry and iconography, philosophy and myth, are interfused. Yet Panofsky, who entitled an address to his American colleagues 'Impressions of a trans-planted European', has always been concerned to identify estrangement from classical art as the dominant theme of the classical tradition. Of Albrecht Dürer, whom he describes as the first Northern artist to feel 'pathos of distance' from the classical world, he writes: 'For him antiquity was neither a garden where fruits and flowers still bloomed, nor a field of ruins the stones and columns of which could be re-used: it was a lost 'kingdom' which had to be reconquered by a well-organized campaign'.

After the garden metaphor, and the metaphor evoking the classical inscription, the campaign is perhaps, for Finlay as well, the analogy which really strikes home.

After Giovanni Francesco Guercino, *'Et in Arcadia ego'*, Rome, Galleria Corsini.[2]

Inv. Giovanni Francesco Guercino   *Del.* Gary Hincks

2 'Et in Arcadia ego' is not a classical tag. Indeed Panofsky suggests that it was in all probability devised by Giulio Rospigliosi, who was born in 1600 at Pistoia in Tuscany and died in 1669, two years after his election as Pope under the title Clement IX. Certainly Guercino's picture, which was painted at Rome between 1621 and 1623, is the first pictorial treatment of the theme of Death in Arcady. It draws upon the idealized Arcady of Virgil's *Eclogues*, peopled by the happy Bucolics of Theocritus' pastoral *Idylls*. Yet in this work, it confronts them with a portent bearing late Medieval associations: the Death's Head as a *memento mori* which reminds the dreaming swains that 'Even in Arcady, I, Death, hold sway'.

Inv. Ian Hamilton Finlay   *Del.* Gary Hincks

In Finlay's version, the rude effect of the Death's Head on mouldering masonry, supplemented by mouse and fly as popular symbols of decay, is replaced by the camouflaged tank which bears the Death's Head (Totenkopf) insignia of the German SS-Panzer division. Hyper-bolically, the medieval symbol is transformed into the terms of modern tank warfare, while the clustering ivy suggests a more con-temporary symbol for insidious decay. In Guercino, the Arcady retrieved by Renaissance poets is brutally interrupted by the over-explicit presence of a skull noticeably larger than life. In the new version, the over-bearing tank, with its crudely stencilled device, casts elegiac musings into the background.

'Footnotes to an Essay', 1977
with Gary Hincks and Stephen Bann
From the catalogue of the 1977 Serpentine Gallery exhibition

After Nicolas Poussin, *'Et in Arcadia ego'*,
Chatsworth, Devonshire Collection.[3]

Inv. Nicolas Poussin   *Del.* Gary Hincks

3 Poussin's first version of the 'Et in Arcadia ego' theme was
probably completed around 1630, in response to a commission from
Rospigliosi and with obvious indebtedness to the earlier work by
Guercino. Yet Poussin has quite transformed the atmosphere of the
previous painting, making the contrast between the idyll and the
Death's Head much less brutal. A shepherdess has joined the two
enquiring shepherds, who neglect the almost concealed skull and
trace out the form of the inscribed letters, a 'telling symptom' as
Panofsky reminds us 'of Poussin's intellectualistic inclinations'. Yet a
didactic element is still present in the work, which was intended as a
counterpart to Poussin's picture of *Midas Washing His Face in the River
Pactolus*. Hence the presence in the foreground of the river-god
Alpheus, balancing Pactolus. The 'Midas' picture condemns the mad
pursuit of riches, whilst the 'Arcady' work casts attention on the
transitory nature of human pleasures.

After Nicolas Poussin, *'Et in Arcadia ego'*,
Paris, Louvre.[4]

Inv. Nicolas Poussin   *Del.* Gary Hincks

4 Poussin's second, and more famous version of the theme was
produced about five or six years after the first version. The formal
scheme which in the other case had been borrowed from Guercino,
with a few significant modifications, has here been completely revised.
And Panofsky reminds us that the possibility of a totally new reading
has been brought about by the compelling character of Poussin's
Arcadian vision. The Death's Head has disappeared altogether, the
tomb has become a simple rectangular block (reminiscent of the 'bel
sasso quadrangulo' instanced in Jacopo Sannazaro's *Arcadia* of 1502).
The pensive Arcadians are no longer confronted with the challenge of
the *memento mori*: they cast their minds back upon the beautiful past –
a transition, as Panofsky suggests, 'from thinly veiled moralism to
undisguised elegiac sentiment'.

Inv. Ian Hamilton Finlay   *Del.* Gary Hincks

In the new version, the anthem of the Waffen-SS 'Wenn alle Brüder
Schweigen' (when all the brothers are silent) appears in the place of
the intimation of mortality. This anthem, based on the patriotic song
composed for the German War of Liberation in 1813 by Max von
Schenkendorf, is itself a noble lament for fallen heroes as well as an
incitement to further heroism. Moreover it casts a shadow back into
the German past, to Schenkendorf's own Romantic patriotism, and to
the initial composition of the tune in 1724 (just a century after
Poussin's arrival in Rome). Each of these stages, from the stark
contemporary reference to the mythical connection with the Roman
journey, forms an additional layer in the cultural dimension.

Inv. Ian Hamilton Finlay   *Del.* Gary Hincks

Finlay chooses to retain precisely the ambiguity of the original
reference. Poussin's picture is the very point from which these two
divergent interpretations of 'Et in Arcadia Ego' – the moralistic and
the elegiac – can be said to arise. It therefore serves the function of an
enigma, simultaneously evoking but not resolving the interplay of two
cultural traditions. In Finlay's version the enigma is the stone tank or
tomb which only partially discloses itself, offering the same equi-
vocation to the interpreter.

After Giovanni Battista Cipriani, *'Death even in Arcady'* (engraving).[5]

Inv. Giovanni Battista Cipriani   *Del.* Gary Hincks

5   With Poussin's second version, the elegiac reading of 'Et in Arcadia Ego' had entered the pictorial tradition. Yet those who knew Guercino's original work would be bound to continue to interpret the tag in the initial, moralistic sense. Cipriani, an Italian artist working in the later 18th century, seems to be aware of both precedents. Like Poussin, he increases the number of figures: by this stage we therefore have five attendant shepherdesses and a frolicking child, not to mention a dog and sheep which nestle into the fallen classical columns. The tomb itself has become an elaborate neo-classical affair, with the Death's Head re-established on a Baroque cartouche. Yet the Italian translation of the text, 'Ancora in Arcadia Morte', leaves us in no doubt that Cipriani saw Death as the original speaker. Indeed part of the purpose of the work, in spite of its florid and decorative elements, seems to be to revive the shock effect of Guercino's painting. The shepherds are struck dumb with astonishment, and even the child flees panic-stricken to his mother.

After Georg Wilhelm Kolbe, *'I too, was in Arcady'* (engraving).[6]

Inv. Georg Wilhelm Kolbe   *Del.* Gary Hincks

6   The two antithetical interpretations of 'Et in Arcadia Ego', oddly reconciled in Cipriani, coexist harmoniously in the Romantic view of the world where there is almost a fusion of what is sweet and what is melancholy. Johann Georg Jacobi anticipates this fusion when he writes in his *Winterreise* of 1769 (the earliest instance of the 'Tomb in Arcady' in German literature): 'Whenever, in a beautiful landscape, I encounter a tomb with the inscription *Auch Ich war in Arkadien*, I point it out to my friends; we stop a moment, press each other's hands, and proceed.' In this picture, the German Romanticist Kolbe uses the appearance of the blank tomb in the fantastic forest simply as a means of underlining the absorption of the two lovers in one another. For Goethe, as Panofsky notes, the reference to Arcadia even came to the point of losing all relationship to the ideas of death and destruction. 'Auch ich in Arkadien' became the motto of his 'blissful journey to Italy', meaning simply, 'I, too, was in the land of joy and beauty'.

Inv. Ian Hamilton Finlay   *Del.* Gary Hincks

The elaborate tomb bearing what Panofsky calls the 'coat of arms of Death' has been reinterpreted by Finlay as a camouflaged tank at the edge of a wood. All the figures have been replaced by foliage, which parts to reveal the unexpected threat (of the Cipriani elements, only a corner of the classical fragment has been retained, testifying to the tank's destructive power). The Cipriani text is as if painted on the side of the tank with white paint, while the superstructure reveals the double 'SS' sign, as if in two parallel strokes of lightning. It is in fact these strokes of lightning which give a new immediacy to the scene, recreating symbolically the panic of the Arcadians before the manifestation of Death.

Inv. Ian Hamilton Finlay   *Del.* Gary Hincks

For Finlay, it is as if the lovers had come upon an abandoned tank, not camouflaged as in previous examples but interwoven with boughs of evergreen in an almost formal way and covered with branches which have the effect of wreaths. The tank therefore loses its threatening quality, its capability to serve as a 'memento mori', and becomes a nostalgic evocation of earlier heroism. This, finally, is the image of remoteness and estrangement from the past. As Goethe came to equate Arcady with the Italy of his nostalgia, so these two images betray a nostalgia for their original model in Poussin, a Romantic yearning for the classical ideal.

ANTICIPATIONS

'And the earth, anchoring in the perfect
harbours of Aphrodite, meets with these
in equal proportions, with Hephaistos
and Water and Gleaming Air. . .'

POEM ON NATURE, FRAGMENT 98

See Burnet, *Early Greek Philosophy*

5. Baroque

6. Barque

7. Bark

8. Baroque

From *Anticipations*, 1983
booklet
We are invited to 'misread' the presocratic fragment, appre-
ciating it as a verbal counterpart of the 'School of Watteau'

From *Woods and Seas*, 1981
booklet

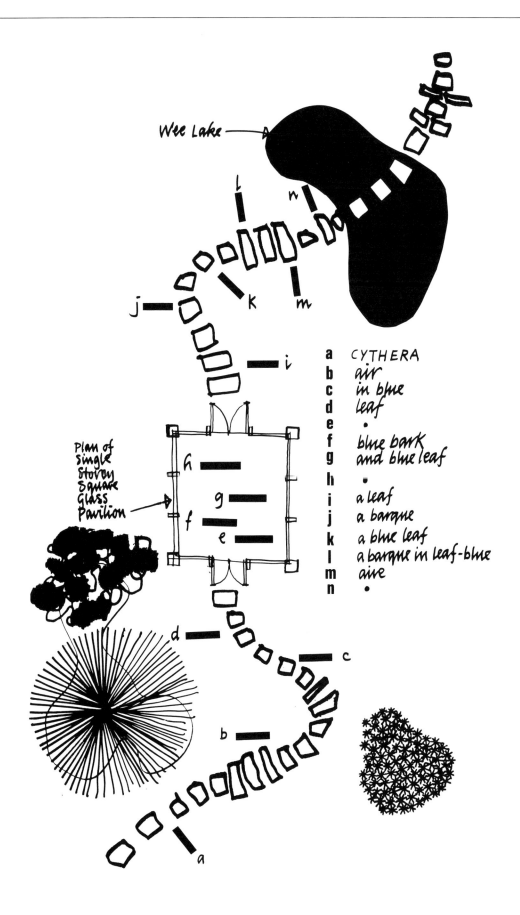

Wee Lake

l   n

j   k   m

i

Plan of
Single
Storey
Square
Glass
Pavilion

h
g
f
e

d

c

b

a

a CYTHERA
b air
c in blue
d leaf
e •
f blue bark
g and blue leaf
h •
i a leaf
j a barque
k a blue leaf
l a barque in leaf-blue
m aire
n •

Cythera – plan for garden version, 1965
with Peter Lyle

can achieve only a partial definition of sublimity. The contrast between an ironic, dialectical negativity (Socrates) and an irredeemable one (Satan) underlines what is at stake in any definition of the economy of the sublime. The globally positive account, moreover, fails to do justice to the historical and political perceptions of Burke and Bradley. If one follows the latter's advice to call to mind sublime figures in history, one may well agree that whether they are radical or gloomy, violent or peaceful, terrible or adorable, they impress the imagination by their immense or even irresistible might. However, the fascination exerted by such figures remains problematical.

The following lines were first published in 1790:

> Their rising was to illumine and beautify the world. Their quest over their competitors was by outshining them. The hand that, like a destroying angel, smote the country, communicated to it the force and energy under which it suffered. I do not say (God forbid) I do not say, that the virtues of such men were to be taken as a balance to their crimes; but they were some corrective to their efforts.[5]

If one did not know that their author was Edmund Burke, one would be tempted to regard such words as prophetic. They seem to anticipate the French Jacobins of the Year of the Terror (1793-4). The Jacobins emerged as the driving force in the Committee of Public Safety (in effect a revolutionary government) at a time when the young republic was close to collapse. The Convention was an indecisive assembly, the economy was in ruins, fractionalism was rife, civil war had broken out, and foreign armies had already crossed the frontiers and were threatening to overrun France. Granted this context, French apologists of the Terror explain its rigours by the needs of the day – an analysis which has only recently been contested with any success. The apologists furthermore point out that the infamous Committee's action was in many ways successful. Indeed, Bonaparte had already declared that it was the only serious government of the revolutionary period, while R. R. Palmer, perhaps the most sympathetic American historian of the Revolution, insists that the Terror was a moment more of creation than destruction.[6] And even Burke's 'destroying angel' prefigures the expression 'archangel of death' applied to Saint-Just, a leading Robespierrist, by Michelet in his *History of the French Revolution*. Completed in 1853, this monumental work is notoriously a celebration of the Revolution.

Burke, however, was implacably hostile to the French Revolution. The lines from his *Reflections on the Revolution in France* do not refer to the Robespierrist faction. They are retrospective, their subject being primarily Cromwell, but also a few figures from earlier French history. Nevertheless, the close kinship between this historical appreciation and Burke's account of the sublime raises yet again the problem of the relationship between aesthetics and politics or historiography: of the figuration of power.

A powerful account of the sublime, together with a helpful historical signpost, is provided by Harold Bloom. Bloom paraphrases Longinus, recalling that as a literary idea the sublime originally meant a lofty style whose verbal power was conceived agonistically, seeking to triumph over all possible competition. He then updates the argument:

> But in the European Enlightenment, this literary idea was strangely transformed into a vision of the terror that could be perceived both in nature and in art, a terror uneasily allied with pleasurable sensations of augmented power, and even of narcissistic freedom, freedom in the shape of that wildness Freud dubbed 'the omnipotence of thought', the greatest of all narcissistic illusions.[7]

Both this modern, catastrophic sublime and the intellectual roots of the French Revolution, with its notorious 'excesses', date back to the Enlightenment. The conjunction is interesting.

Expression is never self-evident, never fully in harmony with itself, so it becomes the sphere of terror. Poetics and aesthetics are inescapably polemical.[8] Aristotle himself sees the figurative energies of language as being pitted against the literal norm (*kurion* or *idion*) which is tantamount to expressive death. One must, however, distinguish between the common concept of terror and the modern idea of Terror with a capital T. The latter is the forerunner of the contemporary notion of terrorism. It is commonly accepted to date no further back than the French Revolution.

Rhetorical theory is dependent on political anthropology. Classical rhetoric granted terror an explicit position in the complex body of rules and genres governing the entire range of discursive practices, by way of Aristotle's account of tragedy. This was a cornerstone of his rhetoric and poetics, and was accorded pre-eminence over the centuries. The tragic mode, as epitomized by *Oedipus Rex*, revolves around the problems of figuration and interpretation, which are the very hub of the complex plots most favoured by Aristotle. If, then, tragedy brings about the *catharsis* of pity and terror, the dramatic structure prescribed by Aristotle can be said not only to constitute the law of a genre which has today disappeared, but also to represent a formalization of the dramatic – or tragic – nature of all expression.[9] Classical rhetoric thus institutionalized the tragic mode as the point of resolution of the tensions and terrors besetting all expression.

It is this safety-valve which disappears with the demise of rhetoric. The terror of expression, no longer integrated within a coherent system of discourses, breaks out at random, occupying the entire poetic enterprise without finding any one stable cathartic point. Modern poetic practice is thus characteristically uncompromising. It is radical, and can even become totalitarian.[10] In romantic and post-romantic literature (taking these to mark the final dismembering of the body of classical rhetoric), a certain madness of expression becomes the norm, together with fantasies of an apocalyptic transformation in the conditions of expression by means of a single act of rhetorical invention.

There is an obvious political parallel. In his *Penser la Révolution Française*,[11] François Furet breaks with the conventional French apology of the 1793–4 Terror as a necessary response to the pressures of the day. Focusing on Robespierre, who tended to remain one step back from the centre of action and decision, Furet explains why the austere and reserved lawyer from Arras is nevertheless the true incarnation of the Revolution. Robespierre marks its rhetorical centre, striving to coincide with the (supposed) voice of the people. The conjunction of language and power which he represents, Furet sees as producing modern democratic culture – but it nevertheless constitutes in his judgement a pathological conception of power. The events of the Year of the Terror can be taken to bear out both sides of the argument.

The modern poetic crisis (or poetics of crisis) is but one indication of the way in which language and signs have gone into turmoil. Victor Hugo draws together modern political and literary culture in an exemplary manner. Declaring war on rhetoric, he identifies with the Terrorists of the Revolution: *'Je suis ce Robespierre'*.[12] Of course, like all terrorists, he sees himself as a counter-terrorist, purging violence by violence. Such is perhaps the modern substitute for catharsis. It is equally evident, as Rimbaud cruelly remarked, that Hugo does

not eliminate rhetoric. He merely displaces it.

This, then, is the context in which Finlay's works referring to Saint-Just and the Robespierrists, and also to the Third Reich, can best be understood. The nineteenth-century artist, d'Angers, who did a portrait of Saint-Just, assimilates his subject to a sublime landscape. Like Coleridge in the anecdote retold above, d'Angers is surveying a cataract:

> There falls as if from the sky an immense cataract, sweeping away immense blocks of granite and the dried trunks of fir trees, uprooting young trees. The cataract is produced by Lake Gaube, on the mountaintop, which has not stopped flowing since the beginning of time. The terrifying sound of the waterfall appears to me as the revolutions of mankind, as plagues, battles, cholera. I see, in the sublime revolution, great men about to be swallowed up. I think of the great names of Christ, Moses, Robespierre, Danton and Saint-Just, etc. And this terrible cataract hurls itself in fury into a profound abyss where a rainbow appears – the Tricolor which was to go to the ends of the earth.[13]

Finlay quotes this description approvingly. However, with the notable exception of a work exhibited at the Hayward Gallery in the summer of 1983 (p. 48), his works on the French Revolution are not in the heroic sublime manner.

The *Present Order* sculpture is monumental. It consists of fragments each weighing approximately one ton. The text inscribed on these also figures on a poem/card which invites its reader to cut them out and arrange the words in order (p. 256). The invitation is physically to gauge the will which makes the Saint-Just tag a sentence, by testing the force required to accomplish the labour of shifting the stone fragments. An explicit challenge to the economy of the sublime.

Finlay's work on the Revolution is frequently in an idiom more closely linked to the eighteenth-century English landscape garden. This has important cultural implications, Milton's epic of redemption being a powerful force behind its growth:

> Milton alone of either Charles's time
> In horticulture hit the true sublime;
> What vary'd beauties in his gardens shine,
> The charms of nature live in every line;
> The powers of fancy cou'd no higher soar,
> His Eden blooms as Eden bloom'd before.[14]

The Miltonic conflation of political, aesthetic and religious realms is perhaps best echoed by the works in Finlay's Sacred Grove (p. 124) at the Kröller-Müller Museum in Holland. The Grove celebrates Corot, Lycurgus, Michelet, Robespierre and Rousseau. By their very structure, the tree-columns to be found there make one meditate on the articulation between classical and natural values. They also recall the age of sensibility which produced, not only the Burkean notion of the sublime, but also the poems of Gray and Collins which hesitate between classical allegory and natural description.

The problematics of the classical and the natural haunted the English garden. The French garden in the style of le Nôtre (of which Versailles is the prime example) represented artifice, and the freely winding and undulating English park, as it emerged in the early 1700s, was overtly a rejection of French authority both in the arts and in politics. It was an endorsement of liberty and tolerance against tyranny and oppression, democracy against autocracy.[15] The historical and political connotations do not stop here. Gardens such as Cobham's at Stowe and Aislabie's at Studley Royal were symbols of liberty created by prominent Whigs forced out of public life. Such gardens did not simply express the idea of freedom by their less contrived scenery. They also included emblems of freedom, justice or goodness, which invoked classical prototypes. The Elysian Fields at Stowe represent an allegory of good and bad government.[16] They contain a Temple of British Worthies, with sixteen busts, and also Temples of Ancient and Modern Virtue. The Temple of Ancient Virtue contained life-size statues of Socrates, Homer, Lycurgus and Epaminondas – exemplary classical instances of a philosopher, poet, lawgiver and general. John Dixon Hunt and Peter Willis insist on the problematical nature of such allusions, which are to be discerned as much in the architecture and inscriptions of the Stowe temples as in the heroes actually celebrated: 'in these matters of English Augustanism, the assimilation of Classical ideas was not merely a question of "imitation", but of "translation", of making Homer (in Pope's phrase) "speak good English", and of registering the difficulties as well as the opportunities of cultural obligations'.[17] This is precisely the point of Finlay's neoclassicism, conceived as a strategy rather than an idiom. The Sacred Grove – and the prototype Pantheon in the garden at Stonypath, where there are also monuments to Saint-Just and Fabre d'Eglantine (p. 260, p. 262) – combines Stowe's temples. Its sweep is trans-

historical. It is also a bold catachresis, combining both grove and temple. As such, it furthermore represents an impressive reworking of the older tradition of the formal garden, with its topiary pyramids (still to be found in Kensington Gardens in the early eighteenth century).

Finlay's tree-columns are informed both by Rousseau's conception of natural man and by the neoclassicism of the French Revolution. Revolution figures implicitly in Finlay's work as early as 1966 when the booklet *Autumn Poem* was published (p. 280). This plays on the expressions 'turning over the earth' and 'the earth turning over' – both being signs of autumn.[18] However, the link between the natural cycle and the political notion of revolution was made much later, with the pun on the name of Fabre d'Eglantine in an inscription at Stonypath (p. 262) and in the booklet *A Litany/A Requiem* (p. 281), in which the crop for Thermidor consists of the executed Robespierrists.

The Anaximander Fragment (p. 281) is in many ways a reworking of *Autumn Poem*. The latter was the first of Finlay's works to include photographs. They were arranged according to a binary rhythm of close-ups and more distant views – a system also adopted in the Anaximander booklet, which furthermore alternates views with and without classical architectural fragments.[19] In both booklets, the text is repetitive and involves minimal variations. *The Anaximander Fragment* cites a philosophical meditation which might have been inspired by the natural cycle. It incorporates all the formal and referential complexity developed by Finlay in the intervening decade and a half. The 'things' of which the philosopher (600 B.C.) speaks may be considered to include the eruptions marked by the architectural fragments. The effect is to underline how the presocratic sentence takes stock of perpetual change both in nature and in culture, the intertextual play between the Autumn and Anaximander booklets evoking different values of the latter term.

The Anaximander Fragment gives eleven different translations of a single philosophical sentence. However, it is only at one point that they differ significantly. What the vast majority of translators render as 'injustice', Kahn says is an 'offence' and Diels, 'recklessness'. These variations underline the catastrophically unstable nature of the affirmative force which I have suggested to be by nature polemological. On what grounds does one come down on the side of one translation or another? Are we moderns not altogether too embarrassed by the notion of power to be able properly to face up to the problem?[20] Finlay's systematic foregrounding of the cultural dimension of the French Revolution or the Third Reich constitutes a hyperbolical statement of this predicament. The invocation of Lycurgus and Saint-Just in a card insisting on the values of fixation, placement and obeisance (p. 262) counterbalances the pre-socratic 'recklessness', while continuing to ponder on those two major myths of authority – nature and the classic. The Arcadian connotations of *A Flute for Saint-Just* (p. 257) are indicative of the ambivalent accomplishment it celebrates, and *He Spoke Like an Axe* (p. 255) adroitly mingles bucolics and menace.

The scythes inscribed with revolutionary sentences and now installed in Finlay's Garden Temple (p. 70) are related to the Saint-Just axe. They powerfully combine the pastoral ideals of the French Revolution with the traditional allegorical representation of death. Their link with an earlier poem/card of Finlay's again demonstrates the complexity of the artist's exploration of cultural forces. *Mower is Less* (p. 282) wittily rephrases Mies van der Rohe's aesthetically purist dictum 'Less is more', finding a formula which brings to mind Andrew Marvell's exquisite pastoral variations on the theme of death the mower. Taken together, the poem/card and the scythes demonstrate how Finlay continues to reactivate traditional motifs in a way which challenges us to evaluate cultural forces, be they the ideals of modern architecture, or the mythical and philosophical notions underlying revolutionary upheaval.

It is only when the cultural dimension is properly established that one can fully appreciate the emblematical importance of the figure of Saint-Just to the Little Spartan War. His name was adopted by the Saint-Just Vigilantes, a loose organization of friends and allies which has carried out a number of spectacular actions in defence of Little Sparta. One could invoke in the Vigilantes' defence the same sense of urgency and danger as historians have used to defend their tutelary genius, who was renowned as a thinker of actions. However, it has been seen that such an apology is at best incomplete. So it is well to recall that the Saint-Just Vigilantes first appeared in a fictional context, in the *Third Reich Revisited*, in a work focusing on the connection between political and natural revolution (p. 144). One should not forget this when reading the Saint-Just quotations that Finlay posted next to his Hayward sculpture, which provides the necessary and in many ways undecidable context.[21]

The *Redemption (Renovation) Scheme* is ambivalently

sublime, as is the *Third Reich* series as a whole. Finlay's 'German' works are indeed characteristically fiercer than most of those referring to the French Revolution. This is the case, not only of the Arcadian *Footnotes to an Essay*, but also in the eruption of a German element in the English landscape garden, as in the booklet *S/F* (p. 283). The inscription on one of a series of *Porridge Bowls for Sans-culottes* reads:

In Revolution, politics become Nature

and *S/F* sombrely invites its reader to ponder over the value of the final term, as Finlay does again in the disturbing *Propaganda for the Wood Elves* (p. 286), or in his works on the theme of camouflage, such as the dryads already referred to (p. 7).

Elves and dryads are not, of course, sublime in the Burkean or Bradleian sense. They do not suggest infinity on the overwhelming scale described by these writers. Rather – like the series of works in which Finlay punningly conflates pansies and panzers (p. 287) – they are uncanny in their combination of the sustaining and disruptive qualities of aura. It is this uncanny quality – the casual panic which invests the whimsy – that distinguishes Finlay's work from the romantic sublime. With Finlay, it is not a question of going out and yielding to a demiurgic force. His problematical proposition is to reinvest his environment and culture with the 'ideas' and the 'strength' without which things exist 'but on sufferance'.[22] If *S/F* sets out the two extremes, *Wildflower* (p. 69) seeks to incarnate one of the intermediate stages which the booklet also invites the reader to allegorize.

Flowers, for Burke, epitomize beauty in the vegetable world. Similarly, for Bradley, they are beautiful, graceful or pretty, but rarely grand – and even less sublime. He adds that in the latter cases one does not think of them as small. Such a scale of values is absent from the memoirs of Albert Speer, who is puzzled by his master's attitude towards nature:

> Hitler's decision to settle on Obersalzberg seemed to point to a love of nature. But I was mistaken about that. He did frequently admire a beautiful view, but as a rule he was more affected by the awesomeness of the abysses than by the harmony of a landscape. It may be that he felt more than he allowed himself to express. I noticed that he took little pleasure in flowers and considered them entirely as decorations.[23]

Hitler (even more than Robespierre, whom historians,

however, still condemn with equal vigour) can be taken to represent the hyperbolically catastrophical sublime which is the extreme instance of the problematical modern relation to strength or power. It is therefore curious to find Speer, so close to the Führer in architectural matters, completely missing the point. How much more perceptive was d'Angers on Robespierre, Saint-Just and Danton. Finlay's *Wildflower* – 'a mean term between revolution and virtue' – strives to bridge the gap that Speer fails even to visualize.

Wildflower is both a concrete poem/object (a vase with plants by no means out of place in the poet's garden) and a text which is obviously relevant to Finlay's dispute with the authorities. It can therefore be taken to condense the features of Finlay's artistic life which have most attracted public attention. Like the codfish featured in the early story 'The Sea-Bed', the Wildflower also demonstrates Finlay's ongoing concern with traditional modes and themes. The difference between the fish and the flower nevertheless illustrates the development of the artist's work. The cod provoked sentiments which were disturbing, but scarcely articulate. If the Wildflower appears enigmatic, it stimulates a process of meditation which takes in a whole range of issues vital to a proper understanding of the energies of European culture. Finlay's oeuvre represents a coherent and important cultural project, in that it seeks to engender a serious consideration of the state of Western civilization. Its triumph is that, by its very disposition (its poetics), it activates the cultural tissue which it so strenuously dissects.

He Spoke Like an Axe, 1984
card, with Richard Healy

Cut around outlines. Arrange words in order.
Louis-Antoine Saint-Just, 1767–1794

Ian Hamilton Finlay · Nicholas Sloan · For The Committee of Public Safety, Little Sparta

The Present Order, 1983
card, with Nicholas Sloan

A FLUTE[1] FOR

ICE[2]
DUST[3]
ICE
DUST
ICE
DUST
ICE
DUST
ICE
DUST
ICE

SAINT-JUST[4]

[1] Among his personal effects, an ivory flute hints at an accomplishment otherwise overlooked.
Geoffrey Bruun, *Saint-Just, Apostle of The Terror*

[2] He carries his head like the Holy Sacrament.
Camille Desmoulins

[3] I despise the dust of which I am made and which is speaking to you; this dust can be persecuted and put to death! But I defy anyone to wrench from me the independent life I have given myself through the ages and in the heavens . . .
Saint-Just, *Republican Institutions*

[4] Louis-Antoine de Saint-Just, 1767–1794; friend of J-L David and Robespierre

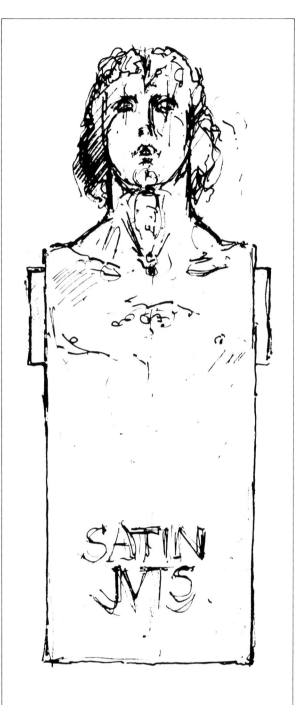

HEROIC ANAGRAMS: SAINT-JUST

Ian Hamilton Finlay
Alexander Stoddart

Wild Hawthorn Press: for the Committee
of Public Safety, Little Sparta

A Flute for Saint-Just, 1983
card

Heroic Anagrams, 1983
folding card, with Alexander Stoddart

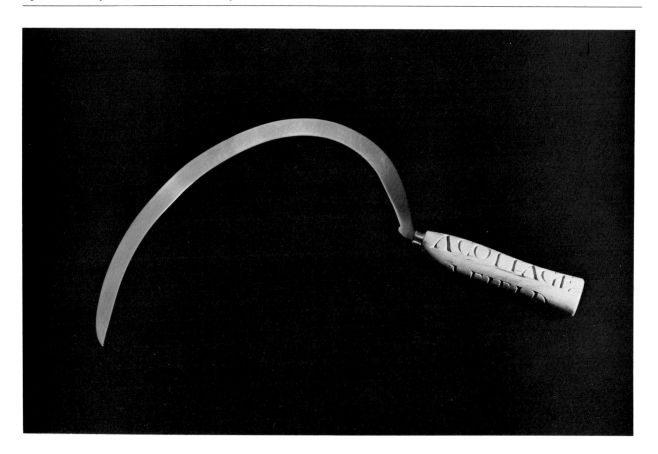

Sickle, 1985
wood and metal, with John Andrew and Keith Brookwell
The inscription is extracted from a speech by Saint-Just and
reads: 'A cottage, a field, a plough.'

The Words We Have Spoken, 1985
stone, with Nicholas Sloan
The sense of Saint-Just's words is dramatized in the 'ruined'
presentation. It is inferred that the inscription might once have
been part of an heroic architecture

Terror/Virtue medal, 1984
bronze, with Nicholas Sloan

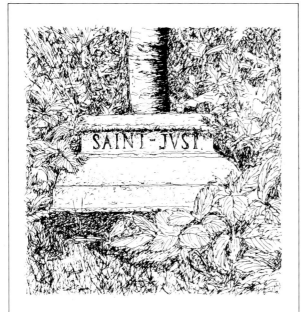

Ian Hamilton Finlay: *Tree Column-Base 'Saint-Just'*, in the garden, Little Sparta. (Louis Antoine de Saint-Just, 1767–1794.) The tree is a silver birch, the plants are strawberries. The 'base' is the upturned capital of a Doric pilaster. The name was cut by Keith Bailey. The drawing is by Andrew Townsend. The Committee of Public Safety, Little Sparta.

Tree Column-Base: 'Saint-Just', 1983
card, with Andrew Townsend

Tree Column-Base: 'Saint-Just', 1981
stone, with Keith Bailey

Against the Hébertists and the Dantonists[1]

all governments lie

all generals lie

all Grecians lie

all gypsies lie

all gymnosophists lie

all grocers lie

all Graces lie

[1] *Roughly, the liberal atheists and the liberal opportunists. The point being made is Robespierre's: 'In the Revolution what is immoral is politically unsound, what corrupts is counter-revolutionary'. In short, cynicism and lack of faith are destructive of order.*

Ian Hamilton Finlay. Wild Hawthorn Press, for The Committee of Public Safety, Little Sparta

Against the Hébertists and the Dantonists, 1983
card

A PLACEMENT
obeisance

It is the case with gardens as with societies: some things require to be fixed so that others may be *placed*. Ian Hamilton Finlay, '*Detached Sentences on Gardening*'.

Tree Column-Bases 'Lycurge' (Lycurgus) and 'Saint-Just', in the garden, Little Sparta. Photographs by Andrew Griffiths. The Wild Hawthorn Press.

A Placement, 1983
folding card, with Andrew Griffiths

Plant trough, 1980
stone and wood, with Keith Bailey

Inscribed Column, 1983
The inscription on the base of the column is taken from Saint-
Just and reads: 'The world has been empty since the Romans.'

Near the column stands the heather-thatched 'Doric Hut' for
the Roman geese; and beyond is the termination of the 'Wild
Garden' and the barren moorland of Strathclyde

SAILORS! REVOLUTIONARIES! LEARN FROM YOUR BOLDNESS!
SAINT-JUST AS TATLIN
Ian Hamilton Finlay and Gary Hincks, after the self-portrait by Vladimir Tatlin
WILD HAWTHORN PRESS

Sailors! Revolutionaries!, 1987
'Sailors! Revolutionaries! Learn From Your Boldness! Saint-Just as Tatlin'
print, with Gary Hincks (after the self-portrait by Vladimir Tatlin)

Saint-Just stood up in the first cart, his head held high, his neck bare, a carnation in his buttonhole, his eyes coolly surveying the crowds that lined the str~~eet~~ The old Saint-Just was restored who said, "I despise the dust that forms me and speaks to you."

R. R. Palmer, *Twelve Who Ruled*.

Carnation, 1987
cards in envelope

After Piranesi, 1991
lithographic print, with Gary Hincks

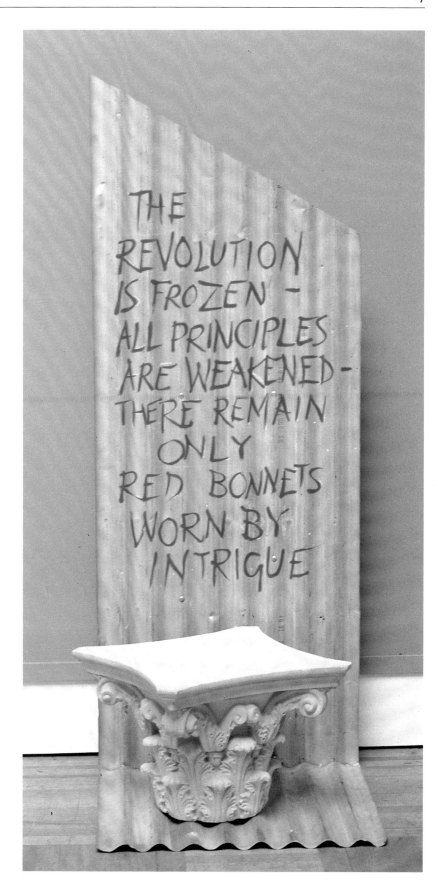

THE REVOLUTION

The Revolution is frozen; all
principles are weakened; there
remain only red bonnets
worn by intrigue.

The waves in the rye grass
never reach the shore.

S-J, IHF

The Revolution, 1990
Poem in folder

The Revolution is Frozen, 1991
stone, corrugated iron

The Sound of Running Water, 1990
wall installation, Christine Burgin Gallery, New York.

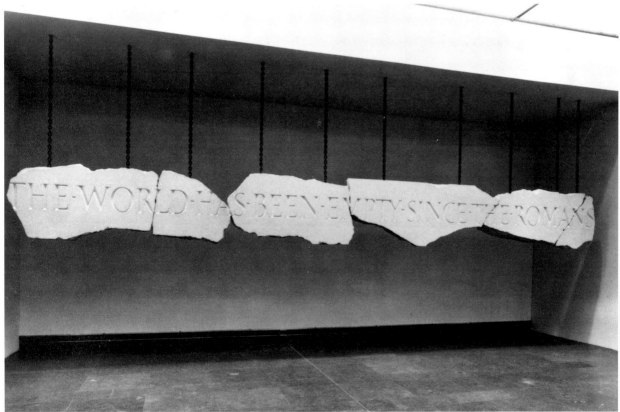

Clay the Life, 1987
marble, with Alexander Stoddart and Nicholas Sloan
The first two lines are often ascribed to the neo-classical
sculptor Canova (1757–1822)

The World Has Been Empty Since the Romans, 1985
stone and steel chain, with Nicholas Sloan

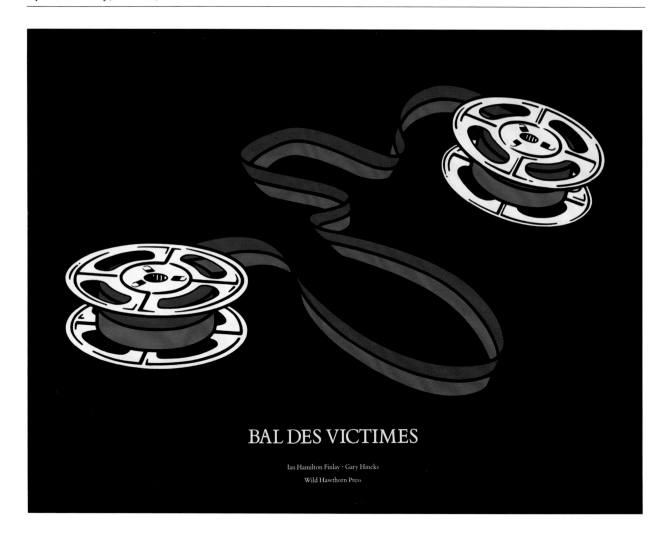

Bal des Sublimes, 1989
screen print, with Gary Hincks

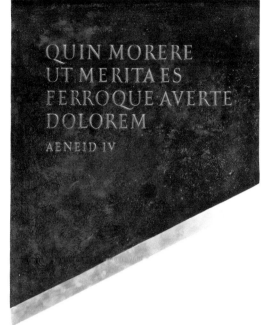

'Quin morere', 1990
bronze, with Nicholas Sloan
The bronze blade is engraved with an inscription from
Virgil's *Aeneid*, relating to the decision of Dido to use her
own death to expiate her guilty love for Aeneas.

La Révolution est un bloc, 1990
bronze, with Nicholas Sloan

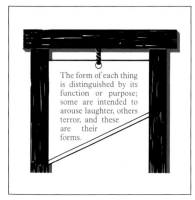

The form of each thing is distinguished by its function or purpose; some are intended to arouse laughter, others terror, and these are their forms.

Frighten me, if you will, but let the terror which you inspire in me be tempered by some grand moral idea.

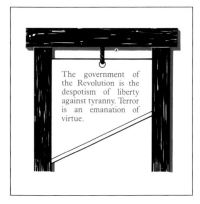

The government of the Revolution is the despotism of liberty against tyranny. Terror is an emanation of virtue.

Terror is the piety of the Revolution.

A View to the Temple, 1987
wood and bronze, with Keith Brookwell and Nicholas Sloan
installed at the Kassel Documenta, 1987

4 Blades, 1987
cards in folder, with Gary Hincks; texts by Nicolas Poussin, Denis Diderot, Maximilien Robespierre, Ian Hamilton Finlay

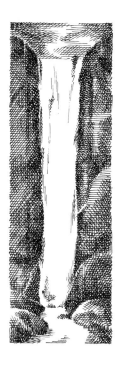

Two Landscapes of The Sublime

Ian Hamilton Finlay   Gary Hincks   Wild Hawthorn Press

KING

ohne
titel

sans
title

without
a head

Two Landscapes of the Sublime, 1989
lithographic print, with Gary Hincks

King, 1990
Poem in folder

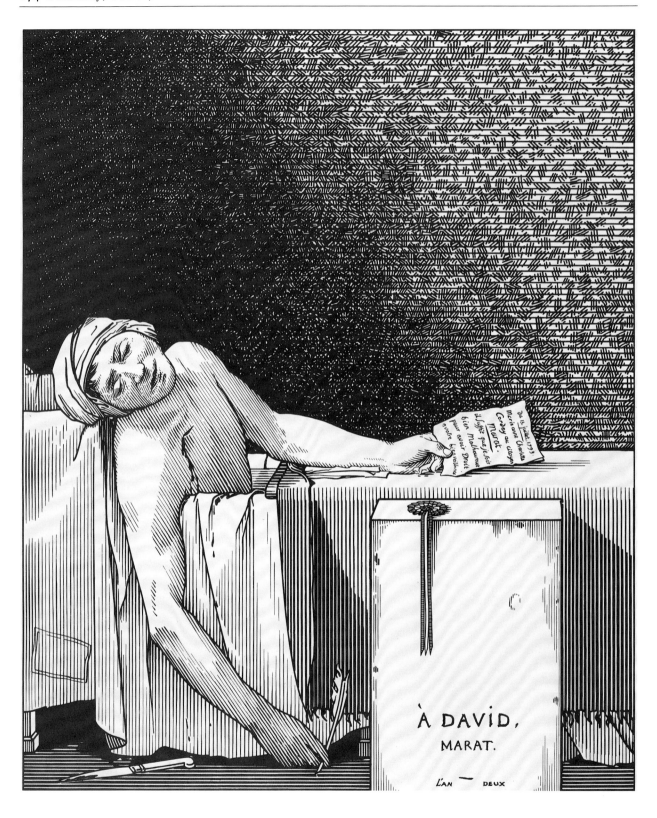

Marat Assassiné, 1986
print, with Gary Hincks

*Both the garden style called 'sentimental', and the
French Revolution, grew from Rousseau. The garden
trellis, and the guillotine, are alike entwined with
the honeysuckle of the new 'sensibility'.*

IAN HAMILTON FINLAY · GARY HINCKS · WILD HAWTHORN PRESS

Both the Garden Style . . ., 1987
print, with Gary Hincks

In the Terror, a red silk thread worn
around the neck intimated that friends
or relatives had been lost to the
guillotine. Aphrodite (or Venus) being
a goddess, the same adornment
signifies the loss of Olympian relatives
and refers not to the Revolution's
'Sublime' Terror but rather to the
subsequent, secular Terror directed
against The Ideal.

Aphrodite of the Terror, 1987
plaster

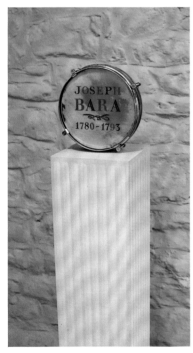

Hommage à Bara, 1987
wood, with Margaret Spencer

Two Drums, after J.-L. David's painting
of the dying drummer-boy Bara, 1987
painted drumheads and wooden
plinths, with Gary Hincks

Monument à Joseph Bara, 1986
stone and bronze, with Keith Bailey

Four Kings for the Republic, 1987
wooden plinths, plaster, metal

Embroideries, 1986–7
with Pamela Campion

3 Pots of Jam, 1987
jampot covers with Michael Harvey

Guillotine Teapot, 1987
Pipe (Le Père Duchesne), 1987

Inkwell, 1987
ceramic, with David Ballantyne

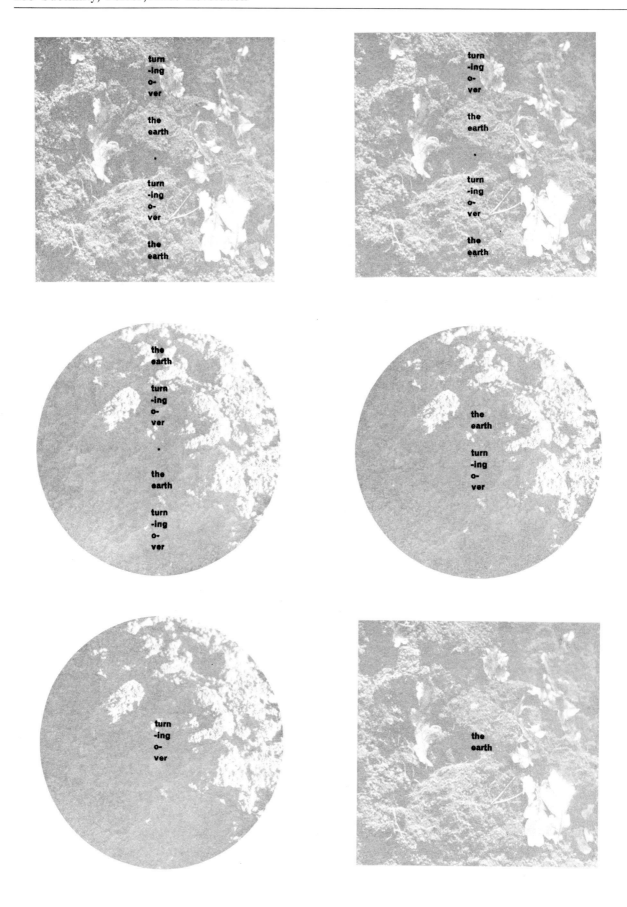

From *Autumn Poem*, 1966
booklet, with Audrey Walker

Whence things have their origin, there they must also pass
away according to necessity; for they must pay penalty and
be judged for their injustice, according to the ordinance of
time. *Nietzsche*

But where things have their origin, there too their passing
away occurs according to necessity; for they pay recom-
pense and penalty to one another for their recklessness,
according to firmly established time. *Diels*

A Litany for Prairial

   Angélique

   Tilleul

   Pavot

   Serpolet

   Chèvrefeuille

   Thym

A Requiem for Thermidor

   Fleuriot

   Hanriot

   Couthon

   Payan

   Robespierre

   Saint-Just

From *The Anaximander Fragment*, 1981
book, with Harvey Dwight

A Litany, A Requiem, 1981
booklet
A list of plants from the month of *Prairial* (French Revolutionary
Calendar) is set against a list of those revolutionaries guillotined
along with Robespierre in the month of *Thermidor*. A note
explains that the fatal day was named *Arrosoir* (Watering-can)

PALLADIAN

PICTURESQUE

CHARM, *n.* a something pleasing in a person or thing; it came in with the Revolution and went out with the War.

Whether people swear on the old altar, before the Holy Sacrament, or take the oath before the cold image of abstract liberty, the true symbol is elsewhere. The beauty, the grandeur, the eternal CHARM of those festivals, is that the symbol is a living one.
Michelet, *History of the French Revolution*

Ian Hamilton Finlay, Laurie Clark.
The Wild Hawthorn Press

Mower is Less

After Thomas Hearne, 1977 card, with Gary Hincks
'Palladian' is transformed into 'Picturesque' by the addition of molehills. According to the eighteenth-century aesthetic theory, broken surfaces are more pleasing to the eye than smooth

Charm, 1984 card, with Laurie Clark

Mower is Less, 1973
card, with Sydney McK. Glen, Graphic Partners, Edinburgh

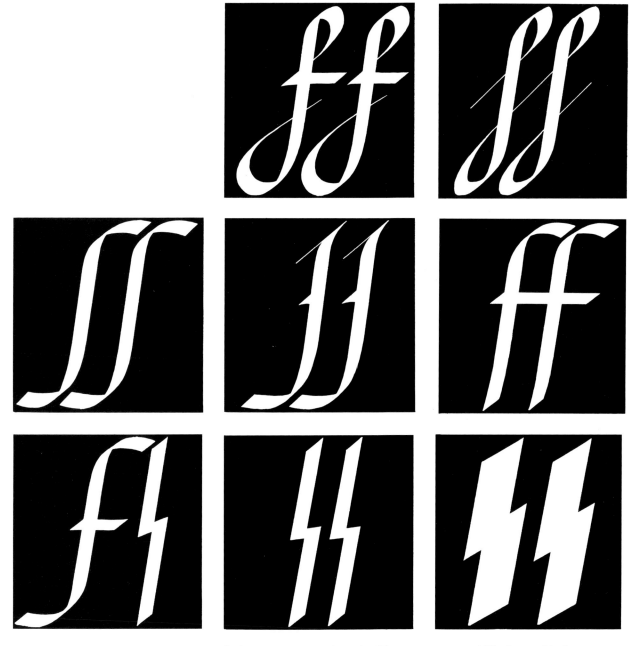

In this sequence, as in the earlier 'Footnotes to an essay' (Catalogue of the Ian Hamilton Finlay Serpentine Gallery exhibition, 1977), and the print-variation on Bernini's 'Apollo and Daphne' (1977), the notorious Nazi-German organisation, the SS, is equated with Nature. That is to say, it signifies the ultimate 'wildness' in a scale whose other, 'cultivated' extreme is the eighteenth century. In tracing the progression (or descent) from the civilised script of this period – in which 'f's' were customarily substituted for 's's – to the runic rendering or double lightning stroke of the SS uniform and banners, we therefore follow the gradation between 'Culture' and 'Nature'. We must ourselves 'allegorise' the letter-forms of the stages which intervene.

From *SF*, 1978
booklet, with George L. Thomson

Classical U-boat pens in wartime. Note
Type IIC U-boats anchored outside the pens.
A section of Albert Speer's Atlantic Wall
can be seen in the background (centre).
An Allied air raid is in progress.

AFTER JOHN FLAXMAN R.A.

Ian Hamilton Finlay.   Gary Hincks.   Wild Hawthorn Press.

After John Flaxman, 1981
card, with Gary Hincks
'The Classics! It is the Classics, and not the Goths nor Monks,
that Desolate Europe with Wars.' William Blake, 'On Homer's
Poetry and On Virgil'

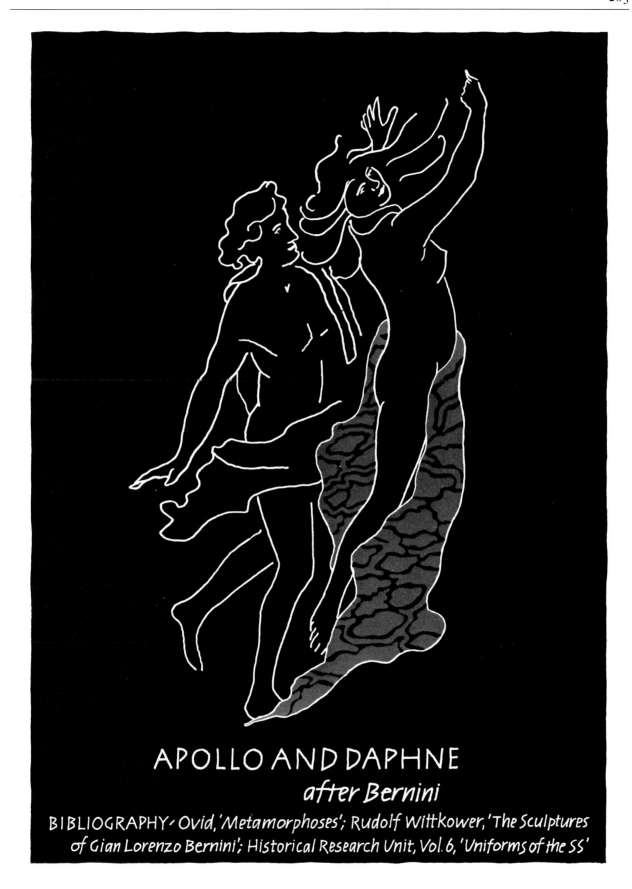

Apollo and Daphne, after Bernini, 1977
screen print, with Ron Costley

PROPAGANDA FOR THE WOOD-ELVES

Propaganda for the Wood Elves, 1981
print in folder, with Harvey Dwight

PANZER VOM WINDE ZERZAUST

PANZER BEI SCHNEEWETTER

From *Taschenbuch der Panzer*, 1981
with Ian Gardner

The Speer Project

A garden is a fragile creation. With only a few exceptions, the great Italian gardens have been reduced to mere shadows of their former splendour. Bomarzo, that memorable Baroque assemblage of stone beasts and temples, is like a string of sentences from which the verbs have been excised. We can hardly begin to reconstruct in our imagination the ordered greenery in which these monsters took their places. Perhaps they were never very much tamer than they seem now, with most of the surrounding vegetation removed. English gardens have often suffered the same fate. The very pair of gardens which seem closest in spirit to Little Sparta – those gardens carefully created over a long period by the poets Pope and Shenstone – have disappeared, leaving hardly a trace. We can still read exhaustively about the design of Pope's garden around his villa at Twickenham, or about Shenstone's modest but influential 'ferme ornée' near Halesowen in Shropshire. But we are aware that the lack of a great landed family to safeguard both house and garden exposed both these poets' gardens to the cumulative effects of exploitation and decay.

Little Sparta, a modern poet's garden, shares this predicament. On occasions its defencelessness against the external world has been strikingly, and starkly, brought home. Having no secure financial basis, it is offered to the visitors as a free and accessible spectacle. But, intermittently, this opportunity has to be withdrawn because of the crude and punitive actions of the regional authority. Little Sparta reverts (as it does in a sense every autumn, when the cold weather sets in) to the status of a 'secret garden', withdrawn into itself and keeping its meaning for a very few. This book, with its splendid photographic documentation of the garden at particular points in time, perpetuates – but to a certain extent misrepresents – the essence of Little Sparta; by giving it an ideal existence, it minimizes the effect of the cold winds which rage around.

How can the 'secret garden' be represented? That is a question which means a great deal more than would appear at first sight. Finlay wants us to sense the contrast between the purity of the vision and the hostile climate which hedges it in. One way is through metaphor, the recasting of the problem in a hyperbolic form which compels us to recognize an original truth about it. The Speer project published here for the first time is just such a hyperbolic metaphor. Imprisoned for a long time in Spandau prison as a result of the Nuremberg trials, the former architect and aide of Hitler, Albert Speer, applied himself to the creation of a 'secret garden' out of the rubble of the exercise yard. This lengthy and absorbing activity, whose 'secrecy' can be measured by the fact that, only by lying on one's stomach on the grass, could the architecture of rubble be interpreted as Speer intended, was in fact the last architectural project of a figure who had, in his early years,

THE WALLED GARDEN

been hailed as the heir to the German neoclassical tradition.

Of course the Speer project, as it is published here, is not a simple documentation of this garden of rubble and ruins. Although they are derived from colour photographs of the garden supplied to Finlay by Speer, the images have undergone a further metamorphosis in the intensely realized water-colours of Ian Gardner. One way of commenting on this track of interpretation, from Stonypath to Spandau, from the photographic record to the artistry of the water-colour, would be to say that the secret garden has found expression in its final, most purely aesthetic form. But this might be an oversimplification, for even the distinctive English quality of Ian Gardner's technique recalls the close connection, in the eighteenth century, between landscape painting and topographical records for military purposes. In just the same way, when we go back to the eighteenth-century garden, we find the closest of connections (and not only for Tristram Shandy's Uncle Toby!) between the earthworks of the gardener and those of the siege engineer. Finlay's strategy, here as elsewhere, is to recall these connections rather than to efface them. Irony, Vico's 'double vision', becomes the other side of the coin to beauty. From this process, not even the secret garden is exempt.

THE MOUNT

Commentary by Stephen Bann

From *A Walled Garden*
with Ian Gardner and J. F. Hendry

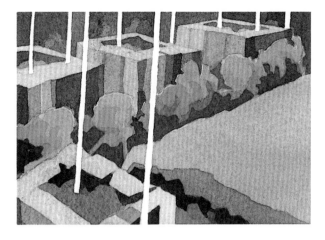

THE SECRET GARDEN

THE SECRET GARDEN

THE STONE GARDEN

THE STONE GARDEN

THE WALLED GARDEN

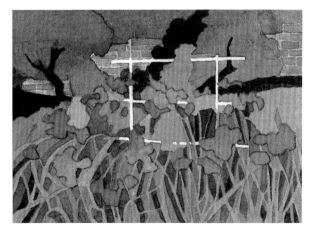

A BED OF ROSES

Inv. Ian Hamilton Finlay   Del. Gary Hincks

ARROSOIR

The Robespierrists were guillotined on Arrosoir, *Watering-can*, in
Thermidor, *Month of Heat*. (Republican Calendar, 1792–1806.)
Babeuf described Robespierre as 'the genius in whom resided truly
regenerative ideas . . .'

Arrosoir, 1984
print, with Gary Hincks

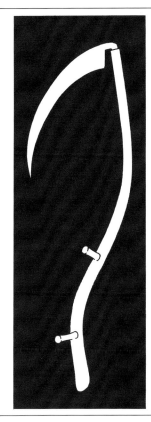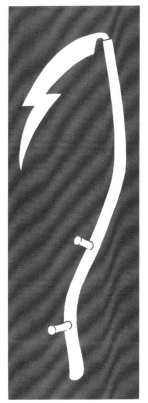

"I have seen that Death is a Reaper, who cuts down with his scythe not only the lowly clover, but also the grass that grows tall; I have seen that Death is a Gardener, who does away with the climbing larkspur as well as the violets that creep along the earth; I have seen that Death is a Player, and indeed a naughty one, for he knocks down the skittles and does not set them up again, and he takes the king as well as the pawns; I have seen that Death is a thunderbolt that strikes not only the tumble-down straw huts, but also the splendid houses of monarchs..."
Abraham a Santa Clara.

3 BANNERS Ian H milton Finlay / Gary Hincks

Plank, *n.* a narrow board on which the victim, bound, is delivered to shipwreck.

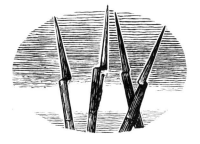

Pike, *n.* a Jacobin plinth.

Cart, *n.* a two-wheeled vehicle for the transport of solitudes.

Guillotine, *n.* the highest peak of The Mountain; and its deepest ravine.

Death is a Reaper, 1991
folding card, with Gary Hincks

From *Jacobin Definitions*, 1991
booklet, with Kathleen Lindsley

Adorno's Hut, 1989
wood and metal, with Keith Brookwell and Andrew
Townsend

12 THE OBJECTS OF ALLEGORY

The recent renewal of interest in allegory can be explained by the way the allegorical figure's obviously artificial nature draws attention to the act of interpretation.[1] Ian Hamilton Finlay exploits this to the full in his variation (p. 297) on Rousseau's tomb in the crypt of the Panthéon in Paris, where the bodies of notable French republican 'worthies' have been put to rest. The torch on the original monument is a standard allegorical prop, and is thus easily interpreted as representing Truth. But what is one to make of the machine-gun with which Finlay balances it? Could this perhaps symbolize Nature, which is mentioned alongside Truth in the inscription on the monument? If that is the case, then Finlay's allegorical transposition of nature clashes with conventional interpretations of Rousseau. Indeed, there is nothing 'noble' in the weapon's 'savagery'. However, in a world in which the ideal is not immanent – where truth and nature are in tension, or even conflict – Finlay suggests that force be also read as Action. His variation on Rousseau's tomb thus belongs with his works juxtaposing Virtue and Terror (as in, for instance, the two sides of a medal shown on p. 259) or with his variations on Bernini's Apollo and Daphne (p. 285), in which Saint-Just's pursuit of the Republic as an Ideal puts in motion the irreconcilable forces of love and fear evoked in Ovid's description of the mythical chase. The allegorical poetics developed by Finlay over the last decade can be seen, then, as an attempt to induce the reader or viewer to step aside from all-too-familiar historical or philosophical frameworks. Its main thrust, however, is to concentrate the attention on conventions and traditions of interpretation that actively involve one in the elaboration of meanings – and indeed to invite one to reflect on this process itself.

After John Flaxman R.A. (p. 284) thus takes a hint from Speer's architectural idiom to revive one of the eighteenth-century artist's famous illustrations of Homer, and Finlay's allegorical celebration of an Allied air raid prompts one to ponder on the relevance of classical culture to the representation of modern warfare.[2] An enigmatic inscription in the garden at Little Sparta discreetly reverses the question of the presence of classical divinities in the modern world. In a shaded corner, an architectural fragment half-buried in the grass reads 'no ripe rasp'. Taken literally, this assertion

that there are no ripe raspberries is perfectly acceptable. Nevertheless, although its prosaic texture underlines yet again Finlay's concern to push reality into the foreground and avoid unconsidered flights of poetic fancy, the inscription teases the visitor who, by playing around with its letters, will find that he can assemble the name of the goddess Proserpina. Proserpina was the wife of Pluto, god of the underworld. She was associated with crops and fertility. The absence of raspberries in this particular corner of the garden is thus related to the disappearance of the goddess, buried in the opacity of her anagram – though, since in the myth of Proserpina her return above ground heralds the arrival of spring, this absence is not definitive.

In Finlay's work, anagram and pun pick up on the artifice inherent in allegory, developing the play of presence and absence and thereby underlining the tenuous nature of the connections that our culture remains capable of weaving together. In his variation on a classical landscape, *Klassische Landschaft*, the artist infuses the entire texture of an image with an ultimately ambivalent play on presence and absence (hail and farewell), while in his anagrammatical busts the Muse astutely associates chance and destiny[3] to define the character of various historical figures in such a way that these become quasi-allegorical expressions of the qualities that they incarnate.

Allegory is a potent tool in the hands of the post-Romantic artist. Its artificiality underlines the historical and cultural fracture that Romantic symbolism sought to overcome by a process akin to denial. At the same time, it suggests formal avenues whereby art and poetry can come to terms with the loss of wholeness that lies at the very heart of the modern artist's enterprise. The notion of art and literature as autonomous concepts can be traced back to the speculations of early German Romanticism, and is thus paradoxically related to the demise of classical harmony as a putatively realizable goal. Finlay, however, has built out of the collapse of classical culture a poetics in which allegory serves to confront the problem of formulating coherent cultural statements. His broad allegorical framework induces what, in a phrase borrowed from Hegel, he calls 'a thinking consideration of objects'.[4]

The artist described his own early work as 'Symbolist'.[5] However, his short stories (for example) demonstrated that the result could prove subjective in the extreme, making it difficult fully to articulate the vision and sentiment informing their symbolic epiphanies. Just as the toys Finlay constructed in the early 1960s allowed him to overcome the aporias of post-Romantic symbolism and pointed the way towards his first, consciously static concrete poems, so his allegorical objects bring the observer to a halt. They force one to call into play diverse strands of knowledge – artistic, literary, philosophical, historical – and induce a meditation on the condition of contemporary culture.

It is, from this point of view, necessary to stress a further aspect of allegory that has become increasingly relevant to Finlay's work. This is the emphatically literal impact of the allegorical 'vehicle'. In order to read an allegory successfully, one is often required to mobilize a considerable number of cultural references. However, the original image or object does not disappear in the process. Frequently, indeed, the figurative dimension of allegory is only obliquely alluded to, and may be indicated on the level of generic expectations alone.[6]

In the ill-fated proposal for a garden at Versailles to commemorate the French Revolution and the Rights of Man (pp. 132–3), the dates 1789–1989 were to be engraved on the gateposts of the site where the Declaration of Human Rights was proclaimed. This would not only have provided a key for identifying as the French nation the collective 'we' (*nous*) cited in the heroic inscription, but would also have underpinned the complex set of visual associations established by Finlay through his careful choice of forms and materials (such as species of trees). The commemorative garden was not designed as a transparent text making some reassuringly explicit ideological statement, but as an invitation to meditate on the cultural texture of a major historical landmark. While the garden's idyllic beauty would have underlined the aspirations of the Revolution, its forms and materials would have prompted the visitor's meditation.

Elsewhere, in a play on the word 'style', Finlay designed actual stiles (p. 296) that punningly summarize the texture of his allegorical poetics. In this case, the object is quite literally an obstacle that must be surmounted, just as, in the process of interpretation, thought may be considered to rise above whatever it encounters on the horizontal plane. There is no gate which can be opened to allow free access to unbridled speculation. On the contrary, it is the opacity of the obstacle that sets off the flight of thought. This, for Finlay, is the very essence of poetic style.

In recent years the artist has at times greatly intensified the literal impact of his allegorical objects, strategically introducing real tension into his work. As Finlay declared with reference to the work he composed *in situ* for 'Documenta 8' at Kassel in 1987:

> A friend very recently said to me that he thought contemporary poetry so boring that he no longer writes serious poems (i.e. prefers or is driven to, humour). I replied that my alternative is a SUPER-SEVERE idiom, which cannot be misunderstood (as pandering to the time).[7]

In the gardens of the Museum Fridericianum in Kassel, then, four guillotines were set up (p. 272). These were not sculptures that evoked at a safe distance the notion of a guillotine, but were constructions on a scale that closely resembled that of actual guillotines. While these formed an archway framing a small neoclassical temple at the far end of the gardens, they remained emphatically instruments of terror and demanded to be seen as such. The bronze of the blades reinforced the classical aspect of the installation, but the high polish of the cutting edge glinting in the sunshine attracted the eye from a distance – just like the real thing.

A View to the Temple invites a figurative reading on various levels. In the first place, by framing the distant temple Finlay establishes an optical perspective which unmistakably suggests a historical one, space here implying time. Also, while the temple is an instance of the beautiful, the terror of the guillotines exemplifies the sublime. A conjunction is thus suggested between historical and aesthetic concerns (underlined by the quotations engraved on the blades) that is wholly relevant to the question of the sublime.[8] In effect, Finlay forces us to reconsider questions that Burke, for example, was unable to confront. The impact of his installation depends on the delicate balance achieved between stark reality and classical beauty, so that the severity of the idiom is indicative of the high seriousness of the artist's concerns.

The cruelty of history is articulated in even more hyperbolical terms in a work first exhibited in Paris in 1987. *Osso* (p. 298) consists of three large marble fragments spelling out the word 'bone' in Italian, its middle letters being realized in the runic script adopted by the Nazi SS. On the second fragment in the sequence, the 'SS' stands alone. Finlay had previously used the SS sign as an allegorical substitute for a premonitory death's head in *Footnotes to an Essay* (p. 245), while in *SF* (p. 283) he had opposed the runic 's' and the elegant 'f'-shaped 's' used by printers as late as the eighteenth century, to invite the reader to allegorize the articulation of civility and savagery. More recently, he has composed a series of variations on scythes and sickles, associating the pastoral motif of 'Death the Mower' (p. 291) with the same evocation of twentieth-century horror.

Since the middle of the 1980s, Finlay has frequently allegorized the opposition between nature and culture. In 1987, he gave the title *Inter Artes et Naturam* to his 1987 exhibition at the municipal museum of modern art in Paris. The theme was illustrated by variations on the sphere and the cube carried over from his *Talismans and Signifiers* (pp. 114–15), but now given the dimensions of the minimal sculptures one might expect to find in an exhibition of contemporary art. These variations were accompanied by meditations on the origins of the Corinthian capital or the classical temple and, most dramatically, by *Osso*.

In 1988, four converging latticed paths were constructed for the Victoria Miro Gallery. Built out of rough branches and rectilinear lengths of wood, this new version of *Inter Artes et Naturam* reconstitutes a notional grove in an eighteenth-century garden, with its open temple protected by trees (p. 17). As one skirts round the sacred grove, regular (i.e. classical) form and irregular (unruly) energy intermingle to provide a picturesque spectacle. However, the viewer is expected to penetrate into the heart of the wood. Unlike the pre-Romantic collector of picturesque vistas, he is not to be content with admiring from a comfortable distance. The work's formal indications invite him to pause in the midst of the 'dark wood' of his life's journey through the disorder of the contemporary world, in order to give form to his perceptions.

Osso allegorizes, more abruptly than any other work of Finlay's, just how difficult a proposition this may be. Nature, as implied by a Grecian landscape with a temple, or again by the neoclassical bucolics associated with the French Revolution, was an idealized force. As an exteriorized sacred dimension, it was the object of reverence (as it again becomes in the Sacred Grove, illustrated on p. 124, that Finlay dedicated to French and Greek culture at the Kröller-Müller Museum in The Netherlands). Modernity, however, is defined by the loss of harmony. For Coleridge, nature thus becomes a demonic allegory, while, by adopting lightning flashes to spell out their initials, the SS catastrophically espoused this new order. *Osso* does no more than graphically take stock of the fact. It suggests, not that human evil can be explained away as 'natural' but rather that – for whoever is prepared to face up to the history of our century – the SS cannot be wished away. It is surely salutary for the ecologist, who sees nature as an uncorrupted source, or the common city-dweller who makes it the object of nebulous reverie, to stumble against the fragments of *Osso* and its jagged allegory. This is especially true if the viewer is not immediately able to summon up an obvious figurative code as a guide towards achieving the necessary 'thinking consideration of objects'. Once again, it is in the conjunction of a tenuous cultural fabric and an extremely harsh reality that the challenge of Finlay's work resides.

STILES I

Thesis: fence

Antithesis: gate

Synthesis: stile[1]

¹ Hegel, *Logic*

STILES II

Do you know, gentlemen, what a city is like? A city is a horizontal tension and a vertical tension. Nothing else.

Theo van Doesburg.

Do you know, gentlemen, what a stile is like? A stile is a horizontal tension and a vertical tension. Nothing else.

I. H. F.

From *A Country Lane, A Proposal for the Glasgow Garden Festival*, 1988
booklet, with Laurie Clark

ICI REPOSE L'HOMME
DE LA NATURE ET DE LA VÉRITÉ

Le Tombeau de Rousseau au Panthéon. L'élévation avec
la mitraillette remplace le plan du dessin original. Si la
lampe est une allégorie de la Vérité, on peut considérer
que l'arme à feu représente soit l'Action soit la Nature.

Tombeau de Rousseau au Panthéon, 1989
print, with Gary Hincks

Rousseau's tomb in the Pantheon, Paris. The elevation with
the sub-machine-gun takes the place of the original design.
If the lamp is an allegory of Truth, the arm with the gun
represents Action or Nature.

Osso, 1987
marble, with Nicholas Sloan

13 TRANSLATING
THE CLASSICS

While the literal impact of allegorical vehicles drawn from modern history enhances the citational texture of the poetics Finlay has favoured since the mid-1960s, the continued use of wordplay and visual rhymes to structural ends complexifies the formal apparatus that the artist began to develop even before the advent of concrete poetry. Furthermore, Finlay's use of allegory is intimately bound up with the transportation (or translation: *translatio*) of classical values into contemporary culture. Allegory not only has a long history as a classical figure (its artifice has emphatically pre- or even anti-Romantic connotations), but also, through transposing ideas or propositions into a figurative idiom, it provides Finlay with a further opportunity to confront classical and modern forms and values.

The wit of a concrete poem from *Telegrams from my Windmill* (1964) provides an early example of classical 'translation' in Finlay's work. *Au-pair girl* consists of the words of its title mechanically repeated to produce a pear-shape. The poet now feels unhappy with this conjunction of contemporary banality (signified by the text) and a form evoking the classical cubism of Gris.[1] However, as Stephen Bann once suggested, the punning paean 'Oh! pear girl!' recalls the Latinate elegance of Horace.[2] The prosaic poverty of the text, the minimalism of which is underlined by the reduced dimensions of the image it forms, may thus be read as an effective economy of artistic means, so that its bathos can be read as litotes. Ultimately, however, the effect remains mixed, and Finlay's pear / au-pair girl can perhaps be taken as the complex muse of his concrete poetry – an embodiment of tensions the artist has never ceased to confront in ways which could only evolve, but which he has never simply wished away.

In the eighteenth century, artists and philosophers were not always so clear-sighted (or firm-hearted). During a trip to Sicily in 1779, for example, the French painter Valenciennes could not help regretting that the laundry girls working in the waters of a fountain famous since antiquity in no way resembled the nymphs who had formerly haunted the spot.[3] And just a few years earlier, Diderot had protested against the groups of people going about their everyday duties in Hubert Robert's paintings of Roman ruins. The effect, according to the philosopher, was to spoil the poetry of the scene.[4] Finlay adopts a radically different strategy, deploying verbal and visual rhymes to simultaneously underline and surmount vast distances in space and time.

In *Apollo in Strathclyde* (p. 302), the barren Scottish moorland 'rhymes' with the Mediterranean Sea celebrated in the *Odyssey*, while in a series of public commissions – such as the grove dedicated to Robert Louis Stevenson in Princes Street Gardens, Edinburgh, or more recently the Ian Hamilton Finlay sculpture garden at Luton (pp. 136–9) – birch trees are treated as notional columns. There is nothing more hyperborean than a turnip field or a birch tree. In either case, however, the 'rhyme' is formally apt and the parallelism, though stretched to an extreme, still holds. Indeed, the analogy is all the more challenging for incorporating such tensions.

Finlay's reinscriptions of cultural landmarks are more often than not mediated by previous assimilations or traditions. Thus, conceived as 'the marble tree',[5] the birch appears as an analogue in the natural world of the writer Walter Pater's north-European reincarnations of classical deities.[6] If the series of tree-plaques exhibited in Basel in 1984 (p. 128) and subsequently installed in a Breton park seem to invoke diverging areas of culture – scientific names for trees and pairs of lovers from literary classics – this initial effect is counteracted by natural science's reliance on the Latin terminology of Linnaeus. Indeed, the coexistence of precise scientific categorization and an easy familiarity with literary classics brings to mind Linnaeus's near contemporary Goethe, perhaps the last exemplar of a truly universal culture, who aptly subtitled his Italian journal, mingling precise observations of natural phenomena and expressions of a high cultural sensibility, *Et in Arcadia Ego*. Finlay's tree-plaques and column-bases are not content enigmatically to register our estrangement from various monuments of our culture, or from the unified sensibility which could encompass them. Entrusted 'to the protection of the trees' (like the Dryads from the Temple at Little Sparta threatened with summary arrest by the Sheriff Officer at the height of the Little Spartan War), our cultural heritage is absorbed into a metaphor of textuality or tradition: in acquiring the status of classics, works of art, literature or science become natural objects of contemplation and veneration.

Finlay's modern translations of classical philosophy or mythology can, however, take an altogether more abrupt turn. A monumental inscription from 1987 thus subsumes the four elements of the Heraclitean flux within the figure of an Exocet missile, while *Heraclitean Variations* (p. 303) recalls the role played by this same missile during the Falklands War. The gilded laurel-crowned head placed in the garden at Little Sparta in the autumn of 1988 has the words *Apollon Terroriste* engraved on its brow (p. 64), bringing up to date Finlay's earlier renderings of the god's lyre/bow as a piece of artillery (pp. 222–3). The figure of Saint-Just as a modern avatar of Apollo is suggested by the use of the French language in the inscription. In each of the cases just cited, hyperbolic images of terror or warfare are used, not to deify violence but – through a 'thinking consideration of objects' – to encourage the reader/observer to ponder on the problematics of power in its earliest philosophical or mythological manifestations. We are only too ready to read the classics on an innocuously metaphorical level. Finlay's contemporary translations, however, insist on the fact that the notion of *polemos*, which goes back to the very roots of our civilization, cannot so readily be disarmed.

Extremely varied and sophisticated translations of this order are the very essence of the artist's neoclassicism, which does not imply a specific idiom but a determination to intervene incisively in the fabric of contemporary culture:

> Romanticism presupposes a person, classicism presupposes a public, neoclassicism presupposes an event.[7]

The events Finlay refers to are far removed from the facile scandals by means of which a moribund avant-garde still periodically strives to revive its flagging fortunes. A work of art that sets out to 'civilize' Dada or Minimalism functions in an altogether different manner. Thus, while so many younger artists struggle to come to terms with the paradoxical heritage of Duchamp, Finlay's *Proposal for a Monument to Jean-Jacques Rousseau* (p. 134) coolly retranscribes the sceptical master's peep-hole aesthetics into a classical idiom. Duchamp's posthumous *Etant donnés* is an enquiry into what has become of the gaze, that expression of visual fascination on which the entire history of western art rests. Finlay responds imaginatively. His monument proposes to reconstruct

our visual imagination, and encourages us to reconsider the way in which we contemplate our environment. The operation was repeated with respect to Minimalist reductionism when Finlay chose to set down in a museum of contemporary art a set of neoplatonic cubes and the 'Virgil bricks' that form his *Shaded Path (1)* (p. 305),[8] thus translating our classical heritage into a contemporary idiom or, vice versa, transporting the aesthetics of late modernism back into the sphere of classical culture.

The events and wars waged by Finlay to reaffirm cultural values in the face of the philistinism of state bureaucracies – and particularly his battles over the definition of architectural follies, or the significance of garden temples – partake of the same logic. The poster campaigns carried out by the Saint-Just Vigilantes in Paris, London and Edinburgh were all militantly neoclassical, as were the various manifestations staged by the French Section of the Vigilantes in the late 1980s.[9]

The pertinence of Finlay's interventions is underlined by the high public profile of some of his more recent permanent installations. Discreetly but strategically situated at the heart of a major sculpture park, the Kröller-Müller Sacred Grove set out to subvert from within the logic of late modernism.[10] The abandoned project for the A86 motorway outside Paris would have been far more visible. Incorporating a large pyramid that would have served as a view-point (fulfilling the function of a ha-ha), it was intended to transpose a contemporary urban landscape into the idiom of the eighteenth-century sublime landscape.

An approach-road to a motorway constitutes a transitional space. Like his contributions to major international exhibitions, which are frequently inscribed in marginal areas,[11] Finlay's permanent installations deliberately occupy such spaces. The major project carried out for the Harris Museum and Art Gallery at Preston in the north of England is, for example, situated at the twin entrances to the building.

Reworking in a classical mode poems dating back to the days of concrete poetry, Finlay's Preston improvements prepare the transition from the everyday outside world into that of the museum by urging upon the museum visitor the reverence such a move implies. Between *wave/rock* (p. 306), situated just outside the entrance, and *how blue? / how blue!*, inscribed round a lantern in the vestibule, the museum is defined as a transitional space between natural fact (rock) and sacred precinct (the original Greek temple open to the sky).

The wave-sign engraved in the glass doors at Preston has a long history in Finlay's work. Originally used in a kinetic booklet in the late 1960s,[12] it re-appeared on a wall in Livingstone new town in Scotland (p. 121), as well as in the artist's first major public commission at the Max Planck Institute in Stuttgart (p. 229). The sign is in fact a proof-readers' convention for inverting the order of letters inadvertently misplaced. Finlay most frequently uses it in conjunction with the word 'wave' in a variety of languages, to establish a permutational wave movement.

A recent version carved in blocks of undressed stone by the Pacific Ocean at the University of California, San Diego (p. 306), underlines the significance of this theme to Finlay's entire enterprise. 'Wave', here, is in Latin: *unda*. The work's classical rigour is inspired by the seascapes of Claude, and is not merely an austerely minimalist hymn to the sea. Strategically placed next to the humanities building, the inscription invites the student or passer-by to meditate on the transfer (translation) of classical values from their distant cradle on the shores of the Mediterranean. Subject, form and context thus converge to exemplify Finlay's most enduring concern.

A considerable distance has been covered by the artist since the numerous cards, prints and booklets which, in the 1960s, took waves and the sea as their theme. The underlying ambition nevertheless remains the same. Finlay's public improvements and installations are powerful formulations of a determination to re-order the elements of our culture. By pursuing a 'great wave of translation', in which his vision of the universe and his analysis of culture are mutually reinforced, Ian Hamilton Finlay doubtless runs the risk of remaining exposed and 'solitary'.[13] However, he simultaneously keeps alive the hope of effecting a sea-change in our sensibility.

This perspective is not entrusted to a hypothetical future. The pastoral or idyllic vein that has always been present in Finlay's work – including many of the pieces based on the French Revolution, an event which the artist describes as a heroic pastoral whose Virgil was Rousseau – predominates in many of his more recent exhibitions,[14] installations or landscape proposals; it appears in the glass poems and embroideries that rework earlier texts and also in his most recent series of neon poems. As ever, the presiding deities are poetry and painting – Lamartine and Matisse, for example, in a celebration of the simple life in a moment of turmoil (p. 152).

Officially opened in the spring of 1991, the Ian Hamilton Finlay Sculpture Garden at Stockwood Park, Luton, is placed under the aegis of paintings and sketches by Claude, a gesture wholly consistent with its inscription within the tradition of the eighteenth-century landscape garden. In this context of overtly interweaved cultural references, the excavated ha-ha in the middle of Finlay's garden is more than an archaeological revival. Marking a notional boundary without however interrupting the view, it underlines the questions of continuity and articulation that are embodied in the very texture of the artist's landscaping. At Luton, the metamorphosis of a flock of sheep into a group of rough-hewn stones (p. 138) is not only a practical expedient that acclimatizes Finlay's painterly subject into a semi-urban environment. It gives the pastoral reference a monumental status consonant with the Pythagorean transcription which induces the stroller to ponder on the significance of Finlay's landscaping in the contemporary context of a de-sacralized culture. Or again, the inscriptions on the Luton caprice (p. 136–9) playfully refuse to sort out levels of vision. They combat any temptation the visitor might have to indulge in a deflationary reading of the classics. For 'errata', one should perhaps read 'metamorphoses' – metamorphoses of the classical tradition. Reading 'Daphne' as laurel, for example, has the effect of naturalizing the fable after the event. However, the paradoxical literalism of 'NARCISSUS'/ 'NARCISSUS' and 'ECHO' / 'Echo' demonstrates that the translation from myth to 'reality' is never quite as simple as it seems. Where is the young man, and where is the flower? Where is the nymph and where the sound? Repetition here actually keeps the Ovidian characters alive.

The park acts as a complex space which is at once actual and notional, woven out of diverse strands that refuse to separate out but act critically to re-contextualize our contemporary environment. As such, it is the ideal locus of Finlay's numerous 'translations' from the classics. The successive versions of *Cythera* bear this out. Originally a poem/booklet (1965) translating Watteau's famous painting into the idiom of concrete poetry, *Cythera* was proposed as a garden project for the Brighton Festival of Concrete Poetry in 1967 (p. 249). In 1991, it formed the centrepiece of a major international exhibition in Berlin (p. 156). In a city that was until recently cut in two by the infamous wall that divided Europe, Finlay built a work in the shape of a pathway that managed simultaneously to suggest past divisions and the desired point of arrival – a notional island (Watteau's 'Cythera') conjured out of the air in a song which, by way of silent variations on just two words ('bark'/'barque'), operated controlled jumps in scale that embodied the variation between two elements (land/water). Spanning some twenty-five years, the metamorphoses of *Cythera* indicate that the space of the artist's idylls is neither his own private domain nor some distant, hypothetical realm. It is a moment of stasis carved out here and now by a trope – or turn[15] – of language that momentarily halts the flow of time, reaffirming the Apollonian principle throughout the evolutions of our culture.

Apollo in Strathclyde[1]

The wine-dark sea, the turnip-marbled field

[1]The Hyperborean Apollo of Walter Pater's *Apollo in Picardy*.
In Little Sparta he is identified with Saint-Just.

From *Monostichs de la Guerre de Petite-Sparte*, Ian Hamilton Finlay. Photograph, Marius Alexander.

Apollo in Strathclyde, 1986
card, with Marius Alexander

Transformations of fire:

first, San Carlos Water; but half
the water is earth, half lightning
storm.

Kahn: 'The reversals of fire; but of sea
half is earth, half lightning storm.'

Burnet: 'The transformations of Fire are,
first of all, sea; and half of the sea is
earth, half whirlwind.'

Fire coming on will discern and
catch up with all things.

Sheffield, 4 May 1982

Kahn.

Burnet: 'Fire in its advance will judge
and convict all things.'

Exocet steers all.

Kahn: 'The thunderbolt pilots all things.'

Burnet: 'It is the thunderbolt that steers
the course of all things.'

Heraclitean Variations, 1986
booklet

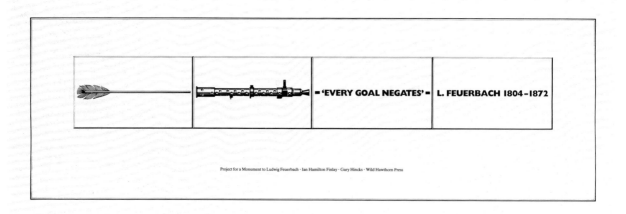

Project for a Monument to Ludwig Feuerbach · Ian Hamilton Finlay · Gary Hincks · Wild Hawthorn Press

"Nature is the Devil in a fancy waistcoat."

Samuel Taylor Coleridge

Translation for our time:
"Nature is a storm trooper in a camouflage smock."

Ian Hamilton Finlay

Wild Hawthorn Press, Little Sparta, Dunsyre, Lanark, Scotland.

Proposal for a Monument to Ludwig Feuerbach, 1986
print, with Gary Hincks

Nature is the Devil in a Fancy Waistcoat, 1987,
card

A Shaded Path, 1987
brick, with David Ballantyne

Stone drums with 'wave/rock', 1989
stone, with Michael Harvey
Museum entrance, Harris Museum and Art Gallery, Preston

Unda, 1987
stone, with Nicholas Sloan
University of California, San Diego

Revolutionary Heads, 1990
plaster and wood
O. M. Ungers' private library, Cologne

The plinths of the identical, traditional classical heads are
inscribed with the names of members of the Committee of
Public Safety, 1793–4

The antient manner of Temples in Groves.

GROVE, n. an irregular peristyle

The gentle neighbourhood of GROVE and spring
Would soon unbosom all their echoes mild . . .

Milton, *The Passion*

Grove, 1987
print, with Gary Hincks (after William Stukeley)

Notes and References

BIOGRAPHICAL NOTES

1 – Or, as Finlay puts it, Arcady (cf. ch. 10).
2 – 'The whole thing is surrounded by a romantic glow.' Finlay, letter to Stephen Scobie, August 1970, in 'Summer Elephants', *White Pelican* Vol. 1, 2 (1971), p. 54.
3 – See the note on the dust-jacket of *The Sea-Bed and Other Stories* (Alna Press, 1958).
4 – Mike Weaver, 'Ian Hamilton Finlay', *Extra Verse* 15 (Spring 1965), p. 19
5 – Finlay, letter to David Brown, March 1976. Quoted in David Brown, 'Stonypath: An Inland Garden'.
6 – Stephen Bann, 'Ian Hamilton Finlay: An Imaginary Portrait', in the catalogue to Finlay's exhibition at the Serpentine Gallery (London: Arts Council, 1977), p. 15.
7 – Sue Finlay, note to the author, October 1984.
8 – Finlay, letter to the author, September 1983.
9 – Finlay, letter to the author, October 1983.
10 – 'The summer of 1971 was indeed a time for taking stock of the garden as it had developed in the previous four years,' notes Stephen Bann, quoting a letter he received from Finlay: 'I have been speculating . . . on the idea of the garden as an enclosed thing. For a while (in my experience) I was greatly perplexed as to why Stonypath did not have a garden-y garden' (letter to Stephen Bann, June 1971) (Stephen Bann, 'A Description of Stonypath', *Journal of Garden History*, Vol. 1, 2 (1981) p. 118.
11 – In the 1970s, Finlay embarked on a series of drawings with Jud Fine (p. 24) – and then had the work of the American modernist transformed into embroideries. He also had a *Marble Paper Boat* made in honour of Max Bill (p. 25). Such are the gaps his collaborations seek to bridge: between modernity and traditional crafts, between noble and trivial materials. The notional collaboration *The Months* (p. 171) pits domestic craftsmanship and traditional motifs against heavily industrialized modern warfare. The reader or viewer also intervenes as a collaborator in *Homage to Seurat* (p. 24) and in Finlay's question booklets (p. 21).
12 – Finlay, letter to the author, October 1983.
13 – Statements to the contrary by various officials of the Region are in contradiction with the correspondence on the subject.
14 – The SAC Charter requires it to 'develop the knowledge, understanding and practice of the Arts; to increase the accessibility of the Arts; to advise our Government and local authorities'.
15 – At one point an official of the Region declared that neither the Region's representatives nor its computer knew what a garden temple was.
16 – I quote from the letter sent by the Vigilantes to the authorities.
17 – Cf. Letter to Ian and Sue Finlay dated 27 April 1988, from Dominque Bozo, then head of the department of the French Ministry of Culture that had commissioned Finlay to present a proposal for the garden at Versailles. This letter represents the official French position on the affair. Hundreds of copies were distributed to journalists and others enquiring about the matter. It was published in *Artefactum*, no. 25 (1988), p. 48.
18 – See letter of 27 April 1988.
19 – The arts journalist Catherine Millet made

the following statement about *Osso* on the French radio station 'Europe 1' (25 March 1988): 'I saw a work, I saw Nazi signs carved on it, *basta* [enough].' The comment was backed up by a misleading description of the work (which Millet did not even name) and a false account of the conditions in which it was exhibited in Paris.
20 – Catherine Duhamel at a meeting with Sue Finlay (in the presence of the author), at which she expressed the Minister of Culture's regrets for the cancellation, 30 March 1988.
21 – The French fracas had certain repercussions in the British press. After initially supporting Finlay, the *TLS* turned against the artist. Finlay was refused the chance to refute allegations which had been made against him on the basis of unspecified 'documents'. *Apollo* and the London *Evening Standard* made out-of-court settlements with the artist after publishing articles concerning him.

CHAPTER 1

1 – Written answer to the author, September 1983.
2 – 'Beauty is the thing. Order and Beauty . . . in the honestest way, given the possibilities of the time.' Finlay, letter to Stephen Scobie, August 1970, in 'Summer Elephants'.
3 – Finlay in conversation with the author, June 1984.
4 – Finlay, letter to Stephen Scobie, August 1970, in 'Summer Elephants'.
5 – See Stephen Scobie, 'Rhymes and Reasons: Kahnweiler, Gris, Finlay, Stein', in the catalogue to Finlay's *Collaborations* exhibition (Kettle's Yard Gallery, Cambridge, 1977), p. 27.
6 – Stephen Bann applies this description to Finlay himself. See 'Ian Hamilton Finlay: An Imaginary Portrait', p. 8.
7 – As well as the model reproduced here, the series includes small sculptures of a glider, also entitled *Pierrot*.

CHAPTER 2

1 – See *The Sea-Bed and Other Stories*.
2 – For Benjamin's discussion of the notion of aura, see especially 'The Work of Art in the Age of Mechanical Reproduction', in *Illuminations*, ed. Hannah Arendt (London: Fontana Books, 1970) pp. 219–53.
3 – Geoffrey Hartman, *Wordsworth' Poetry 1782–1814* (New Haven & London: Yale University Press, 1971), p. 3.
4 – Geoffrey Hartman, *Criticism in the Wilderness: The Study of Literature Today* (New Haven & London: Yale University Press, 1980) p. 69. Hartman notes that Wordsworth's 'Intimations of Immortality' ode opposes the disruptive and the sustaining qualities of such visionary gleams.
5 – Finlay now disowns 'Catch 23', calling it 'a dreadfully bad poem' (written answer to the author, October 1983). See also Mike Weaver, 'Ian Hamilton Finlay', p. 17. 'Catch 23' dates from 1965:

    fish
      fish
        fish
oddfishoddfishoddfish
oddfishoddfishoddfish

çodfishçodfishçodfish

oddfishoddfishoddfish
oddfishoddfishoddfish
      fish
        fish
          fish

6 – See for example the typescript poems of Dom Sylvester Houédard, English representative on the concrete poetry movement's international committee.

7 – Finlay himself discusses the wider significance of 'Fir/far' in his commentary on the drawing *Friedrich and the Motorway*, from the *Third Reich Revisited*. This, together with the entire *Third Reich* series, can be found in *New Arcadians' Journal* 15 (Autumn, 1984).
8 – Letter to Pierre Garnier, September 1963, in *Image* (December 1964) pp. 9–10.
9 – The 'Little Fields' construction no longer exists. It was in wood, even if Finlay would have preferred low brick walls with letters in wrought iron protruding slightly from the surface.
10 – This observation is made by Bernard Lassus in his Preface to Finlay's *Selected Ponds* (Reno, Nevada: West Coast Poetry Review, 1976), no pagination.
11 – Finlay's 'Unnatural Pebbles', amongst which figures *peras/pears* perform the same function on a different scale.
12 – Quoted by Stephen Bann in *Footnotes to an Essay*, in the Serpentine catalogue, p. 37.
13 – See Stephen Bann, 'L'oeuvre d'art dans la ville: le talon de Saint Thomas', *Revue d'esthétique*, 3–4 (1977) p. 132.

CHAPTER 3

1 – See Stephen Bann, 'Kinetic Art and Poetry', *Image* (Winter/Spring 1966), p. 4.
2 – 'Isolated, single letters are pattern but letters joined in words (as these are) are direction. Those in the "Acrobats" poem are both, behaving like the real circus acrobats who are now individual units, now – springing together – diagonals and towers ' Finlay, in Emmett Williams, ed., *An Anthology of Concrete Poetry* (New York: Something Else Press, 1967), no pagination.
3 – M. L. Rosenthal, *The New Poets* (New York: Oxford University Press, 1967), p. 205.
4 – Cf. Stephen Bann, *Ian Hamilton Finlay – An Illustrated Essay* (Edinburgh: Scottish National Gallery of Modern Art, 1972), p. 15.
5 – James Joyce, *Stephen Hero* (London: Jonathan Cape, 1969), p. 218.
6 – In *Taschenbuch der Panzer* (Wild Hawthorn Press, 1981).
7 – On the question of hieroglyphs, see also ch. 7.
8 – See *The Tate Gallery 1974–76: Illustrated Catalogue of Acquisitions*, p. 83.

CHAPTER 4

1 – See the letter from Finlay to Stephen Bann, quoted in Stephen Bann, 'Introduction' (to an anthology of concrete poetry), *Beloit Poetry Journal*, vol. XVII, 1 (1968), p. 5.
2 – For Aristotle on metaphor, see *Poetics* 1457b ff.
3 – Finlay, letter to the author, October 1984.
4 – 'The Thorn' is a celebrated instance which can usefully be cited here, since Wordsworth's defence of his poem revolves round the personality of a narrator not dissimilar to Finlay's English colonel.
5 – Stephen Bann has noted the importance of the 'indication of style' implied by Finlay's choice of Patrick Caulfield to execute this work. He observes that 'Caulfield's sophisticated reworking of Cubism serves precisely to introduce a Cubist reference, in the context of which Finlay's equation of the lemon and the fishing-boat becomes more charged with meaning' (Stephen Bann, 'Ian Hamilton Finlay: Engineer and Bricoleur', *Ceolfrith* 5 [1970], p. 4).
6 – See *30 Signatures to Silver Catches* (Tarasque Press, 1970), in which Finlay describes fishing vessels from Fife, in Scotland, as 'sturdy, plump, pointed, *lemon-shaped*' and adds a bibliographical note which further complicates any efforts one might make to attribute the 'lemon' metaphor to a single source: see Gloria Wilson, *More Scottish*

Fishing Craft (Fishing News (Books) Ltd) 1968.
7 – The hand of an artist. Finlay is referring here to the habit artists have of adding colour notes in pencil to their sketches. (Letter to the author, 4 October 1984).
8 – See ch. 2, note 4.
9 – Finlay, letter to the author, March 1984.
10 – Stephen Bann goes so far as to suggest that 'There is no economy of the essential and the inessential which could govern [the] process'. See Finlay's *Heroic Emblems* (Vermont, USA: Z Press, 1977), p. 36.
11 – Cf. Antoine Compagnon, *La Seconde Main: le travail de la citation* (Paris: Editions du Seuil, 1979), p. 279.
12 – See Jonathan Culler, *Structuralist Poetics* (London: Routledge & Kegan Paul, 1975), *passim*.
13 – The term 'documentation' is used by Finlay.
14 – Finlay, letter to Stephen Bann, June 1970, quoted in 'Ian Hamilton Finlay: Engineer and Bricoleur', p. 3.
15 – Pierre Fontanier's definition of metaphor, quoted by Compagnon, *op. cit.*, p. 19.

CHAPTER 5

1 – 'The fields and forests, mosses and springs of an ancient pastoral landscape.' Finlay, quoted in Stephen Bann, 'Ian Hamilton Finlay's *Ocean Stripe 5*', Scottish International (March/April 1967) p. 47.
2 – For an analysis of this set of figures, see Tzvetan Todorov, 'Recherches sur le symbolisme linguistique: le mot d'esprit et ses rapports avec le symbolique', in *Poétique*, Vol. V, 18 (1974), pp. 304–11.
3 – Quoted in Stephen Bann, 'Ian Hamilton Finlay's *Ocean Stripe 5*', p. 47.
4 – Finlay later incorporated the question form in the very structure of some of his work. See for example the 'test booklets'.
5 – See *The Tate Gallery 1978–80: Illustrated Catalogue of Acquisitions*, p. 93.
6 – For a detailed analysis, see the article by Stephen Bann cited in note 1, to which I am indebted here.
7 – See Stephen Bann, *loc. cit.*, p. 50.
8 – See Stephen Bann, 'Ian Hamilton Finlay: Engineer and Bricoleur', p. 5.
9 – See ch. 2.

CHAPTER 6

1 – See Terry Eagleton, *Walter Benjamin or Towards a Revolutionary Criticism* (London: Verso Editions, 1981), p. 101.
2 – Aristotle, *Rhetoric*, 1358b.
3 – Quoted in Pierre Pachet, 'Georg Büchner: paroles dans le trouble', in *Passé/Présent* 2 (1983), p. 97.
4 – See for example the homages to Gris and Kahnweiler.
5 – Written answer to the author, September 1983.
6 – Stephen Bann, 'A Description of Stonypath', p. 142.
7 – Paul Overy, *The Times*, Tuesday 3 May 1977.
8 – The *Sunday Times*, for example, found the original exhibition 'ludicrous and distasteful' (29 August 1982). For a more complete evaluation of the *Third Reich*, see *New Arcadians' Journal* 15 (Autumn 1984).
9 – Miles Orvell, 'Poe and the Poetics of Pacific', *Collaborations* catalogue, p. 22.
10 – See Douglas Hall, 'The Finlay/Fine Collaboration', *Collaborations* catalogue, p. 15.
11 – Philippe Lacoue-Labarthe & Jean-Luc Nancy, *L'Absolu littéraire: théorie de la littérature du romantisme allemand* (Paris: Editions du Seuil, 1978), p. 75.

12 – K. W. F. Solger, *Erwin: dialogues on beauty and art* (1815), quoted in Tzvetan Todorov, *Théories du symbole* (Paris: Editions du Seuil, 1977), p. 257.
13 – See Todorov, *op. cit.*, p. 257.
14 – By the citation of an area of (official) culture – traditional names – in which warships are allegorical virtues.
15 – Atheneum I; 2 (1798), fragment no. 383.
16 – In Greek: *krisis*.
17 – See Finlay's letter to Pierre Garnier quoted in ch. 2.
18 – Piet Mondrian quoted in *Tout l'oeuvre peint de Piet Mondrian* (Paris: Flammarion, 1976) item no. 289. See plates 287, 289, 289(1), 289(2), 289(3).
19 – Quoted in Jean-Claude Lebenstejn, 'Mondrian: la fin de l'art', in *Critique* XXXIX; 438 (1983) pp. 893–912. I am indebted to this article for much of the information concerning Mondrian reproduced here.
20 – Lebenstejn suggests a parallel between Mondrian's historical logic and the politics of the tyrannous regimes he denounces – and over which he imagines this logic will triumph. Replacing the Dutch artist in the context of the 'chronic folly' of the avant-gardes of his time, Lebenstejn says of the dissolution or uplifting of art into life, transcending the framed painting and the walls of the museum: 'Therein lies the folly [or madness] – in the desire to Mondrianize the whole world'.
21 – See Lebenstejn, *loc. cit.*
22 – Cf. Jean-Luc Nancy, 'Menstruum Universale, la dissolution littéraire', in *Aléa* 1 (1981) p. 81.
23 – The logic of the avant-garde and Harold Bloom's 'anxiety of influence' are perhaps the most eloquent symptoms of this violence.

CHAPTER 7

1 – See Stephen Bann, 'An Imaginary Portrait', p. 27.
2 – See 'The work of art in the age of mechanical reproduction', p. 229.
3 – Stephen Bann, 'Introduction' to Finlay's *Heroic Emblems*, pp. vii–ix.
4 – On the aesthetics and structure of emblems, see the essays by Stephen Bann and Friedhelm Kemp in J-M. Benoit, ed., *Figures du Baroque* (Paris: Presses Universitaires Françaises, 1983); also Yves Giraud, ed., *L'Emblème à la Renaissance* (Paris: Sèdes, 1982).
5 – See E. H. Gombrich, 'Icones Symbolicae' in *Symbolic Images* (London: Phaidon Press, 1972), pp. 113–95.
6 – In his 'Theses on the Philosophy of History', Benjamin insists that the past has to be retrieved: 'only a redeemed mankind receives the fullness of the past – which is to say, only for a redeemed mankind has the past become citable in all its moments. Each moment it has lived becomes a *citation à l'ordre du jour* – and that day is judgement day' (*Illuminations*, p. 256). The apocalyptic moment for Finlay is the present moment of judgement, with its flash of wit. And for this, too, there is an echo in Benjamin. The sixteenth of his 'Theses' insists on the present as a moment in which time stands still, and celebrates the virility of the historian who 'remains in control of his powers, man enough to blast open the continuum of history' – a gesture which recalls Finlay's celebrations of the values of heroism in the arts.
7 – Cf. Paul Veyne, *Comment on écrit l'histoire, suivi de Foucault révolutionne l'histoire* (Paris: Editions du Seuil, 1978). See for example pp. 186 and 230.
8 – See note 2.
9 – See ch. 6.
10 – Text of the Saint-Just Vigilantes' communiqué.

CHAPTER 8

1 – Cesare Ripa, 'Introduction à l'Iconologie', French translation with an introduction by Hubert Damisch, *Critique* 315–16 (1973), p. 807.
2 – See Damisch's commentary on Ripa.
3 – Robert Klein, 'La théorie de l'expression figurée dans les traités italiens sur les *imprese*, 1555–1612', in *La Forme et l'Intelligible* (Paris: Gallimard, 1970) pp. 138–9.
4 – See, for example, the way *Ocean Stripe Series 5* (analysed in ch. 5) stresses the idea of 'soundness'.
5 – Alistair Fowler, 'Short, Sharp and to the Point', *Times Literary Supplement* (23 September 1977), p. 1490.
6 – *ibid*.
7 – Quoted in Finlay's Serpentine catalogue, p. 1.
8 – Gombrich, 'Icones Symbolicae', p. 165.
9 – See *Heroic Emblems*, p. 29.
10 – See *Unnatural Pebbles* (Edinburgh: Graeme Murray Gallery, 1981).
11 – Gardening, camouflage, weather, revolution, exile, metaphysics, as well as pebbles.
12 – The common definition of the word 'sentence' as a grammatical unit only comes in sixth place in the *Oxford English Dictionary*, following others (some of them obsolete) which insist on the sentence as a way of thinking, an opinion, an authoritative decision, a judicial judgement, a quoted, pithy or pointed saying, an apophthegm, aphorism or maxim, a passage of Scripture.
13 – See chapters 3 & 5.
14 – Letter to Pierre Garnier. See ch. 2, note 8.
15 – Finlay's word is 'lollygarchs'.
16 – Letter to Mike Weaver, August 1963, in Weaver (see Biographical Notes, note 4).
17 – Letter to author, September 1983.
18 – 'Consecutive sentences are the beginning of the secular.' Finlay, *Detached Sentences on Metaphysics*.
19 – See ch. 6, note 5.
20 – See ch. 2.
21 – Cf. the German version of this inscription, done for the gardens of the Max Planck Institute, Stuttgart (p. 228). The original version is reproduced and discussed in Stephen Bann, 'Ian Hamilton Finlay – The Structure of a Poetic Universe', *Studio International*, LLXXVII (1969), p. 80.
22 – Compare, for example, 'Ring of Waves' (p. 81) with 'Chant for a Regional Occasion' (p. 225) produced two decades later.

CHAPTER 9

1 – In these sundials, 'The work itself is no more than a central reference point in a network of signs and implications. Stephen Bann, 'Afterword' to Finlay's *Honey by the Water* (Los Angeles: Black Sparrow Press, 1973), p. 56.
2 – By Stephen Bann, on a card published by the Scottish National Gallery of Modern Art.
3 – See *Romances, Emblems, Enigmas* (Wild Hawthorn Press, 1980).
4 – See also 'Lux Umbra Dei' rewritten as Gomringer's 'das schwarze geheimnis', in *Imitations Variations Reflections Copies* (1976).
5 – 'It is totally determined by the exigency of correlating human time with solar time. Hence we have in the work an image of a self-contained dynamic system; land and sea placed in mutual relationship according to the movement of the sun. The pattern convincingly reproduces the philosophical world of Heraclitus, in which the perpetual state of flux is maintained by the single mobile principle of fire.' Stephen Bann, *Ian Hamilton Finlay: An Illustrated Essay*, p. 20.
6 – See ch. 2. Stephen Bann says that *Azure & Son* 'is itself a representation of that tension between the infinite and the finite, the limitless

and the limited, the numberless and the numbered, which is exemplified in the planning of Stonypath.' Stephen Bann, *Ian Hamilton Finlay: An Illustrated Essay*, p. 23.
7 – For the classical dimension of this sundial, see also the drawing in *A Sailor's Calendar*.

CHAPTER 10
1 – In the earlier *Arcady* (p. 198) and *Arcadian Sundials*, the militaristic element is missing.
2 – The group publishes the quarterly *New Arcadians' Journal*.
3 – See Erwin Panofsky, '*Et in Arcadia Ego*: on the conception of transience in Poussin and Watteau', in R. Klibansky and H. J. Paton (eds.), *Philosophy and History, Essays Presented to Ernst Cassirer* (Oxford: Oxford University Press, 1938), pp. 223–54, and '*Et in Arcadia Ego: Poussin and the elegiac tradition*', in *Meaning in the Visual Arts* (New York: Doubleday Anchor, 1955) pp. 295–320. Much of the material concerning Arcadia to be found in the present chapter is provided by Panofsky.
4 – Finlay, letter to Ad. Reinhardt, 1966. Quoted in David Miller, 'Magical Effects', *London Magazine* XVII; 3 (1977), pp. 82–3.
5 – A famous picture by Signorelli commemorated this 'alluring fiction' (Panofsky).
6 – If it also informs a painting by Giovanni Callista Cipriani, this can be attributed to the fact that Cipriani was active in England from the end of his apprenticeship to the time of his death.
7 – *Detached Sentences on Metaphysics*.
8 – See *Footnotes to an Essay*, 1 and 2.
9 – Cf. Stephen Bann in *Footnotes to an Essay*, 1.
10 – In the first of his two essays, Panofsky observes that the change effected by Poussin 'gives us an insight into the mental processes of a great genius who, like Shakespeare in his Shylock, subconsciously conceives an entirely new idea while consciously keeping to a traditional formula; moreover it throws light upon Poussin's attitude towards the fundamental problems of life and destiny'.

'The transformation of a mere *memento mori* into the revelation of a metaphysical principle which connects the present and the future with the past and overthrows the limits of individuality, means that 'Life' is conceived as transitory yet blessed with indestructible beauty and felicity; on the other hand, 'Death' is seen as a preserver as well as a destroyer. From this emerges the magnificent conception of a cyclical succession which subordinates the existence of individuals to the inexorable laws of cosmic principles, both natural and moral, endowing every stage of this existence, however transitory, with a substantial value of its own.'
11 – *Detached Sentences on Metaphysics*.
12 – '. . . Yet, harmony is a content . . . And yet, what is the content of harmony?' Ian Hamilton Finlay, *More Detached Sentences on Gardening in the Manner of Shenstone*.
13 – See also *Monument at Little Sparta* in Finlay's *Third Reich Revisited, New Arcadians' Journal*, 15.

CHAPTER 11
1 – A. C. Bradley, 'The Sublime' (1903), in *Oxford Lectures on Poetry* (London: Macmillan, 1965 ed.), pp. 37–65. All further references to Bradley are to this essay.
2 – Quoted by Mike Weaver, *op. cit.*, p. 17.
3 – See ch. 6, note 8.
4 – See the Miltonic poem/print *Of Famous Arcady Ye Are*.
5 – Edmund Burke, *Reflections on the Revolution in France* (Harmondsworth: Penguin Books, 1968), p. 137.

6 – See R. R. Palmer, *12 Who Ruled: the Year of the Terror in the French Revolution* (Princeton, New Jersey: Princeton University Press, 1941).
7 – Harold Bloom, *Agon: towards a theory of revisionism* (New York & Oxford: Oxford University Press, 1982), p. 101. It comes as no surprise when Bloom equates the sublime with Benjamin's aura. *Ibid.*, pp. 228 ff.
8 – See Laurent Jenny, *La Terreur des Bignes: poétiques de rupture* (Paris: Gallimard, 1982). The first part of Jenny's book (pp. 7–68) is particularly relevant to my argument here.
9 – Cf. Jenny, *op. cit.*
10 – *Ibid.*
11 – Paris: Gallimard, 1978.
12 – Victor Hugo, 'Réponse à un Acte d'Accusation', in *Les Contemplations*.
13 – From the Notebooks of d'Angers. Quotation supplied by Finlay.
14 – Anon., *The Rise and Progress of the Present Taste in Planting Parks* (1767).
15 – Cf. John Dixon Hunt & Peter Willis, *The Genius of the Place* (London: Paul Elek, 1973), p. 8.
16 – Cf. Patrick Eyres, 'Gardens of Exile: cultural hedgehogs', *New Arcadians' Journal* 10 (Summer 1983), no pagination.
17 – Hunt and Willis, *op. cit.*, p. 34.
18 – In Stephen Bann's words, 'the preparation of the soil for the next season and the inclination of the earth away from the sun'. *Ian Hamilton Finlay's Ocean Stripe 5*', p. 49.
19 – In *Autumn Poem* the distant 'planetary' views are formal illusions induced by the round format and the lighting.
20 – The Scottish authorities, at least, would seem to be so. The differing translations cited in *The Anaximander Fragment* may be taken to put in a nutshell the essence of Finlay's dispute with Strathclyde Region. A gesture which the Region has failed to properly condemn as falling foul of the law, it continues to punish as an offence against itself. Being unable to motivate its refusal of mandatory rates relief to Finlay's *Temple* by referring to the letter of the law (as opposed to its own interpretation of the law), it justifies its behaviour by claiming not to understand what a temple is. To continue to employ the term can therefore be taken as an offence against their limited literacy and, in view of the heavy financial consequences, may almost be considered a sign of recklessness.
21 – Some of Finlay's own *Detached Sentences on Metaphysics* were pasted onto pillars in a disaffected church, housing an exhibition of contemporary art, at the Pierre et Marie Curie Institute, Paris, Autumn 1983.
22 – 'What has neither idea nor strength exists but on sufferance', Michelet, quoted by Finlay on one of his *Porridge Bowls for Sans-culottes*.
23 – Albert Speer, *Inside the Third Reich* (London: Sphere Books, 1971) pp. 83–4.

CHAPTER 12
1 – See above, chapter 7.
2 – In 'The Atlantic Wall' (*New Arcadians' Journal* 14, 1984), Finlay conducts a picturesque tour of the German fortifications, juxtaposing watercolours by Ian Gardner and extracts from the eighteenth-century writings of William Gilpin.
3 – 'Anagrams are the Muse playing Patience' 'A man's anagram is his Fate' (Adapted from Heraclitus). I. H. Finlay, 'Anagrams: a Postscript', *Poursuites Révolutionnaires*, exhibition catalogue, Fondation Cartier, Jouy-en-Josas, 1987, p. 61.
4 – 'Philosophy can initially be characterized as a thinking consideration of objects.' Hegel, quoted by Finlay in the catalogue to his exhibition of *Works*, Butler Gallery, Kilkenny Castle, Ireland (1989).

5 – Cf. the biographical note on the dust-jacket of *The Sea-Bed and Other Stories* (1958).
6 – As frequently, for example, in allegorical readings of biblical texts.
7 – Letter to the author, 28 December 1986.
8 – For a more detailed examination of *A View to the Temple* from the point of view of the sublime, see Yves Abrioux, 'Visibilité et figurativité: le sublime', *Fabula* 9 (1987), pp. 101–9.

CHAPTER 13
1 – It will be recalled that Finlay regards the pear as 'the ideal fruit, on the cubist tree (or table), suggest[ing] a perfect limited form'. Cf. chapter 1.
2 – See Stephen Bann, 'Introduction', *Concrete Poetry, an International Anthology* (London: London Magazine Editions, 1967).
3 – Geneviève Lacombe, 'Pierre-Henri de Valenciennes en Italie: un journal de voyage inédit', *Bulletin de la Société de l'histoire de l'art français* (1978), p. 150.
4 – Diderot, *Salon de 1767*. See Diderot, *Œuvres esthétiques* (Paris: Editions Garnier, 1968), p. 643.
5 – Cf. *A Remembrance of R.S.L.*, 1987.
6 – See especially 'Denys l'Auxerrois' (1886) and 'Apollo in Picardy' (1893).
7 – Ian Hamilton Finlay, *Detached Sentences for Prospect '89, Frankfurt*.
8 – ARC, Municipal Museum of Modern Art, Paris. See chapter 12.
9 – See *Digraphe*, 43, 45, 46 (1988).
10 – For a detailed analysis of this work, see Yves Abrioux, 'Dissociation: on the poetics of Ian Hamilton Finlay's Tree/Columns', *Word & Image*, IV, 1 (1988), pp. 338–44.
11 – Like, for example, *View to the Temple* (p. 272), which was intended to draw the eighteenth-century park and temple at Kassel into the context of 'Documenta'; or the memorial to the poet Annette Droste-Hülshoff, fixed to a tree in an old graveyard in Münster.
12 – *Wave* (1969).
13 – Cf. the card *Wave* (1979): 'Wave/Solitary Wave/Great Wave of Translation'.
14 – Such as *Pastorals*, Claire Burrus Gallery, Paris, 1987, and *Idylls*, Victoria Miro Gallery, London, 1990.
15 – *Trope*: etymologically *tropos*, from *trepein*, to turn; also formerly used to indicate the turning of the sun (Apollo) at the solstice (hence 'tropics', 'tropical').

Bibliography

Compiled by Pia Simig
All printed works were published by Wild
Hawthorn Press, unless otherwise stated.

1   POOR. OLD. TIRED. HORSE.
Nos 1–25, 1961–7

2   BOOKS AND BOOKLETS

The Sea-Bed and Other Stories, 1958, Alna Press,
1st and 2nd edition
The Dancers Inherit the Party, Migrant Press,
1960, 2nd ed. 1962, 3rd ed. (wrongly
described as 1st), Fulcrum Press, 1969
Glasgow Beasts, An a Burd, 1961, 2nd ed.
February 1962, 3rd ed. June 1962, 4th ed.
December 1962, 5th ed. Fulcrum Press, 1965.
Papercuts by John Picking and Pete McGinn
Concertina, with John Picking and Pete McGinn,
1962
Rapel, 1963, ten fauve and suprematist poems
Canal Stripe Series 3, 1964, kinetic booklet/poem
Canal Stripe Series 4, 1964, kinetic booklet/poem
Telegrams from My Windmill, 1964
Futura 7, Editions Hansjorg Mayer, 1965, five
poems, folding print
Ocean Stripe Series 2, 1965, kinetic booklet/poem
Ocean Stripe Series 3, 1965, kinetic booklet/poem
Cythera, 1965, kinetic booklet/poem
Canal Stripe Series 8/699I, 1965, handmade
booklet
Und Alles Blieb Wie Es War (one-act plays
translated into German), 1965, Universal
Editions, Vienna
Picture Book, Christmas 1965
Autumn Poem, photographs by Audrey Walker,
printed by The Salamander Press, 1966
6 Small Pears for Eugen Gomringer, 1966
6 Small Songs in 3's, with linocuts by Zeljiko
Kujundzic, 1966, printed by The Salamander
Press
Tea-leaves and Fishes, printed by The Salamander
Press, 1966
Ocean Stripe Series 4, design and drawings by
Emil Antonucci, 1966
Headlines Eaveslines, Openings Press, 1967
Stonechats, one-word poems, hand-printed by
The Salamander Press, 1967
Ocean Stripe Series 5, Tarasque Press, 1967
Canal Game, Fulcrum Press, 1967 (1st edition
designed by the Goliard Press)
Headlines Pondlines, 1968
The Collected Coaltown of Callange Tri-kai,
Screwpacket Press, 1968
Air Letters, drawings by Robert Frame, Tarasque
Press, 1968
The Blue and the Brown Poems, with Atlantic
Richfield, calendar, twelve poem prints with
commentaries by Stephen Bann, Jargon Press,
1968
3/3's, 1969, 3 poems/3 photographs
After the Russian, with John Furnival, Openings
Press, 1969
A Boatyard, printed by Shenval Press, 1969
Lanes, drawing by Margot Sandeman, hand-
printed by The Salamander Press, 1969
Wave, hand-printed at The Salamander Press,
1969
Rhymes for Lemons, with Margot Sandeman,
handwriting by Gordon Huntly, 1970
Fishing News News, concertina, drawings by
Margot Sandeman, hand-printed at The
Salamander Press, 1970
Ceolfrith 5, with photographs by Diane Tammes,
Bookshop Gallery, Sunderland, Ceolfrith
Press, 1970

Allotments, visualized by Ian Gardner, poems by
Ian Hamilton Finlay, Stuart Mills and Simon
Cutts, Tarasque Press, 1970
30 Signatures to Silver Catches, cover drawing by
Margot Sandeman, published by Tarasque
Press, printed by Shenval Press, 1971
Poems to Hear and See, The Macmillan Company,
New York, USA, 1971
A Sailor's Calendar, with Gordon Huntly,
Something Else Press, New York, USA, 1971,
with interleaves and ring binding
The Olsen Excerpts, photographs by Diane
Tammes, Verlag Udo Berger, D-Göttingen,
1971
A Memory of Summer, with Jim Nicholson, 1971
From 'An Inland Garden', drawings by Ian
Gardner, 1971
Evening / Sail 2., with Michael Harvey, 1971
screen print by Girdwood
*The Weed Boat Masters Ticket, Preliminary Test
(Part Two)*, drawings by Ian Gardner, printed
by hand at The Salamander Press, 1971
Sail / Sundial, 1972
Jibs, photographs by Diane Tammes, Christmas
1972
Kamikaze Butterflies, 1973
A Family, with bookmark, 1973
Straiks, with Simon Cutts, drawings by Sydney
McK.Glen, 1973
Honey By The Water, afterword by Stephen Bann,
Black Sparrow Press, Los Angeles, 1973
Exercise X, with George L. Thomson, 1973
Three Sundials, Rougement Press, 1974
Homage to Robert Lax, 1974
A Pretty Kettle of Fish, photographs by Diane
Tammes, 1974
Silhouettes, with Laurie Clark, 1974
Snow – Sail – Drop – Flake, Moschatel Press,
1974
So You Want to be a Panzer Leader, drawings by
Laurie Clark, 1975
Airs Waters Graces, with Ron Costley, 1975
The Wild Hawthorn Wonder Book of Boats, with
Martin Fidler, 1975
A Mast of Hankies, with photographs by David
Paterson, 1975, nine postcards in folder
The Axis, with Alexander Finlay, 1975
Trombone Carrier, 1975, card in folder
Textbooklet 1, 1975, concertina
Imitations, Variations, Reflections, Copies, with John
Andrew, photographs by Norman Dixon, 1976
The Wild Hawthorn Art Test, with Martin Fidler,
1977
The Boy's Alphabet Book, photographs by David
Paterson, Coach House Press, Toronto, 1977
Homage to Poussin, with John Borg Manduca,
1977
Peterhead Power Station Projects, with Ian
Appleton, 1978
Trailblazers, with C. Tissiman, edited by
Waterman Arrowbile, 1978
SF, with George L. Thomson, 1978
Woods, with Ron Costley, 1978
Peterhead Fragments, with Margot Sandeman,
1979
Dzaezl, with John Borg Manduca, 1979
Textbooklet 2, 1979, concertina
Textbooklet 3, 1979, concertina
Two Billows, 1980
Woods and Seas, 1980
Romances, Emblems, Enigmas, 1980
A Small Classical Dictionary, handprinted, Parrett
Press, 1980
Table-talk, a Selection, designed by Crispin
Elsted, Barbarian Press, Vancouver, Canada,
1981
Taschenbuch der Panzer, with Ian Gardner, 1981
A Litany, A Requiem, 1981
Two Epicurean Poems and an Epicurean Paradox,
1981
The Anaximander Fragment, with Harvey Dwight,
1981

An Improved Classical Dictionary, Parrett Press,
Christmas 1981
Little Sermons Series: Cherries, with Ian Gardner,
1982
Little Sermons Series: Volume Makes Beauty, with
Ian Gardner, 1982
Three Developments, 1982
The Mailed Pinkie, with Gary Hincks,
Verlaggalerie Leaman, Alsbach, W. Germany,
1982
Midway 3, with Grahame Jones, 1982
Anticipations, 1982
A Mixed Exhibition, Barbarian Press, Vancouver,
Canada, 1983, two booklets
The Errata of Ovid, 1983, eight cards in folder
Interpolations in Hegel, Christmas 1984
Epicurus at Chatou, with Ron Costley, Exempla,
Firenze and Exit, Lugo, Italy, 1985
4 Blades, with Gary Hincks, six cards in folder,
1986
Heraclitean Variations, 1986
Thoughts on Waldemar, 1986, 16 cards in folder
Detached Sentences on Weather, with decorations
by Jo Hincks, Christmas 1986
Loaves, with Howard Eaglestone and Antonia
Reeve, 1987
Swastika, n., 1988
A Concise Classical Dictionary, Christmas 1988
After, screen, with Grahame Jones, printed by
John Tetley, 1989
3 Texts, with Stephen Raw, 1989
Thermidor, drawings by Laurie Clark, 1989
5 Proverbs for Jacobins, illustrated by Kathleen
Lindsley, Christmas 1989
Blades, 1989
Bicentenary Texts, 1989
Woodpaths, decorations by Solveig Hill, 1990
4 Baskets, with Kathleen Lindsley, 1990
Flakes, with Gary Hincks, Christmas 1990
3 Stitches, with Kathleen Lindsley, 1991
Jacobin Definitions, with Kathleen Lindsley, 1991
Scud, 1991
Picturesque, with Humphrey Repton, 1991
Myths, illustrations by Solveig Hill, 1991
Detached Sentences on Friendship, with Kathleen
Lindsley, 1991
Four Monostichs, 1991
The Old Stonypath Hoy, illustrations by Gary
Hincks, Christmas 1991

3   CARDS AND FOLDING CARDS

Standing Poem 1 (Pear/Appear), 1963
The Star in its Stable of Light, 1964
Standing Poem 2 (Apple/Heart), 1965 (2 versions)
Standing Poem 3 (Hearts), 1965, card in folder
First Suprematist Standing Poem, 1965, folding
card
Earthship, 1965, paper sculpture in box
Star / Steer, Brighton Festival publication, 1967
3 Blue Lemons, handprinted at the Salamander
Press, 1968
2, From the Yard of . . ., 1968, handprinted at the
Salamander Press
Sea-poppy 1, 1968
Sea-poppy 2, set by Peter Grant, 1968
The Land's Shadows, set by Ann Stevenson, 1968
From 'The Analects of Fishing News', 1968
Pole Night (opening 3), John Furnival, 1969,
folding card
From 'The Illuminations of Fishing News', 1969
From 'Ta Mythika of Fishing News', 1969
Net / Planet, printed by hand, The Salamander
Press, 1969
Barges, with Margot Sandeman, 1969, printed at
The Salamander Press
Point-to-Point, with Jim Nicholson, 1969
4 Sails, photographed by J. W. Lucas, 1969
Xmas Star, with John Furnival, 1969, Christmas
card
Skylarks, 1969, folding card
Valses pour Piano (Water Music), 1970

Arcadian Sundials, with Margot Sandeman, 1970, folding card
From '*The Metamorphoses of Fishing News*', 1970
A Waterlily Pool, with Ian Gardner, 1970
Still Life with Lemon, 1970
Azure & Son, with Michael Harvey, 1970, descriptive leaflet for Sundial, High Street, Biggar
Les Hirondelles, with Ron Costley, 1970, screen print
A Patch . . ., with Margot Sandeman, 1970, screen print
Sheaves, 1970, folding card, screen print
A Use for Old Beehives, with Richard Demarco, 1970, folding card
Boats of Letters, Tarasque Press, 1970
Xmas Rose, with John Furnival, 1970, Christmas card
Zulu 'Chieftain', with American typographer A. Doyle Moore, 1971, screen print
A Sea Street Anthology, photograph by Gloria Wilson, 1971
Homage to Donald McGill, 1971
Flags, with acknowledgements to Simon Cutts, 1971
The Sign of the Nudge, with Michael Harvey, 1971, 2nd edition by Morning Star Publications
The Harbour, photograph by Diane Tammes, 1971
The Old Nobby, photograph by Diane Tammes, 1971
Sails / Waves 1, with Ron Costley, 1971, screen print
Sails / Waves 2, with Ron Costley, 1971, screen print
I Saw Three Ships, with Ron Costley, 1971, screen print
A Heart-Shape, with Ron Costley, 1971
Birch-Bark, photograph by Diane Tammes, 1971
Daisies, with Ian Gardner, 1971, screen print
Book-Flag, with Ron Costley, 1971
The Land's Shadows, with Michael Harvey, 1971, Christmas card for Daedalus Press
Kite: Willing Wings, photograph, New Year folding card, 1971
Tree Shells, with Ian Gardner, 1971, folding card
Catches, with Margot Sandeman, 1971, screen print
Unicorn, I. H. Finlay yacht-model, photograph by Diane Tammes, 1971, folding card
Elegy for Whimbrel and Petrel, with Ian Gardner, Sepia Press 1971
Xmas Morn 1965, with Michael Harvey, 1971, Christmas card
A Pittenweem Fancy, 1972, folding card
Is There a Ship Named the Wave Sheaf?, with Michael Harvey, 1972
Homage to E. A. Hornel, photograph by Ian Hamilton Finlay, 1972
F 1, photograph by John Roberts, 1972, folding card
The End, with Ian Gardner, 1972, 1st edition folding card, 2nd edition card, Morning Star Publications, 1989
Homage to Seurat, with Ron Costley, 1972, screen print
Homage to Walter Reekie's Ring Nettes, with Ron Costley, 1972, screen print
Kite Estuary Model, with Ian Gardner, 1972, screen print
Iron Ship, with Ian Gardner, 1972
Homage to Jonathan Williams, with Michael Harvey, 1972
Blue / Water's / Bark, photograph by Diane Tammes, 1972, folding card
Homage to Kandinsky, with Ron Costley, 1972
Homage to Kahnweiler, with Stuart Barrie, 1972
Tye Cringle, Christmas 1972, folding card
Der Tag, with Ron Costley, 1972

Estuary Cupboards, with Michael Harvey, 1973, folding card
The Sea's Waves, with Stuart Barrie, 1973, folding card in folder
Trim Here, with Michael Harvey, 1973, folding card, cream or grey
Mid-Pacific Elements, 1973, folding card
Tea-cards, with Simon Cutts, 1973, three cards (O.A.P.T., A.F.V.T., M.F.V.T.)
Bath Roundels, photograph by George Oliver, 1973
Homage to Pop Art, with Sydney McK. Glen, 1973
Mower is Less, 1973
Homage to Victor Sylvester, with Michael Harvey, 1973
Wild Hawthorne Weapon Series No 1, with Susan Goodricke, 1973
Landscape / Interior, with Karl Torok, 1973
'A Calm in a Tea-cup', with Richard Demarco, after Kate Greenaway, 1973, folding card
Schiff, with Ron Costley, 1973, folding card
The Mexican Navy, with Martin Fidler, 1974
Harlequin, with Karl Torok, 1974, folding card
The Last Norfolk Wherry, with Michael Harvey, 1974, folding card
Definitions of Lawns 2, with Michael Harvey, 1974, folding card
Bookmark, with Laurie Clark, 1974
Bobbin, with Karl Torok, 1974, folding card
Swans, with Ron Costley, 1974, screen print, folding card
Wild Hawthorn Weapons Series No 2, Homage to Max Bill, 1974, photograph
National Flags Series: Arcadia, with Ron Costley, 1974, screen print
National Flags Series: Cythera, with Karl Torok, 1974
Flotte de Pêche, with Ron Costley, 1974
Rotkehlchen, 1975, photograph
Lullaby, with John Andrew, 1975
Sail / Stamp, 1975
Panzer am Waldrande, with Jim Nicholson, 1975
Cherry Stones, models by I. H. Finlay, photograph by Dave Paterson, 1975
Marine Prototypes, photograph by Vic Smeed, 1975, two photos on card
'The Divided Meadows of Aphrodite', with Ron Costley, 1975, screen print
Pierrot, photograph by David Paterson, 1975, folding card
Homage to the L. A. Doust Art Manuals, 1975, folding card
A Homage to Simon Cutts, photograph by David Paterson, 1975, folding card
Eastertide, with Laurie Clark, 1975, folding card
Horloge de Flore, with Laurie Clark, 1975, folded leaf
Tea-Kettle-Drum, with Georg L. Thomson, 1975, folding card
National Flags Series: Valhalla, with Michael Harvey, 1975
National Flags Series: Utopia, with Michael Harvey, 1975
Stonypath Garden and Gallery Series: 'The Great Piece of Turf', photograph by Michael McQueen, 1975
Stonypath Garden and Gallery Series: 'U.S.S. Nautilus', photograph by Michael McQueen, 1975
Stonypath Garden and Gallery Series: 'Elegiac Inscription', photograph by Michael McQueen, 1975
Calendar, with Laurie Clark, 1975, folding card
Small is Quite Beautiful, with Ron Costley, 1976
Lyres 1, model by I. H. Finlay, photograph by Carl Heideken, 1976
Motoring Chocolate Soldier, photograph by Carl Heideken, 1976
'Adventurer', with Laurie Clark, 1976

Scottish National Gallery of Modern Art Sundial, photograph by David Paterson, commentary by Stephen Bann, 1976
Et in Arcadia Ego, with John Andrew, 1976
Lyres 2, model by I. H. Finlay, photograph by Carl Heideken, 1977
In Memoriam 'The Roberts', 1977
Achtung! Minen, with Michael Harvey, 1977
After Thomas Hearne, with Gary Hincks, 1977
Betula Pendula, with Gary Hincks, 1977
Battle of the Atlantic, Livingston, 1977, three photos on card
Tree-Shells 3, with Bernard Lassus, 1977, folding card
Improvisation No. 1, photograph by Carl Heideken, 1977
Homage to J. M. Synge, with John Borg Manduca, 1977
Wordsworth / Wadsworth, with Jim Downie, 1977
Marionette 1, model by I. H. Finlay, photograph by Dave Paterson, 1978
Marionette 2, model by I. H. Finlay, photograph by Dave Paterson, 1978
Betula Pendula 2, with Gary Hincks, 1978, folding card
Persevere, 1978
Counter-Argument, 1978
'Auch ich war in Arkadien . . .', 1978, photograph
Some Versions of Pastoral, with Gary Hincks, 1978
Leaf / Bark Bookmark, 1978, 2nd edition Morning Star Publication, 1989
Handley Page Heyford, with Gary Hincks, 1978
A Woodland Flute, with Ron Costley, 1978
Reply Card, with John Borg Manduca, 1978
Erratum (for mind read void), 1978
Butterfly, with Ivy Sky Rutzky, 1979, folding card
'Cythera' plan, with Peter Lyle, 1979
'And How Many Divisions Has Arcady?', with John Borg Manduca, 1979
Wave, 1979
Blue Water's Bark, with Ron Costley, 1979, folding card
Snow Bark, 1979
Arbre (Tree), 1979, 2nd edition Morning Star Publications, 1989, bookmark
Landscape with Woods . . ., with Ian Gardner, 1980
After John Flaxman, R. A., with Gary Hincks, 1980
Camouflage flag flak, with Jud Fine, Italy, 1981
'In the Back of Every Dying Civilisation . . .', with Claude Chimerique, 1981
Ripple, 1981, folding card
Capital, n. A Republican Crown, with Lucius Burckhardt, 1981, folding card
Two Trees, with Richard Healy, 1982, two sheets to be folded into rectangular columns
From '35 One-Word Poems': *Curfew – Curlew*, with Ian Gardner, 1982, from the exhibition 'Presences of Nature'
From '35 One-Word Poems': *Deep-V-Hull – geese*, with Ian Gardner, 1982, from the exhibition 'Presences of Nature'
From '35 One-Word Poems': *Drip-Dry – May*, with Ian Gardner, 1982, from the exhibition 'Presences of Nature'
From '35 One-Word Poems': *Moorland – Marquetry*, with Ian Gardner, 1982, from the exhibition 'Presences of Nature'
From '35 One-Word Poems': *Osiris – Osiers*, with Ian Gardner, 1982, from the exhibition 'Presences of Nature'
Temple of Apollo Facade, with Nicholas Sloan, 1983
Attack Letter-dart, with Nicholas Sloan, 1983
Shock Tropes, with Nicholas Sloan, 1983, folding card
A Column A Day, with Gary Hincks, 1983, folded leaf

Two Prospects, with Ian Gardner, 1983, The New Arcadian Press
A Dryad Discovered, with Grahame Jones, 1983, folding card
Wildflower, 1983, pressed flower in folder
Hommage à David (1), with Ron Costley and Gary Hincks, 1983, folding card
Hommage à David (2), with Ron Costley, 1983, paper cut-out
'The Present Order', with Nicholas Sloan, 1983
Tree Column-Base 'Saint-Just', with Andrew Townsend, 1983
A Flute for Saint-Just, 1983
'Pink Melon Joy' – and More, 1983, text card
Against the Hébertists, 1983
Liberty, Terror and Virtue, with John Stathatos, 1983
Lexical Diversions, with Mark Stewart, 1983
A View on the Hedgehog Garden, with Norman Lockhart, 1983
A Placement, photographs by Andrew Griffiths, 1983, folding card
'Within the System . . .', with Mark Stewart, 1983
Join the Saint-Just Vigilantes (1), 1983
Join the Saint-Just Vigilantes (2), 1983
Saint-Just Vigilantes – Secret:, 1983
'Daddy, What Did You Do in the Little Spartan War?', 1983
'Neoclassicism Needs You', 1983
Football Match, Christmas 1983
Two Translations, 1983
Closed, 1983
Heroic Anagrams: Saint-Just, with Alexander Stoddart, 1983, folding card
Arrosoir: A Regeneration, with Gary Hincks, 1984, folding card
He Spoke like an Axe, with Richard Healy, 1984, folding card
Charm, with Laurie Clark, 1984
Temple, with Mark Stewart, 1984
The Marble Arrow, 1984
Names on Trees, with Mark Stewart, 1984
Christmas Card, 1984, folding card
Dovecote, with John Tetley, 1984
Every Goal Negates: Second Anniversary of the First Battle of Little Sparta, 1985
Arrow, with Ron Costley, 1985, folding card
Fewer sculptures . . ., 1985
Windmills Winding Waters, 1985, concertina
The S.A.C. is Now Discovering the Price . . ., 1985
The Desire of Towing, Christmas 1985, folding card
Card for the Third Anniversary of the Battle of Little Sparta, February 4, 1986
Card for the Third Anniversary of Strathclyde Region's raid on the Garden Temple, Little Sparta, March 15, 1986
Wreathing of Rockets, 1986, folding card
Pear, with Stephanie Kedik, 1986, folding card
Nettles, with Stephanie Kedik, 1986, folding card
Other and Still Other . . ., 1986, folding card
5 Words, 1986, folding card
The Name of the Bow . . ., 1986, folding card
How Will One Hide . . ., 1986, folding card
Even the Oatmeal Drink . . ., 1986, folding card
Somewhere in the Wood . . ., 1986, 1st edition: Christmas folding card, 2nd edition: Peter Knee letterpress, 1989
'I was a Member of the National Trust', 1986
'I was Published by Jonathan Cape', 1986
Strawberry Hill, The Hermetic Press, 1986
A Modest Hero, with Gary Hincks, 1986
Marat, 1986, folding card
Forget-Me-Not, with Stephanie Kedik, 1986, folding card
River, Ocean, Lake, The Hermetic Press, 1986, folding card
Le Silence Eternel de Checkpoint Sandy, photograph Antonia Reeve, 1986
Apollo in Strathclyde, photograph Marius Alexander, 1986

Reed-Pipe, 1986
Card for the 4th Anniversary of the First Battle of Little Sparta, 1987
Card for the Fourth Anniversary of Strathclyde Region's raid on the Garden Temple at Little Sparta, 1987
Sticker for Victory, 1987
The National Trust Follifies . . ., 1987
Follies War Special, 1987
Dialogue, 1987
Mr Greene and the White Brigands, 1987
Menu à la Carte, 1987
According to the National Trust . . ., 1987
Wild Hawthorn Weapons Series: Saint-Just Vigilantes Celebrate . . ., 1987
Head-ley, 1987
Jeunesse Dorée of the Counter-Revolution, 1987
Dim Wim in his Crazy Windmill, 1987
The Enlightenment, 1987
Waldemar is the Venom . . ., 1987
When the World Took to Tolerance . . ., 1987
Justice for the Fat Stupid Kids, 1987
Liberal Democracy . . ., 1987
He was the First Schoolmaster . . ., 1987
The Difference Between a House . . ., with Mark Stewart, 1987
Imprisoned in Every Italian Battleship . . ., with Mark Stewart, 1987
Arbre de la Liberté, 1987
Les Sans Culottes, with Laurie Clark, 1987, folding card
Art Press, Paris, Announces, 1987
A One Word Poem for the Ladies of Art Press, 1987
Advertising Fascism, 1987
Louis Treize, 1987
Myriam Salomon Owns . . ., 1987
Brount, 1987
Head of Gwyn Headley, 1987
Head of Waldemar Januszczak, 1987
La Tricoteuse, 1987
A Young Blade, 1987
From 'Clerihews for Liberals', 1987
The Garden is Open, 1987
Poppy, n. the Phrygian Flower, with Jo Hincks, 1987
Socle, 1987
Memory, 1987, folding card
Heraclitean Variations, Christmas 1987, collection in a box
To All Saint-Just-Vigilantes, Christmas 1987
A Proposal for the Furka Pass, with photographs by Marco Schibig, 1987
Rowan, 1987
Willow, 1987
Nature is the Devil, 1987
Cruel and Ingenious Sophists . . ., 1987
Paris is the Sink of All Vices, 1988
Monostitch for the Revolution, 1988
1930 / 1980, 1988
The Case of the Intellectual Terrorist, 1988
Ligue des Droits, 1988
Ligue, 1988
Blades, for Michael Blum, Jonathan Hirschfeld, Yves Hayat, with Gary Hincks, 1988, concertina
Riff-raff, 1988
Within this Ticket . . ., 1988
Hedgehog Garden Hint, 1988
Basta, 1988
Néoclassicisme Révolutionnaire, with Gary Hincks, 1988
Summer Poem, 1988
Bark / Barque / Baroque, with John R. Nash, 1988
After Basho, 1988
'When Pleasures are like Poppies Spread', 1988, folding card
A Definition for Michael Blum. Ambiguous, n., 1988
The Desmoulins Connection, 1988, ten assorted folding cards in envelope
Picabia Series (2), 1988, set of three cards
A Fragment, 1988, folding Christmas card

De Man, 1989
Birds Fly. Waterfowl Ply., with Gary Hincks, 1989, folding card
Fête Champêtre, with Stephen Duncalf, 1989, Morning Star Publications
Bicentary Tricolour, with Gary Hincks, 1989
Januszczak, 1989
The Flageolet's Surname, with Kathleen Lindsley, 1989
Aphrodite of the Terror, photograph by Marco de Valdivia, 1989, Galerie Jule Kewenig
Order is Repetition, 1989, folding card
A Proposal for the Celebration of the Bicentenary . . ., 1989, folding card
Voysey Stile, with Mark Stewart, 1989
Little Sparta, 1989
The perfect sentence . . ., with Kathleen Lindsley, 1989, concertina
For Simon Cutts, 1989, folding card
Martin Waters, 1989, folding card
Matisse chez Duplay, with Julie Farthing, 1989
The Temple of Apollo, photograph by Andrew Griffiths, 1989
From the Collected Dictionaries, 1989, Morning Star Publications, two bookmarks
Snow, n., with Gary Hincks, 1989, folding Christmas card
Installation, 1990, folding card
3 Dates, 1990, folding card
Two Milestones, 1990, folding card
Matisse chez Duplay, photograph by Elke Walford, 1990, published by Glasgow Museum and Art Galleries
A Rose is a Rose is a Rose, 1990, folding card
A Tree of Liberty, 1990, folding card
Water-lilies, with Gary Hincks, 1990
Christmas Card, 1990
Gate Fold, with Gwyneth Leech, 1991, folding card
Abraham à Santa Clara, with Gary Hincks, 1991, folding card
A Model of Order . . ., with Gary Hincks, 1991
Abraham à Santa Clara, with Gary Hincks, 1991, concertina
A Reflection on the French Revolution, 1991, folding card
Two Landscapes, with Ian Gardner and John Robert Cozens, 1991, concertina
Bouleau/Birch, with Caroline Webb, 1991
Joseph Bara, with Laurie Clark, 1991, published by Galerie Stadtpark Krems
Shepherds – Bath Towels, Christmas 1991, folding card

4 POEMS / PRINTS

Pear – Appear – Disappear, 1963, paper sculpture poem
Poster Poem (Red Boat), 1963, screen print
Poster Poem (Le Circus), 1964, screen print
4 Sails with typography by Ed Wright, 1966, folding poem in blue, yellow or red
Acrobats, Tarasque Press, 1966, screen print
Star / Steer, Tarasque Press, 1966, screen print
Sea-poppy 1, Tarasque Press, with Alistair Cant, 1966, silkscreen
Summer Poem, with Jim Nicholson, 1967, screen print
Ajar, 1967, screen print
La Belle Hollandaise, with Herbert Rosenthal, 1967, screen print
Land / Sea, with Herbert Rosenthal, 1967, screen print
Marine, with Patrick Caulfield, 1968, screen print
Sea-poppy 2, 1968, screen print
Fauve Poem, with John Furnival, 1969
Poem / Print No 11, with John Furnival, 1969, screen print
Seams, 1969, screen print
Evening / Sail, 1970, 2nd edition by Graeme Murray Gallery, 1991, screen print

Errata, with David Button, 1970, two prints in folder

Catameringue, with Peter Grant, 1970, screen print

Poem / Print No 14, with John Furnival, 1970, screen print

The Little Seamstress, with Richard Demarco, 1970, screen print

Homage to Mozart, with Ron Costley, 1970, screen print

Scottish Zulu, with David Button, 1970, screen print

Archangel, with Sydney McK. Glen, Christmas 1970, calligramme

Seven Plates from Edgar J. March's 'Sailing Drifters', printed for Ceolfrith Press, Sunderland, 1970, folding print

Shenval Christmas Poem / Print, 1971, folding print

Sailing Barge Redwing, with Ian Gardner, 1971, screen print in folder

A Rock Rose, with Richard Demarco, 1971

Glossary, with Richard Demarco, 1971, print in folder

Seashells, with Ian Procter, 1971, print in folder

The Little Drummer Boy, with Ron Costley, 1971, screen print

Homage to Vuillard, with Michael Harvey, 1971, screen print in folder

Prinz Eugen, with Ron Costley, 1972, screen print

Sail Wholemeal, with Jim Nicholson, 1972, screen print

Homage to Modern Art, with Jim Nicholson, 1972, screen print

HMS Illustrious, Aircraft Carrier sculpture project, with Richard England, 1972, screen print

Spiral Binding, with Ron Costley, 1972

Di, with Michael Harvey, 1972, two prints in folder

The Washington Fountain, with Karl Torok, 1972, print in folder

Topiary Aircraft Carrier, with Ian Gardner, 1972

Copyright, with Ron Costley, 1973, screen print

Stationary, with Ron Costley, cover drawing by David Button, 1973

Family Group, with Karl Torok, 1973, print in folder

Necktank, with Michael Harvey, 1973

Arcadia, with George Oliver, 1973

Homage to Malevich, with Michael Harvey, 1974, lithograph in folder

Gourd, with Ron Costley, 1974, screen print in folder

Venus of the Hours, with Ron Costley, 1975, screen print

Sundial print: Umbra Solis . . ., with Michael Harvey, 1975, screen print

A Panzer Selection, with David Button, 1975

L'Embarquement pour l'Ile de Cythère – Homage to Watteau, 1975, print in folder

Lullaby, with John Andrew, 1975, screen print

Luftwaffe – After Mondrian, with Jud Fine, 1976, lithograph

Homage to Agam, with David Button, 1976, two prints in folder

At the Field's Edge, with John Borg Manduca, 1976, in folder

Are Aircraft Carriers Urban or Rural?, with John Borg Manduca, 1976

'Someone . . . Somewhere . . ', with Jim Nicholson, 1977, screen print

Battle of Midway I, with Ron Costley, 1977, screen print

Battle of Midway II, with Ron Costley, 1977, screen print

Porphyry, with Ron Costley, 1977, print in folder, published by Graeme Murray Gallery, Edinburgh

Apollo and Daphne, after Bernini, with Ron Costley, 1977

'Flowers', with Jim Downie, after Tom and Laurie Clark, 1977, print in folder

'Of Famous Arcady Ye Are', with Michael Harvey, 1977, poster for the Ian Hamilton Finlay exhibition at the Serpentine Gallery, London, September 1977

Christmas folder, with Ron Costley, 1977

The Harbour at Gravelines, with Gary Hincks, 1978, screen print

Bois d'Amour – Homage to Serusier, 1978, print in folder

Ulysses was Here, with Ron Costley, 1979

Nude / Draped Nude, with Gary Hincks, 1980

Sub Specie Aeternitatis, with John Borg Manduca, 1980

Les Cimétières des Naufrages, 1981, print in folder

A Classic Landscape, with Ian Gardner, 1981

Lettre de Cachet, with Gary Hincks, 1981

Angélique et Médor, with Nicholas Sloan, 1981, print in folder

Propaganda for the Wood-Elves, with Harvey Dwight, 1981, photograph in folder

Penny Browns, with Ian Gardner, 1982

The Months, with Nicholas Sloan, 1982

The Epictetus Text, with Grahame Jones, 1982, original watercolour in big folder

The Illustrated Esoteric Dictionary, with Ian Gardner, 1982, print in folder, The New Arcadian Press

4 Posters Against the Scottish Arts Council, with Nicholas Sloan, 1982, in black or red

A Chant for a Regional Occasion, 1983, folding print

Temple, n. (after Claude), with Mark Stewart, 1983, folding print

Saint-Just Posters, 1983, set of four

Ian Hamilton Finlay Posters, 1983, set of four

Arrosoir, with Gary Hincks, 1984

Three Kings for the Republic, with Gary Hincks, 1984

Corinthian Capital, n. with Nicholas Sloan, 1985, paper cut-out

Reap the SAC Faction, 1985

Proclamation, 1985, in red or blue

Saint-Just Cube, with Nicholas Sloan, 1986, paper cut-out

Urn (Garden Poem), 1986, folding print

Marat Assassiné, with Gary Hincks, 1986

Seven Seed Packets, with Gary Hincks, 1986

Revolution, n., with Gary Hincks, 1986, print in folder

Twilight, 1986, print in folder

Chanson d'Automne, 1986, two prints in folder

Two Visions, 1987

Follies – A Little Spartan Guide to the National Trust, 1987

Head of the Dead Marat, with Gary Hincks, 1987

Sailors! Revolutionaries!, with Gary Hincks, 1987

Joseph Bara, after Gris, with Gary Hincks, 1987

And Even As She Fled . . . (1), with John R. Nash, 1987

And Even As She Fled . . . (2), with John R. Nash, 1987

After Bernini, with Gary Hincks, 1987

Now the Names of the Twelve . . ., with John R. Nash, 1987

Oh! Nature . . ., with Gary Hincks, 1987

Both the Garden Style . . ., with Gary Hincks, 1987

Knitting was a Reserved Occupation, 1987

Le Tricot Etait une Occupation Reservé, 1987

From the Nabis Series: Filiger, 1987, print in folder

From the Nabis Series: Der Untergang des Abendlandes, 1987, print in folder

From the Nabis Series: Poire / Loire, 1987, two prints in folder

Fountain, 1987, calligramme in folder

Classical / Neoclassical, with Gary Hincks, 1987

Rowan, 1987

Willow, 1987

Millet: Pseudo-Moralist, 1987

The Poor Fisherman, with Gary Hincks, 1987

The Medium is the Message, 1987, screen print

Laconic, with Ron Costley, 1987, screen print

Ligue des Droits de l'Homme, 1987

Grove, n., with Gary Hincks, 1987, print in folder

Delegation without Response, 1987

Lasciate ogni Speranza, 1987, in red or black

Clay the Life . . ., with Alexander Stoddart, 1987, folding print

Néoclassicisme Révolutionnaire, with Gary Hincks, 1988, screen print

Personnes Intéressées, 1988

Picabia Series (1): The French Attaché is Papier Maché, 1988, red or black

Picabia Series (1): Art Press is Part Cress, 1988, red or black

Picabia Series (1): All that Glitters is not Aryan, 1988, red or black

Picabia Series (1): Parisians Spoil the French, 1988, red or black

Picabia Series (1): The League of Rights Intrigues in Tights, 1988, red or black

Picabia Series (2): Don't Put All Your Heads in one Basket, 1988, red or black

Picabia Series (2): Spare the Blade and Spoil The Factions, 1988, red or black

Picabia Series (2): Don't Cast your Revolutions before Swine, 1988, red or black

'Brailed', with Grahame Jones, 1988, print in folder

'Every Effect   ', with Jo Hincks, 1988, screen folding print

A Memory of the 90's, 1989

Sundial, illustrated by Kathleen Lindsley, 1989

Still-life, drawing by Carlo Rossi, 1989

Bicentenary Tricolour, with Gary Hincks, 1989

L'Ami du Peuple, 1989, lithograph

Seven Definitions Pertaining to Ideal Landscape, with John R. Nash, 1989, seven prints in folder

Matisse chez Duplay, with Julie Farthing, 1989

Countercomposition, with Gary Hincks, 1989, screen print

Callimachus, with Gary Hincks, 1989, invitation to the Kilkenny Castle

Quin Morere, with Gary Hincks, 1989, lithograph

Swallows Little Matelots, with Michael Harvey, 1989, screen print

Tombeau de Rousseau au Panthéon, with Gary Hincks, 1989

Two Landscapes of the Sublime, with Gary Hincks, 1989, lithograph

The Sound of Running Water, 1989

Dove, . . ., with Julie Farthing, 1989, screen print

Two Still-Lifes, for the exhibition 'Nature Morte' at the Galerie Philomene Magers, 1989, folding print

Bal des Victimes, 1989, screen print

10 prints for Sandwich Boards, 1989: *Girondism is Not a Faith . . . 1989 Belongs to the Public and the Politicians . . . Nous Regarderons la Révolution Française . . . Le Geste Girondin . . . The Life of Saint-Just . . . Qui Croit au Compromis . . . The Girondist Perceives the Blade . . . Une Révolution qui Employait Quotidiennement . . . Le Couperet n'est pas une Icone de la Mort . . . The Blade Stained with Blood is no More . . .*

Rose Pettigrew, with Kathleen Lindsley, 1989, poem folder

Water-Cooled Water Cress, with Julie Farthing, 1990, silkscreen print

The Revolution is Frozen . . ., with Gary Hincks, 1990, lithograph

His Bed a Meadow, 1990, lithograph with fold-out

3 Sailboats, with Gary Hincks, 1990

Two Poems, 1990

Mystic, 1990, poem in folder

King, 1990, poem in folder

The Revolution, 1990, poem in folder
1794, 1990, poem in folder
The Jacobin Vasarely, with Gary Hincks, 1990, two prints in folder
Decal Sheet 62, with Gary Hincks, 1990
Decal Sheet 23, with Gary Hincks, 1990
Sickle/Lightning Flash, with Gary Hincks, 1990
Two Scythes, with Gary Hincks, 1990
Scythe/Lightning Flash, with Gary Hincks, 1990
The Sound of a Single Swallow, with Gary Hincks, 1990, poem in folder
Golden Age, with Gary Hincks, 1990, poem in folder
Prinz Eugen, with Gary Hincks, 1990, poem in folder
Two Examples, 1991, poem in folder
After Magritte, with Gary Hincks, 1991 poem in folder
'2', 1991, poem in folder
Diamond Studded Fishnet, with Julie Farthing, 1991, silkscreen
Capital – Ship, with Michael Harvey, 1991, silkscreen
Stem and Stern, with Julie Farthing, 1991, silkscreen
Gulfs and Wars (Prinz Eugen), 1991, published by Kunstverein Friedrichshafen, Germany
Poverty, with Julie Farthing, 1991, screen print
3 Spaces, 1991, folding poem
Sackcloth, 1991, poem in folder
Broken/Bent, 1991, poem in folder
Morning/Rill, 1991, poem in folder
After Piranesi, with Gary Hincks, 1991, lithograph
Ventôse, with Gary Hinks, 1991, published by Overbeck-Gesellschaft Lübeck, colour lithograph
Two Adaptions, 1991, poem in folder
Autumn, 1991, poem in folder
Idylle, illustration by Gary Hincks, 1991, poem in folder
Column-Drum to Drum, with Gary Hincks, 1991, screen print
3 Columns, with Catherine Lovegrove, 1991, lithograph
Reedpipe, photograph by Martyn Greenhalgh, 1991, published in 1990 by Exempla Firenze & Exit, Lugo, folding print in envelope

5   PROPOSALS

A Walled Garden, with Ian Garden and J. F. Hendry, 1979, watercolours
The Monteviot Proposal, with Nicholas Sloan, originally published in 1979, reproduced in 'Mr. Aislabie's Gardens', 1981, The New Arcadian Press
A Proposal for the Restoration of the Heriot-Watt University Sundial, with Nicholas Sloan and Liz Owen, 1979
The Celle Proposal (A Celebration of the Grove), with Nicholas Sloan, 1984, made for Giuliano Gori
The Tower of the Nets, with Mark Stewart, 1984, crayon / ink
Project for the Schweizergarten, Vienna, with Nicholas Sloan, 1984, hand-coloured photocopy in folder
The Temple of the Ideal Republic, with Mark Stewart, 1985, loose-leaf folder, hand-coloured photocopy
Sundial Garden, with Mark Stewart, 1985, crayon / ink
Three Monuments, Pyramids of the Revolution, with Mark Stewart, 1985, loose-leaf folder
The Temple of Bara, with Mark Stewart, 1985, loose-leaf folder, hand-coloured photocopy
Saint-Just Pyramid, with Nicholas Sloan, 1985
Sea Coast, after Claude Lorrain, with Gary Hincks, 1985, lithographic print

Proposal for a Wall, with Gary Hincks, 1985
Klassische Landschaft, with Gary Hincks, 1985, print/folder
Gateway to a Grove, with Michael Harvey, 1985, two lithographic prints in folder
The Temple of Bara, with Mark Stewart, 1986, two colour lithographs
Proposal for the Stuart Collection at the University of California, San Diego, 1986, loose-leaf folder of lithographic prints, plans, texts and photographs
L'Idylle des Cerises, with Michael Harvey, 1986, booklet
Six Proposals for the Improvement of Stockwood Park Nurseries in the Borough of Luton, with Gary Hincks, 1985 and 1986, six print/folders
A Variation on Lines by Pope, 1986, lithograph in folder
4 Colonnes, 8 Affiches pour L'Abbaye Cistercienne de l'Epau, 1986, eight prints in folders
Proposal for a Monument to Jean-Jacques Rousseau, with Gary Hincks, 1986, lithographic print with fold-outs, in folder
Proposal for a Monument to Ludwig Feuerbach, with Gary Hincks, 1986, print
A Shaded Path (1), 1987, folded print
A Remembrance of R. L. S., with Gary Hincks, 1987, print in folder
A Proposal for the R. L. S. Club, with Michael Harvey, 1987, print in folder
A Remembrance of R. L. S., illustrated by Kathleen Lindsley, 1987
Erinnerung an Annette (1), the Ruschhaus Proposal, with Gary Hincks, 1987, concertina print, proposal for Münster
Erinnerung an Annette (2), with Gary Hincks, 1987, concertina print, proposal for Münster
A Proposal for the Garden of Pauline Karpidas, with Andrew Townsend, 1987, folding print
A Proposal for the Furka Pass, with Wouter Weijers and Kathleen Lindsley, 1987, folded print
A Country Lane, A Proposal for the Glasgow Garden Festival, illustrated by Laurie Clark, 1988
Proposal for a Sundial to be Placed on Marat's House in Paris, with Eric Marland, 1988, lithographic print
Projet pour un Parc Républicain, with Gary Hincks, 1988, print in folder
Six Tree Column Bases, with Iain Stewart, 1988, three coloured lithographs in folder
A Proposal for the Forest of Dean, with Gary Hincks, 1988, lithographic print in folder
Un Jardin Révolutionnaire, with Alexander Chemetov, introduction by Stephen Bann, 1988, book/proposal for The Ministry of Culture and Communication, Paris
Proposal for the Camouflaging of a Type 22 Pillbox in a Classical Park, with Grahame Jones, 1988, coloured lithographic print
A Proposal for Arne, with Gary Hincks, 1988 and 1989, booklet, coloured lithograph
A Proposal for a Private Garden in Germany, for Dr M. Hanstein, with Robert Johnston, 1989
Crate Furniture for Sansculottes, with Neil McLeish, 1989, screen print in folder
A Shaded Path (2), 1989, folding print within folder
Into the Forest, with Andrew Townsend, 1989, folding card
Five Signposts, with Kathleen Lindsley, 1989, print/folder
The Sacramento Proposal, with Neil McLeish, 1990, folding print
A Project for a Promontory, with Kathleen Lindsley and Malcolm Fraser, 1990
Proposal for a Pair of Gate Piers and Finials, with Andrew Townsend, 1990, folding lithograph
Six Milestones, A proposal for Floriade, The Hague, Holland, with Michael Harvey, 1991

Beautiful Kydippé, A proposal for the garden of Dr and Mrs Herkenhöner, Hennef, Germany, with Michael Harvey, 1991, print in folder
Proposal for a Tree-Plaque: MD, with Michael Harvey, 1991, print in folder
For Klaus Werner Proposal for a Postscript to 'The Present Order', 1991, folder

6   MISCELLANEOUS

Partisan Gallery Handout, 1963, for an exhibition by Peter Stitt which included contributions by Rothenberg and Finlay
Arcady ABC (Some Questions on the Poem), 1968, Tarasque Press
The Weed Boat Master's Ticket Preliminary Test (Part One), 1970, Tarasque Press
Land/Sea, Indoor Sundial, with description of 'Land Weathercock' by Stephen Bann, 1970, leaflet
Ceolfrith Street Handout Number Four, 1971, Ceolfrith Press
The Wild Hawthorn Press, New Publications, 1971, Autumn, with descriptions and commentaries by Ian Hamilton Finlay
Four Medallions (1): Kleiner Kreuzer Sonata, with Ron Costley, 1975, made in copper and brass-plated aluminium
Four Medallions (2): Thunderbolt – Steersall, with Ron Costley, 1975, made in copper and brass-plated aluminium
Four Medallions (3): Midway – Through a Dark Wood, with Ron Costley, 1975, made in copper and brass-plated aluminium
Four Medallions (4): A Celebration of Earth, Air, Fire, Water, with Ron Costley, 1975, made in copper and brass-plated aluminium
'Pacific', 1975, board wargame for two players
Homage to Watteau, 1976, invitation to the Graeme Murray Gallery exhibition
Jampot Covers (sundials), 1977
In World War 1, Many Ships were Sunk . . ., 1977, invitation to Ian Hamilton Finlay exhibition at the Serpentine Gallery, folding card
Sundial Badges, 1978
SAC / ACGB / KGB – Badge, 1978
ACGB Errata slip, 1978
ACGB card, 1979
A Butterfly Garden, with George L. Thomson, 1979, 12 cards in envelope
'Words as Objects – Objects as Words', Scottish Arts Council Director's 'documentation' of this event (photocopies only), 1979
'A Spoken Space', with Ronnie and Henriette Duncan, 1979, cassette for Galerie Gaetan, Geneva
Ex Libris 'Light Comes after Me', with Michael Harvey, 1979, made for the V&A
Ex Libris (Barge), with Michael Harvey, 1979, made for the V&A
Ex Libris 'Ronnie Duncan', 1979
Woods and Seas: A Selection, 1980, two booklets, four cards and two bookmarks in envelope
Arcadian Gliders, with Steve Wheatley, White Lies Publications, 1981, nine gliders in a box
Arts Video film: Ian Hamilton Finlay, 1981
Re-Use Trees, 1981, postal label
The Forest and the Revolution, 1981, invitation
An Open Letter, 1981, The New Arcadian Press
Saint-Just Sundial badge, 1981
Stamps: Kingdom of Fife, Arcadia, Strathclyde Region, Little Sparta, 1982
Inter Artes Et Naturam, 1982, invitation
Diamond-Studded Fishnet, 1982, folded invitation to the exhibition 'A Pittenweem Fancy', Pittenweem Arts Festival
The Third Reich Revisited, 1982, invitation to the exhibition at the Tartar Gallery, Edinburgh
Jampot covers: Let us Invite Nature and . . ., 1982, in red or blue or white

I only know what is just, with Calder Stewart, 1983, paper cut-out sundial

Manifesto for February 4, 1983

Second Front Now!, 1983, folding leaf

Strathclyde Times, 1983, Friday, June 17

Strathclyde's Miles Worse, 1983, sticker

Badge: Too Many Laws, 1983

Jampot covers: Too Many Laws, 1983

The First Battle of Little Sparta, 1984, medal

Terror / Virtue, 1984

Feuersprüche, 1984, The New Arcadian Press

Little Sparta & Kriegsschatz in Paris, The Saint-Just Vigilantes, Little Sparta, 1985, acknowledgement to the exhibition at the Eric Fabre Gallery, Paris

Marat Assassiné, Vitruvius/Augustus – Vitruvius/ Robespierre, Ideological Accessories, 1986, invitation, Victoria Miro Gallery, London

Ian Hamilton Finlay: announcement for Unda, with Sue Finlay and Nicholas Sloan, 1987, folding card, The Stuart Collection, University of California, San Diego

Ian Hamilton Finlay, photograph by Gail Ridgwell, 1987, folding card, Victoria Miro Gallery, London

Carnation, 1987, card cut-out in envelope

Pastorales, 1987, invitation to the Galerie Claire Burrus

Digraphe (Section Française des Vigilants de Saint-Just), 1988, discussion by Jean Ristat, Yves Abrioux, Denis Fernàndez-Recatalà . . .

Ex Libris, RH 202 Lyre, 1989

1789 – 1794, photograph by Martyn Greenhalgh, 1989, folding invitation to the exhibition at the Hamburger Kunsthalle

Callimachus, with Gary Hincks, 1989, invitation to the Kilkenny Castle

Matisse chez Duplay, 1990, mug

Two Flutes for Saint-Just, music by Peter Davidson, 1990, cassette

Twine is Jacobine, 1990, two labels in envelope

I Sing for the Muses and Myself, 1990, a compendium of reprinted and new material on Ian Hamilton Finlay and the garden at Little Sparta, published by Longhouse, Vermont

Les Petites Nativités, with Ron Costley, Christmas 1990, published by Victoria Miro Gallery, cut-out card

Gulfs and Wars, 1991, invitation, Kunstverein Friedrichshafen

Dove . . ., 1991, invitation by Malerisamling/ Lillehammer Art Museum

Small is Quite Beautiful, 1991, invitation, Frankfurter Kunstverein

Evening/Sail, 1991, invitation, Graeme Murray with the Fruitmarket Gallery, Edinburgh Festival

Novalis, 1991, invitation Galerie Sfeir-Semler

Ventôse, 1991, invitation, Overbeck-Gesellschaft Lübeck

The Poor Fisherman, 1991, invitation, Talbot Rice Gallery, Edinburgh

Grove, 1991, invitation, Victoria Miro Galleria Firenze

Fête Champêtre, 1991, Tate Gallery T-shirt

Evening/Sail, produced by Graeme Murray Gallery, 1991, enamelled metal brooch

Evening/Sail, 1991, sweatshirt

Little Drummer Boy, 1991, sweatshirt

Matisse Draughts, with Ron Costley, 1991, produced by Galerie Sfeir-Semler

Mondrian Draughts, with Ron Costley, 1991, produced by Galerie Sfeir-Semler

7 BOOKS AND EXHIBITION CATALOGUES

Akzente, Zeitschrift für Literatur. Carl Hanser, Munich, 1969. Year by year account by Ian Hamilton Finlay of Wild Hawthorne Press

1964–9, with photographs of works and poem prints

Ian Hamilton Finlay, exhibition catalogue, Richard Demarco Gallery, Edinburgh, 1969

Ian Hamilton Finlay, An Illustrated Essay by Stephen Bann, exhibition catalogue, Scottish National Gallery of Modern Art, Edinburgh, 1972

'Aggie Weston's view of Stonypath', *Spring*, no. 2 (1973)

Epitaphs for Lorine, The Jargon Society, Penland, North Carolina, 1973. Collected contributions, including 'Wind Wood Song' by Ian Hamilton Finlay

Ian Hamilton Finlay, exhibition catalogue, with essay by Stephen Scobie, Southampton Art Gallery, 1976

Homage to Watteau, Essay by Stephen Scobie. For the exhibition 'Homage to Watteau', Graeme Murray Gallery, Edinburgh, 1976

Selected Ponds. Photographs of the poet's garden at Stonypath by David Paterson. Introductions by Stephen Bann and Bernard Lassus. West Coast Poetry Review, Reno, Nevada, USA, 1976

Zzzzzz, anthology edited by Kenward Elmslie including 'Carrier Strike!' by Ian Hamilton Finlay with Carl Heideken, Z Press, Calais, Vermont

Collaborations exhibition catalogue, with essays by Stephen Bann, Douglas Hall, Miles Orvell and Stephen Scobie, with a poem 'Stonypath' by Kathleen Raine. Kettle's Yard, Cambridge, 1977

Heroic Emblems, by Ian Hamilton Finlay (with Ron Costley). Introduction and commentaries by Stephen Bann. Z Press, Calais, Vermont, USA, 1977

Ian Hamilton Finlay. Exhibition catalogue, text by Stephen Bann. Serpentine Gallery, London, 1977.

Ian Hamilton Finlay: Gnomique et Gnomonique, by Francis Edeline, published by Atelier de l'Agneau, Liège, 1977

Nature Over Again After Poussin, exhibition catalogue, Collins Exhibition Hall, Glasgow, 1980

Coincidence in the Work of Ian Hamilton Finlay, exhibition catalogue, Graeme Murray Gallery, 1980

Unnatural Pebbles, exhibition catalogue, printed by The Stellar Press with Richard Grasby, photographs by Hani Latif, Graeme Murray Gallery, 1981

'Mr. Aislabie's Gardens', reprint of the Monteviot proposal, New Arcadians, 1981

A Description of Stonypath, by Stephen Bann, photographs by Andrew Griffiths and Harvey Dwight. Friends of Stonypath Garden, 1981. Reproduced from the *Journal of Garden History*, Taylor and Francis Ltd.

'Persiflage', *Aggie Weston's* no. 19, published by Stuart Mills, 1983

Gardens of Exile, New Arcadians' Journal No. 10, Summer 1983. Essays by Patrick Eyres and Ian Hamilton Finlay (Detached Sentences on Exile), with Ian Gardner, John Tetley, Howard Eaglestone and Grahame Jones

Liberty, Terror and Virtue, exhibition catalogue, with essays by Yves Abrioux, Jonathan Buckley and Patrick Eyres. Southampton Art Gallery (*New Arcadians' Journal*, no. 15), 1984.

Talismans and Signifiers, exhibition catalogue, Graeme Murray Gallery, 1984

Blinds, Adrian Harding, 'Little Sparta & Kriegsschatz', Sarkis and Ian Hamilton Finlay, Editions Lebeer Hossmann, Brussels, 1985

Ian Hamilton Finlay – A Visual Primer, by Yves Abrioux, Reaktion Books, 1985

Marat Assassiné & other works at the Victoria Miro Gallery, Victoria Miro Gallery, 1986

Inter Artes et Naturam, ARC, Paris, 1987

Homage to Ian Hamilton Finlay, Victoria Miro, 1987

Pastorales, Galerie Claire Burrus, Paris, 1987

Poursuites Révolutionnaires, Fondation Cartier, Paris, 1987

Ian Hamilton Finlay, press release folder for Paris exhibitions, 1987, Claire Burrus Galerie, Fondation Cartier, Bibliothèque Nationale, The British Council

Ian Hamilton Finlay, by Francis Edeline, French reprint of 1977 edition, 1987

Un Paysage, ou 9 vues du jardin de Ian Hamilton Finlay, exhibition catalogue by Daniel Boudinetin, Fondation Cartier, Jouy-en-Josas, 1987

Ian Hamilton Finlay, exhibition catalogue, Victoria Miro Gallery, London. Introduction by Christopher McIntosh and Katherine Kurs. Published in *The Little Critic*, no. 4, 1988

Exhibition on Two Themes, Galerie Jule Kewenig, 1988

Ian Hamilton Finlay: Arbeiten zur Französischen Revolution, exhibition catalogue, with introduction by Harald Siebenmorgen, Städtische Galerie am Markt Schwäbisch Hall, 1989

Works – Ian Hamilton Finlay, exhibition catalogue, with text by Ian Hamilton Finlay and ten photographs by Martyn Greenhalgh, Butler Gallery, Kilkenny Castle, 1989

The Garden on the Hill, exhibition catalogue, Christine Burgin Gallery, New York, 1990

Ian Hamilton Finlay, exhibition catalogue, with text by Thomas Kellein, Kunsthalle Basel, 1990

'1789–1794', exhibition catalogue, Kunsthalle Hamburg, 1990

Catalogue of Finlay Exhibition, with essays by Giovanni Damiani and Francesca Alfano Miglietti, Galleria Acta, Milano, 1990

A Wartime Garden, with Ron Costley and John Andrew, photographs by Antonia Reeve, Graeme Murray Gallery, Edinburgh, 1990

'Ästhetische Aufrüstung', by I. Conzen-Meairs, in *Künstler, Kritisches Lexikon der Gegenwartskunst*, no. 12, Munich

Holzwege, exhibition catalogue, with texts by Hans Backes and Pia Simig, Neuer Aachener Kunstverein, Aachen, 1990

Ian Hamilton Finlay, exhibition catalogue, Lillehammer bys malerisamling, 1991

Ideologische Äusserungen, exhibition catalogue, with text by T. Kellein, R. C. Kenedy, S. Bann and P. Weiermair, and a bibliography by Pia Simig, Frankfurter Kunstverein, Germany, 1991

Poet in the Woodland, photographs by Martyn Greenhalgh, Galerie Stadtpark Krems, Austria, 1991

Evening will Come . . ., exhibition catalogue, with two essays by Edwin Morgan, Graeme Murray with the Fruitmarket Gallery, Edinburgh, 1991

The Poor Fisherman, text by Duncan Macmillan, Talbot Rice Gallery, University of Edinburgh, 1991

Seven Definitions, with John Nash, Galerie Sfeir-Semler, Kiel, 1991

Ian Hamilton Finlay/Matrix 116, Wadsworth Atheneum, Hartford, USA, 1991

Instruments of Revolution, ICA London, 1992, designed by I. H. Finlay and P. Simig, with Paul Khera, photographs by A. Reeve and S. White

Index

This index refers to Yves Abrioux's texts:
Biographical Notes and Part II

anagram 293
analogy 190
Anaximander 253
Andre, C. 4, 183
Aphrodite *see* Venus
Apollo 159, 168, 213, 214, 219, 299–300; as
    Saint-Just, 300
Aquinas 182
arcady 198, 199, 232, 241–3, 254
Aristotle 189, 190, 192, 193, 198, 204, 218, 251,
    252
aura 165, 166, 167, 168, 182, 183, 189, 191,
    214, 220, 254

Bann, S. 7, 167, 182, 191, 199, 204, 213, 219,
    220, 242
Baudelaire, C. 199
Benjamin, W. 165, 166, 182, 213, 214
Bernini, G. 293
Bloom, H. 251
boats and ships 4, 167, 190
    fishing boats 6, 167, 190, 220
    warships 6, 167, 191, 192, 204, 213, 220, 221,
        232
boat names and registrations 4, 190, 191, 198, 199
booklet poems 2, 167, 198, 253
Bradley, A. C. 165, 250, 251, 254
Burke, E. 250, 251, 253, 254, 294

camouflage 182, 214, 254
Cézanne, P. 191
Chavannes, P. de 17
Christo 183
citation 189–93, 198, 214, 219, 221, 230, 233
classicism *see also* neoclassicism 13, 159, 167,
    168, 190, 191, 192, 198, 205, 213, 219,
    241, 242, 243, 253, 295, 300, 301
'Claude' *see* Gelée
Coleridge, S. T. 165, 189, 250, 252, 295
collaborations 4, 6, 7, 13, 182
concrete poetry 2, 4, 5, 159, 166, 167, 182, 189,
    190, 207, 219, 241, 299, 300–1
Corot, J. 253
cosmology, poetic 219, 220, 221
cubism 1, 159, 166, 191, 219

dada 1, 198–9, 206, 213, 300
d'Angers, P.-J. D. 252, 255
Danton, G.-J. 252, 255
dictionary works 159, 221
d'Eglantine, F. 253
Diderot, D. 299
Droste-Hülshoff, A. von 14
Duchamp, M. 300
Dürer, A. 167, 168

emblem 7, 191, 192, 213, 214, 218, 219, 220,
    221, 232
epigraph 218

fauvism 159, 166, 182, 183, 189, 190, 191, 199,
    204, 221, 232
Feuerbach, L. 14
Ficino, M. 232
Fine, J. 6, 166, 182, 204, 206
Flaxman, J. 293
Fragonard, J. 168
French Revolution 9, 13, 14–15, 192, 232, 233,
    250, 251, 252, 253, 254, 294
'French War' 15
Furet, F. 252

Garden at Stonypath (*see also* Garden Temple) 4,
    5, 6, 13, 167, 168, 214, 221, 293, 300

Garden Temple *see* Temple, Garden
Gelée, Claude, *called* 'Claude', 'le Lorrain' 168, 301
glass poems 2, 198, 233, 301
Gods, Greek and Roman 190, 214
Goethe, J. W. 191, 299
Gombrich, E. H. 213, 219
Gomringer, E. 4
Gris, J. 159, 189, 214, 299
Guercino, G. 241, 242

Hartman 165, 166, 191
Hegel, G. W. F. 205, 293
Heine, H. 190
Heraclitus 207, 218, 220, 221, 232, 243, 250
Hesse, H. 191
hieroglyph 213, 214
Hitler, A. 167, 199, 254–5
Hodler, F. 14
homages 159, 182, 204, 205, 206, 207, 214, 219, 250
Horace 299
Hugo, V. 252
Hunt, J. D. 253
Hussey, E. 7, 218–9

impresa *see* emblem
inscriptions 5, 10, 167, 168, 182, 221, 232, 233, 253
intimisme 182, 219

Joyce, J. 1, 182

Kahn, C. H. 253
Kahnweiler, D.-H. 159, 189
Kandinsky, W. 206
Kemp, F. 213
Kenner, H. 250
Kooning, W. de 214
Kraus, K. 182
krisis 205, 213

Lacoue-Labarthe, J., & Nancy, J.-L., *quoted* 205
Lamartine, A. 301
Lax, R. 207
le Nôtre, A. 253
Lessing, G. E. 218
Linnaeus, C. 299
Little Sparta (*see also* Garden) 4, 5, 6, 8, 9, 10,
    13, 166, 167, 168, 204, 220, 221, 232, 233,
    242, 253, 254, 299, 300
    Follies War 14
    Little Spartan War 7, 9, 13, 214, 220, 254,
        299
    First Battle of Little Sparta 10, 243
    Budget Day Raid 10, 214
Longinus 250, 251
'Lorrain', *see* Gelée

MacDiarmid, H. 189
Malevich, K. 166, 182, 206
Matisse, H. 301
Medici, Lorenzo dei, *called* 'the Magnificent'
    241, 242
metaphor 2, 167, 189–93, 198, 204, 213, 218,
    219, 220, 221, 232, 233
Michelet, J. 251, 252
Milton, J. 242, 250, 252–3
modernism 1, 166, 176, 190, 191, 192, 193, 198,
    199, 206, 213, 219, 250, 252, 295, 300
Mondrian, P. 206, 214
Muses, The 214

Nancy, J.-L., & Lacoue-Labarthe, J. *quoted* 205
neoclassicism 6, 7, 10, 167, 168, 190, 206, 214,
    218, 219, 220, 221, 233, 241, 243, 300
neon poems 6, 182
neopresocratic 218–21, 233, 243
New Arcadians 242
Nietzsche, F. 214, 219, 220, 221, 242

one-word poems 5, 198
Ovid 19, 241, 242, 293, 301

Pan 205
Panofsky, E. 167, 241–3
pastoral 2, 13, 165, 166, 233, 241, 254
Pater, W. 220, 299
Planck, M. 221
Plato 232, 233
Plotinus 213
plurality 219, 220
Plutarch 213
Pluto 293
poem/cards 2, 5, 190, 206, 219, 220, 252, 254
poem/prints 2, 6, 190, 233
poetics *see* poetry; *see also* metaphor, rhetoric
poetry 166, 182, 189–92, 219–20 (*see also* booklet
    poems, neon poems, poem/cards, poem/
    prints)
Pollock, J. 214
Polybius 242
Poor. Old. Tired. Horse. 1, 4, 5
Poussin, N. 10, 168, 241, 242
presocratic philosophy 207, 218, 219, 220, 221,
    233, 253, 254
Proserpina 293
pun 198, 219, 232, 243, 253
Pythagoreans 159, 301

Reinhardt, A. 241
rhetoric 189, 190, 192, 193, 198, 204, 213, 218,
    251, 252
Ripa, C. 218, 219
Robert, H. 299
Robespierre, M. 251, 252, 253, 254
Rodchenko, A. 214
romanticism 168, 190, 300
Rousseau, J.-J. 233, 253, 293, 300

Saint-Just, L.-A. de 9, 10, 233, 251, 252, 253,
    254, 255, 293
Saint-Just Vigilantes 9, 10, 14, 214, 233, 254, 300
Schlegel, F. 205, 250
Schwitters, K. 199
Scottish Arts Council 7, 8, 9
Shenstone, W. 219
short stories 1, 165, 166, 182, 219, 294
Socrates 250, 251
sound poetry 199
Speer, A. 9, 254, 255
Stephenson, R. L. 299
Stonypath *see* Little Sparta; Garden at Stonypath
Strathclyde Region 8, 10
sublime 165, 233, 250–5
sundial 232–3
suprematism 166, 182, 191, 198, 199, 204, 206,
    232, 241
Sylvester, V. 206, 207
symbolism 191, 294

Temple, Garden 4, 7, 8, 9, 10, 13, 15, 168, 213,
    214, 254, 299
Theocritus 141
Third Reich 9, 13, 166, 167, 199, 204, 206, 214,
    232, 233, 242, 250, 252, 254, 294–5
toys and models 2, 219, 250
tree-columns 253
typescript poem 166, 182

Valenciennes, P. H. 299
van der Rohe, Mies 254
Vaughan, H. 232
Venus 214, 232
Veronese, P. 214
Virgil 241, 243, 300

Watteau, A. 214, 241, 301
Wild Hawthorn Press, 1, 6, 17
Willis, P. 253
wit 204–5, 206–7, 213
Wordsworth, W. 165, 189

Zeus 214